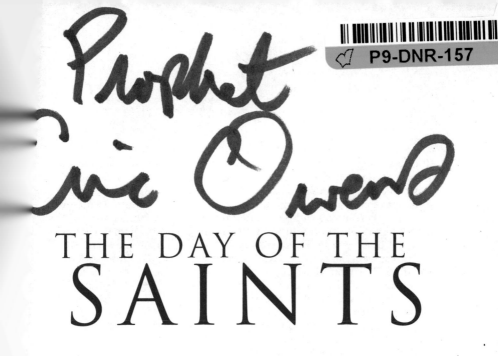

THE DAY OF THE
SAINTS

EQUIPPING BELIEVERS FOR THEIR
REVOLUTIONARY ROLE IN MINISTRY

DR. BILL HAMON

Destiny Image® Publishers, Inc.
P.O. Box 310
Shippensburg, PA 17257-0310

"We Publish the Prophets"

ISBN 0-7684-2166-7

For Worldwide Distribution
Printed in the U.S.A.

This book and all other Destiny Image, Revival Press, MercyPlace,
Fresh Bread, Destiny Image Fiction, and Treasure House books are
available at Christian bookstores and distributors worldwide.

For a U.S. bookstore nearest you, call **1-800-722-6774**.
For more information on foreign distributors, call **717-532-3040**.
Or reach us on the Internet:
www.destinyimage.com

ENDORSEMENTS

Dr. Bill Hamon is a student of the Word. He brings 48 years of ministry experience to this project. Committed to the development and equipping of fivefold ministry, ministers, and saints, the book you now hold is extensive in its research and comprehensive in its scope. From the foundation of "Called to be Saints" through restoration, equipping, activating, and calling, *The Day of the Saints* points the reader to the day "when the saints take the Kingdom and establish God's glory throughout God's new Earth."

Tommy Tenney
Author, GodChaser

The Day of the Saints has my vote for the book of the year in the current apostolic reformation! Bill Hamon has outdone himself by combining sound history and theology with prophetic illumination, all molded by an ear that is hearing clearly what the Spirit is currently saying to the churches. This book will help launch the Body of Christ into a dynamic, exciting era unknown since the days of Jesus and the apostles.

C. Peter Wagner
Chancellor, Wagner Leadership Institute

Bill Hamon has been on the cutting edge of prophetic revelation for years. Not only has he pioneered in the area of the prophetic and apostolic movements, but he also has been instrumental in launching the growing marketplace ministry movement. Now, with this new book, he takes the Church to a place where she can begin to operate in the last-days events. His style of teaching combined with revelation makes this a landmark book for all who are interested in the Day of the Saints: "preaching the gospel, demonstrating the kingdom, and manifesting God's glory throughout the earth."

The Day of the Saints is a benchmark book for the Body of Christ with regard to training and releasing the last-days harvest force. I look forward to its impact on marketplace ministry.

Rich Marshall
Author of *God@Work*

I'm enjoying my dear friend and brother, Bill Hamon's, new prophetic book, *The Day of the Saints*. I've preached with Bill Hamon and believe in his gifts from God, his integrity with God's Word, and the miraculous results of his powerfully anointed ministry. He and his lovely and anointed wife, Evelyn, are dear to Evelyn and me. They have blessed and uplifted us with words of knowledge and discernment of the Holy Spirit.

I believe this most unusual book could very well propel its readers into a new dimension of the prophetic ministry of our Savior and the apostles and prophets of the Bible for our time. Thank you, Bill, for giving the Body of Christ this book from the spirit of a prophet of God.

Oral Roberts
Founder/Chancellor, Oral Roberts University

The Day of the Saints is one of the most revelatory books that I have read in a long time. Dr. Hamon gives us a road map to help us on our way to understanding what God is saying to the Church in this new millennium. Every believer should read it.

Cindy Jacobs
Generals of Intercession

As a successful consultant with a client list that includes AT&T, Aramark, IBM, Kodak, MCI, Phillips Petroleum, Southdown, Sun Control Systems, Sylvan Learning Systems, U.S. Navy, U.S. Treasury Department, United Airlines, US Airways, and Wal-Mart Corporation, I thought I had arrived until I met Dr. Bill Hamon in 1989. His revelation of ministry in the marketplace changed my life forever. His prophetic covering enhanced my thoughts and insights into the business world.

To hear the voice of God in business changes everyone and everything you touch. For example, while working with a major oil company, God gave me an idea that literally saved them millions of dollars. Another God-given idea for one of the largest learning companies in the world will help over a million children a year learn better. Another prophetic insight provided a hiring program that will help thousands of companies over the next years hire right the first time.

Thank you, Bishop Hamon, for the life-changing revelation of ministry in the marketplace.

Sanford G. Kulkin, Ph.D.

Dr. Hamon is one of the earliest pioneers when it comes to the place and the purpose for Christians in the marketplace. He has been used by God through his previous writings and his extensive international ministry to help the Church realize the centrality of the marketplace and the role of believers in it. In *The Day of the Saints* Dr. Hamon brings all this into sharp focus, and he does it at a time when this message is urgently needed. A definite must-read book.

Ed Silvoso
Author of *Anointed for Business*

Dr. Hamon's latest work challenges the Church to see the fertile grounds of ministry that lie all around us, echoing the call for the church to be the Church. Dr. Hamon underscores the need in these days in which we live for the Church to equip and activate Christians for ministry, not only in the Church, but also in the marketplace and the public square as well. Dr. Hamon has a very timely message.

Tony Perkins
Louisiana State Representative

Wow, what an on-time word! All creation is standing on tiptoes groaning, travailing for the manifestation of the saints empowered, activated, and manifested.

The truth of this book aptly describes what is absolutely necessary to fulfill God's promises that the whole earth will be filled with His glory and that Jesus will return when the gospel of the Kingdom is preached to all nations. That day is fast approaching. This truth is unlimiting—it takes the gospel off the platform and on the road of God's ultimate intention to reclaim the world He owns. Saints, let's go for it!

Thanks, Dr. Hamon, for your greatest work yet.

Emanuele Cannistraci
Apostolic Missions International

Dr. Bill Hamon defines the coming movement as the "Saints Movement." He does a thorough study on previous movements the Church has experienced. He declared that this movement of the saints would be the most widespread of them all.

Dr. Hamon is not merely on the "cutting edge"; he is on the "leading edge." Through the eyes of the prophet, he sees those things that are not as though they are.

This movement of the saints will be led by the fivefold ministry. They are the ones to equip the saints for this mighty move of God. This not only prepares the saints for their ministry, but it also clearly defines the role of the apostle, prophet, evangelist, pastor, and teacher.

Read this book with an open mind and be a part of this "coming movement." I can heartily recommend this book!

Earl Paulk
Bishop, Cathedral at Chapel Hill

Awesome! This extraordinary book is revolutionary as it calls for a Church-shaking paradigm shift in our mind-sets on how churches should be structured.

Dr. Bill Hamon has an uncanny revelation anointing like the "sons of Issachar" (1 Chron. 12:32) for knowing the seasons and times we live in and what God's people ought to do.

As Bishop Hamon builds indisputable arguments for fivefold ministry teams equipping God's end-time army of saints for ministry and warfare, he systematically shows what every church must do if they believe they have a promised land (destiny, promises) to possess and enemies (principalities) to conquer. He warns that those who fail in this mandate will condemn their ministries to be "wilderness wanderers."

This timely treatise is a trumpet call for wimpy "love boat saints" to get off their carnal cruise lines, become trained as warriors, and board God's battleship to blow satan's forces out of the water!

Gary L. Greenwald
Apostle, Eagle's Nest Ministries

I have always enjoyed Dr. Bill Hamon's books. Ever since I read his first book, *The Eternal Church*, I have eagerly anticipated each new book. Each one has been a forerunner for its time. With hindsight the revelation in each of the volumes has been validated. The most life-changing book I ever read on the prophetic was *Prophets and Personal Prophecy*, written by Dr. Hamon in the mid-1980s, which has now become the accepted manual for the prophetic around the world. It has been translated into many languages and has brought us an advanced blueprint for pioneering in the prophetic. *The Day of the Saints*, I believe, will be to the Saints Movement what *Prophets and Personal Prophecy* was to the Prophetic Movement. Each chapter has an urgency from God challenging us to get into position and to equip others to partner with God. This book was definitely written with a "sons of Issachar" anointing, communicating the times and seasons of God for us in advance.

Sharon Stone
Director, Christian International Europe

As an ex-NFL player and now CEO of Promise Vision, I know how important it is for God's people to stand up in a society that is drifting away from its moral foundation. I also know how vital it is to get God's people out of the church and into the world. The Kingdom of God must be taken into the marketplace. For this reason, I recommend Dr. Bill Hamon's book, *The Day of the Saints*. This is a clear call demanding a response from every believer to not sit on the sidelines, but to get into the game and give themselves to the purposes of God for this generation.

Reggie White
CEO, Promise Vision

CONTENTS

**Special Points Regarding *The Day of the Saints*
That Will Be Covered in This Book**

The Day of the Saints has great significance and will produce many things to fulfill God's purpose. Many Scriptures will be used to prove each point.

- The Day of the Saints is the next scheduled end-time event.
- The whole creation is earnestly awaiting the Day of the Saints.
- The great cloud of witnesses in Heaven is longing for the Day of the Saints.
- To participants the supernatural will become the norm during the Day of the Saints.
- Every Saint will become a minister in the Day of the Saints.
- Every fivefold minister will become a full expression of Christ Jesus.
- The Day of the Saints will bring the greatest revolutionary restoration truth since the Protestant Movement's revelation and teaching on the priesthood of every believer.
- The Day of the Saints is the next major event in God's full restoration of the Church.
- It is the beginning of the end for the existence of mortal men.
- The Day of the Saints will prepare the way for the Kingdom Establishing Movement.

- It will reveal and activate prophets and apostles in the marketplace.

- Ministers in the marketplace will become as revolutionary an idea to the twenty-first century Church as gentiles becoming Saints was to the first century Church.

- Saints activated in the marketplace will demonstrate the gospel of the Kingdom of God.

- Saints will demonstrate the lordship of Christ as a Kingdom witness to every nation.

- The Day of the Saints will bring the revelation and activation of every Saint into supernatural manifestations.

- Its finalization will cause the glory of the Lord to fill the earth as waters cover the sea.

- It will bring the revelation of God's progressive and ultimate purpose for His Saints, the Church.

- It will prepare the Omega-Transition Generation for their predestinated, victorious destiny.

- The greatest harvest of souls ever recorded in Church history will occur during the Day of the Saints.

- Jesus is excited about this coming Day when He will be fully glorified in His Saints.

INTRODUCTION

In many ways, this is the most important book I have written. Most of my 48 years of ministry have been focused on biblical research, seeking Holy Spirit revelation regarding God's plans for His Church, and equipping God's people in their giftings and callings. This has all been working toward the goal of preparing God's people for a divine movement of restoration that I prophetically sense the Holy Spirit is bringing to the Church. Very shortly, the Saints of God will begin demonstrating the supernatural works of Jesus on a scale that is unprecedented. Millions of born-again, Spirit-filled believers who have been trained and equipped will prophetically speak the words of Jesus and apostolically demonstrate His miraculous power as witnesses of the Kingdom of God.

Those who are familiar with the ministry of Christian International know that our major role is to help raise up apostles and prophets in the Body of Christ to their biblical place as foundational ministries in the Church, built upon the Chief Cornerstone, Jesus Christ. But this is not the end goal in itself. The Book of Ephesians clearly tells us that Christ gave fivefold ministers, including apostles and prophets, to the Church for the purpose of equipping the Saints for the work of the ministry.

This book will scripturally reveal that there is a last-days ministry for the Saints to fulfill. Its purpose is to enlighten the reader concerning what the Holy Spirit has been commissioned to accomplish within the Church during the next several years, and to show how each and every believer is called to participate. As the fivefold ministry gets into place in the Church, the Saints will be equipped and released to demonstrate the gospel of the Kingdom throughout the whole world.

Many Christians are looking for "the Day of the Lord"—the return of Jesus Christ. In recent decades, great emphasis has been placed on the "rapture" of Christians out of this world. However, Scripture indicates that many things will happen before the return of the Lord. The Saints will reap the greatest harvest of souls ever to come into the Kingdom. We will seek to scripturally prove the reality of that "Day" on God's timetable and prophetic agenda—before the coming of the Lord—when the Saints will fulfill all the Scriptures regarding Christ's Church.

This book will show that Jesus is committed to co-laboring with His Church, through the Holy Spirit, until we are fully walking in all that He has prophesied. One of my greatest passions is to help each believer fulfill his or her personal ministry as a member of the Body of Christ. We are not just accidents going somewhere to happen! God has a purpose and destiny for every one of us. Each of us has certain things we are supposed to accomplish on this earth. I have been in ordained ministry for nearly 50 years, yet each one of you reading this book is just as called and appointed as I am to serve God in some form of Christian ministry. Your ministry platform may not be the pulpit of your local church, but rather your business headquarters, realty agency, or local school.

I sincerely believe that this book is being written with apostolic-prophetic revelation concerning God's purpose for His Church—the Saints. My special anointing is like that of the "sons of Issachar who had understanding of the times, to know what Israel ought to do" (1 Chron. 12:32a). My gifting is to reveal the overall picture of the Church from its origination to its ultimate destination, especially dealing with the past, present, and coming moves of God. I am trusting the Lord for new and broader revelation while pulling upon accumulated wisdom and knowledge to fully present the reality of the coming Day of the Saints. We will describe the character, principles, ministry to be manifest, and work the Day of the Saints is to accomplish in God's progressive restoration process, which must continue "until the times of restoration of all things, which God has spoken by the mouth of all His holy prophets since the world began" (Acts 3:21b).

In order to give a clear vision of what the Holy Spirit is getting ready to do, we will spend some time reviewing the process of Church restoration. Many New Testament truths that were understood by the first-century Church were lost in subsequent generations, until the Holy Spirit began enlightening these truths to His people at the time of the Protestant Reformation. Those of you who have read my other books, particularly those relating to the history and destination of the Church, will be familiar with some of this material. However, I ask that you read with an open heart, allowing the Holy Spirit to renew your vision and to quicken to you new insights regarding God's future plans and purposes for us as His Body.

If you are unfamiliar with the restoration process of the Church or have found Church history uninteresting in the past, I trust you will allow the Lord to build an excitement in your spirit. We will see that Jesus really has been faithfully building His Church, and we will see what remains to be accomplished before He can come back. Looking back to see where the Church has come from also prepares us to move forward into our eternal destiny. I trust that these truths will impart vision for the greatest day ever in the life of the Church.

After we describe where the Saints are headed, we will give practical wisdom that relates to every believer. Prophetic clarity and biblical directives will be given for proper preparation and participation in the Day of the Saints. We will seek to explain the ministry the Saints will manifest, the equipping that fivefold ministers are to provide for the Saints, and the maturity that will be required of the Saints. We hope to reveal the principles that need to be practiced and the pitfalls that need to be avoided in order for the Day of the Saints to properly accomplish its purpose. Later chapters will cover how Saints are to operate as ministers in their places of employment in the marketplace and in the arenas of government. We will look at how to be equipped to hear from God prophetically and how to become activated in supernatural giftings and abilities.

Notes at the end of each chapter give more information on the topics covered. Most of the notes reference Scripture verses for those who want to research further. I encourage you to be like the Bereans in Acts 17:11b who "received the word with all readiness, and searched the Scriptures daily to find out whether these things were so."

A "Day of the Saints" is coming in which God is calling every believer to participate. This will be the greatest time in history for those who hunger to fulfill God's will for their lives, especially those who are 100 percent committed to glorify Christ, overcome all things, reap the great harvest, and see God's Kingdom come and His will be done on Earth as it is in Heaven. If you desire to be a part of all that Christ is doing in the Church today, you will want to read with great interest, asking the Holy Spirit both to intensify your desire to participate and to reveal your individual role in His great plan. You have been called for such a time as this! *Lord, I ask that You give all who read this a spirit of wisdom and revelation to know what the Holy Spirit is saying to the Church today and to understand their part in Your great plan and purpose. Amen.*

Now, let us venture into all that is involved in fulfilling God's purposes for us as those "called to be Saints." The whole creation is anxiously awaiting the Day of the Saints, when the Saints take the Kingdom and establish God's glory throughout God's new Earth.

CHAPTER 1

CALLED TO BE SAINTS

THE GREATEST CALLING

The greatest calling in Heaven or Earth is to be a Saint of the Most High God.[1] There is no greater privilege or position than that of being a child of God through Jesus Christ our Lord and Savior. Jesus told the multitudes who listened to His teaching that among those born of women there had not arisen anyone greater than John the Baptist. Then He added that the least Saint in the Kingdom of Heaven is greater than he.[2] The apostle Paul wrote to the Saints at Ephesus that he was praying for them:

> *That the God of our Lord Jesus Christ, the Father of glory, may give to you the spirit of wisdom and revelation in the knowledge of Him, the eyes of your understanding being enlightened; that you may know what is* **the hope of His calling, what are the riches of the glory of His inheritance in the saints, and what is the exceeding greatness of His power toward us who believe.**[3]

The Saints of God are those who have been given the privileged opportunity to be conformed to the image of Jesus Christ. This means not only the conforming of our inward character, attitudes, and desires, but also becoming like Jesus in all our behavior and interactions with those around us. It includes being empowered by the Holy Spirit to operate in power and miracles to bring God's Kingdom to this earth. We are quickly coming to the point in history where average Saints will demonstrate the supernatural works of Jesus Christ. Just as Jesus spoke only what He heard His Father speaking and did only what He saw His Father doing, the Saints of God are being trained and equipped to manifest the words and deeds of Jesus as they go about their daily business.[4]

Definition of the Word *Saint*: Of the many words used in the Bible to identify God's chosen people, the term *Saint* is used most frequently (96 times) and carries some of the greatest revelations of God's purpose for His people both in this age and in the ages to come.[5]

The Greek word *hagios* is translated 62 times as "Saint."[6] It is translated 101 times as "holy" and 93 times as "Holy Spirit" (*hagios pneuma*). It is translated "sanctuary" three times.[7] The word means "holy, separate, set apart." A true Saint is one who has become holy through the righteousness of Christ. Like the tabernacle of Moses and all its furnishings, Saints are separated from the world's use and set apart strictly for God's use and glory.[8] Saints are the Lord's "holy ones." They are sanctified and anointed ones who have become set apart from the ways of the world to live Christ's life and demonstrate God's Kingdom.[9]

During the Dark Ages (approximately A.D. 500–1500) the common use of the word *Saint* was discontinued. It became a term for those to whom the Catholic church granted sainthood—customarily someone who had already died. This is the reason the old King James Version of the Bible refers to each of the Gospels by the name of the person who wrote it, such as Saint Matthew, Saint Mark, etc. Both the Roman Catholic and Eastern Orthodox churches also established patron saints.

However, the Bible presents Saints as simply being those whose sins have been washed away by the blood of Jesus, who have been born of the Holy Spirit, and who have been translated out of the kingdom of darkness into the Kingdom of God's dear Son, which makes them children of God.[10] Other commonly used terms are *Christians*, *believers*, or, occasionally, *the brethren* (brothers and sisters in the Lord). In this presentation we will primarily use the name found most often in Scripture, the *Saints*.[11]

THE CORPORATE BODY OF SAINTS—THE CHURCH

As a corporate group, the Saints, these redeemed people who are called out from the world, separated and dedicated unto God, are called *Ecclesia*, translated as "the Church." Other corporate names are the *Body of Christ, God's building, Christ's Bride*, etc.[12] The apostle Paul described the Church as the Body of Christ. He declared that there is only one Body of Christ on Earth, yet it has many members with various and diverse functions. In First Corinthians 12 he explained that each person who receives Christ as personal Savior is born of God and baptized into the Body of Christ as a particular member. The totality of those members are built together through the Spirit as the corporate Body of Christ, which becomes the habitation of Christ on earth. Just as the physical body of Jesus was the habitation of God the Father while He was on Earth, so now the Body of Christ, the Church, has become the dwelling place and headquarters of Christ upon Earth.[13]

God the Father, the Son, and the Holy Spirit are one, yet each plays a particular part in building the Church. Jesus said that He was sending the Holy Spirit to convict of sin, convert people to Christ, sanctify the believers, empower the Saints, speak the truths concerning Christ, and reveal the future purposes of God. After Jesus had purchased the Church with His own blood, He then birthed the Church and filled it with His Holy Spirit. The Holy Spirit then began baptizing believers as members into the Body of Christ, the Church. The Holy Spirit has gifts that He gives to every member of the Body of Christ.[14] Jesus has gifts that He gives to certain members of the Body of Christ.

Fivefold Ministers: After Jesus ascended back to Heaven, He took His ministry of building the Church and divided it into five categories that He gave as gifts to certain members of His Church. Jesus gave specific names to these gifted ministries. "And He Himself gave some to be apostles, some prophets, some evangelists, and some pastors and teachers."[15] Several terms are used to describe these five gifts that are given to men and women of God: the ascension gifts of Christ, fivefold ministers and fivefold ministry, the governmental and administrative offices of the

Church. Throughout this book you will see them referred to as the "fivefold." Technically speaking, they are not gifts of the Holy Spirit but gifts of Christ Himself to His Church.

Each of the fivefold ministers has received one-fifth of the whole ministry of Christ Jesus. Though the fivefold ministries are equal proportionally, they are not the same in their divine abilities, functions, and ministries. The passage in Ephesians 4 quoted earlier goes on to say that they are all given for the equipping of the Saints. There is no particular Scripture that states what specific things evangelists, pastors, or teachers do. However, there are several Scriptures that state what apostles and prophets do. Ephesians 2:20 explains that they have the foundation-laying ministry in the Church. The Church is not a physical building; it is a "building" made of living blood-washed people. The apostles and prophets are foundational members upon which the rest of the members of the Church are built. They provide a structure for the equipping of the Saints.

God Puts Priority on Saints, Not Leaders: I am a bishop over several hundred churches. I strongly teach the governmental structure of the local church and the apostolic structure of the corporate Church, and I have spent much of my ministry helping to raise up and train those God has called as prophets and apostles. However, I believe that we who are in leadership need to take a new look at where God puts His priorities. The Day of the Saints will not do away with the government and leadership structure of the Church, but it will cause a paradigm shift in the way

Church leaders view the Saints. Instead of being preoccupied with our leadership titles, positions, and authority, we will become more Saints-oriented.

Fivefold ministers were given for the Saints, not the Saints for the fivefold ministers. Too many pastors feel that God gave them the Saints in their congregation to make them successful and to pay tithes so the pastors can be supported in the ministry, build greater buildings, be on television, and take missions trips. There is nothing wrong with all of these activities taking place, but the perception and motive of such a minister is contrary to God's purpose for giving apostles and pastors to His Church. For the Saints to be activated and effective, many ordained ministers will have to make some radical and revolutionary attitude adjustments. The Saints themselves must also receive revelation concerning their calling, privileges, and responsibilities to Christ and His leadership team.

THE NEW TESTAMENT WAS WRITTEN TO THE SAINTS

Apostle Paul addressed many of His epistles to those **"called to be Saints."**

> *Unto the church of God which is at Corinth, to them that are sanctified in Christ Jesus, **called to be saints**, with all that in every place call upon the name of Jesus Christ our Lord....*[16]
>
> *To all that be in Rome, beloved of God, **called to be saints**: Grace to you and peace from God our Father, and the Lord Jesus Christ.*[17]

*Paul, an apostle of Jesus Christ by the will of God, to the **saints** which are at Ephesus, and to the faithful in Christ Jesus.*[18]

The authors of the 27 books of the New Testament addressed their writings as follows:

- **To the Saints**, including the saved, sanctified, faithful in Christ Jesus:

    Romans, Ephesians, Philippians, Colossians, 2 Peter, Jude

- **To Hebrews**, the 12 tribes, pilgrims of the dispersion:

    Hebrews, James, 1 Peter

- **To "*my little children*":**

    1 John

- **To a named individual** and one "*to the elect lady*":

    Luke, Acts, 1 Timothy, 2 Timothy, Titus, Philemon, 2 John, 3 John

- **To the church** at a particular city and "*To the seven churches in Asia*":

    Galatians, 1 Corinthians, 2 Corinthians, 1 Thessalonians, 2 Thessalonians, Revelation

- Three of the Gospels were addressed **to no particular individual or group**:

    Matthew, Mark, John

As I analyzed each book, I was amazed to discover that all the Books of the New Testament were written to Saints, not to church leadership. It would not be proper protocol today for me or any other minister to send a letter to a local church and not address it to the local pastor. It would be seen as ministerially unethical to seemingly bypass the pastor or ignore his position by addressing a letter and greetings "To the Saints." Nevertheless, ten of the New Testament Epistles are so addressed. It is amazing that not one book is addressed to an individual with a fivefold ministry title.

A Pentecostal minister preached a message seeking to lessen the validity of present-day prophets and apostles in the Church. He suggested that there were no continuing prophets and apostles of the Church. One of his main points was the fact that none of the Books of the New Testament were addressed to an apostle or prophet. He neglected to mention that neither are any addressed to an evangelist, teacher, or pastor. Based on his logic and reasoning, we would have to question the validity of the ministry of pastors in the present-day Church, since no Books of the Bible were addressed to a pastor.

Even the Epistle to Ephesus is addressed to the Saints. This is the book in which the apostle Paul did the most teaching on the ministry of apostles and prophets and brought forth the revelation of the fivefold ministries that Christ gave, calling them apostles, prophets, evangelists, pastors, and teachers.[19] The Book of Philippians is the only one that mentions anyone in an overseeing position, and that is after the Saints are mentioned: "To all the saints in Christ Jesus who are in Philippi, with the bishops and deacons."[20]

Relationship Is More Important Than Position: When Paul addressed his letters to individuals such as Timothy, Titus, and Philemon, he did so based more on their relationship to him than on their position in the Church. Paul did not write, "To Pastor Timothy" or "To Timothy, pastor of the local church." He wrote, "To Timothy, a [true and] beloved son [in the faith]."[21] Let us all be open to the Spirit of truth and biblical revelation knowledge to set us free from some of our mind-sets and traditions that are not biblically accurate. As Christ aligns His Church, we will have to embrace truths that will seem revolutionary.[22]

THE MINISTRY OF ALL BELIEVERS

The Day of the Saints will bring revelation of truths that are as revolutionary as some of the major truths of the Protestant Movement. For example, during the Protestant Movement Martin Luther taught the revelation truth of "the priesthood of the believer."[23] This may not sound revolutionary to people who have been Protestant Christians all their lives and do not understand how the Catholic church functioned in those days. However, prior to the Protestant Movement, launched in 1517, the only two representatives of Christendom were the Eastern Orthodox churches and the Roman Catholic church. Members in those churches were not allowed to have a Bible to read. The priests, including all clergy in the Catholic church from the pope to the "father" of each local parish, were the only ones qualified to read the Bible and interpret its meaning. Church members could not go directly to God but had to come before the throne of God through their priest. Sins were confessed to the priest and not directly to God. Church members were completely dependent upon the priest for their relationship with God. Mother Mary and the priests were the mediators between the people and Jesus Christ. Average church members did not even expect direct access to Heaven when they died. The best they could hope for was to shorten their purifying time in the fires of purgatory by doing penance, paying for indulgences, and performing other good works.

The Priesthood of All Believers: The Protestant reformers taught that every Christian believer was a **"priest" unto God** and could approach the throne of God by the blood of Jesus and the grace of God, without the clergy of the church. Any person could confess sins to God and be forgiven without confessing to the priest or having the blessing of the pope or the intercession of Mary, "the Mother of God." In other words, in a personal relationship with God, every believer had the same rights and priestly privileges as the ordained priest of the church. You can see why the hierarchy of the Catholic church branded them as heretics and excommunicated them from the denomination. Catholic leaders declared that the Protestant teachings were anti-church and caused rebellion against the doctrine and delegated authority of the pope, God's vicar, and the priests and fathers who were his appointed religious leaders and mediators for the church members.

The Ministry of All Believers: In the Day of the Saints, the revelation truth that every Saint is a minister of the Lord Jesus Christ will be preached and practiced. This is another way of saying that every believer is a priest unto God. In the first-century Church, the word *minister* did not refer to a title of a clergy position but to a service rendered by the believer. Every Saint has the calling, privilege, and power to minister the Holy Spirit, the Word of God, and the graces of God to others. Every local church should be a congregation of ministers. We are going to see a mighty spiritual army of professionals, laborers, students, home-makers, and retirees demonstrating Christ Jesus' ministry and overcoming power over all the forces of darkness. In Chapter 8 the topic of Saints in the marketplace and public square (government) will be covered in more depth.

All Ministers Require the Same Things: One can better understand and accept this truth by asking the following questions. What does a Saint called to minister in the pulpit need that is different from what a Saint called to minister in the marketplace or public square needs? Nothing! Do the Christian businessperson, government official, and ordained clergy all need their sins washed away by the blood of Jesus? Do they all need to know Jesus as their personal Savior? Should they all be filled with the Holy Spirit and have a workable knowledge of the Word of God? Should they all have Christlike character, practice biblical principles, and be sold out to Christ for His own glory and purpose? The answer is YES! The calling and special divine enablement to fulfill one's calling is different for each Saint, but the needed biblical attributes are the same.[24]

The attributes a person needs to be a good president of a nation are the same attributes a person needs to be a good citizen of a nation. However, the calling to be president requires more preparation in specific skills and ability than the calling to be a citizen who does common labor. Each member of the human body being formed in the womb has a DNA that directs its formation to enable it to fulfill its membership calling. Every member of the natural body partakes of the 11 chemical elements and life-giving blood of the body, but these elements enable each member to perform a different function.[25] Likewise, every Saint participates in the biblical attributes of the Body of Christ, but each ministers differently according to individual calling and membership ministry.[26] In later chapters we will look at more specifics of how Saints can be equipped to function in their personal areas of responsibility.

Divine Church Structure Will Remain: The Saints must understand that the Day of the Saints will not release them to become a law unto themselves. God does everything in divine order. A proper foundation has to be laid before a building can be built. God is restoring the foundational ministries of the prophet and apostle before He fully builds the building of matured and activated Saints.[27] The Church is in the midst of a Prophetic-Apostolic Movement that is restoring the prophets and apostles back to the proper ministry, position, and authority in the Church that they originally had when Christ established His Church.[28] The last five decades of the twentieth-century Church re-emphasized and restored the fivefold ministers back into active ministry within the Church. Those who have Christ's vision, heart, and ministry to the Saints will be the generals and other officers leading God's great army of Saints.

    The first decade of the twenty-first century will see the Holy Ghost bringing revelation and proper alignment of the fivefold ministers according to Christ's original pattern so that Christ may fulfill His purpose in and through

His Church. I believe God's major purpose for the recognition, activation, and unity of the fivefold ministers is for them to fulfill their divine commission of equipping the Saints. Then the Saints may fulfill their membership ministries and be prepared to participate in the Day of the Saints. Please keep in mind that Church structure and divine order are as eternal as Christ and His Church.[29] The Church will always have different levels of God's delegated authority throughout eternity. The Day of the Saints will not lessen the leadership authority and importance of the local church, but will bring divine application that will make it more effective because it will be functioning according to God's full divine pattern.[30]

SAINTS ARE SAVED *TO* GOD'S PURPOSE

Why Human Beings Are Called to Be Saints: We want to reveal some of God's major reasons for calling people from the human race to be His Saints. Much more is involved than just saving them from hell and making them candidates for Heaven. Escaping God's punishment of the wicked in the eternal lake of fire, by accepting Christ's blood for the cleansing of sin and by receiving eternal life with Jesus Christ, is the foundational benefit of being a Saint of God. We who are Saints should never forget what Jesus saved us from and should always keep an attitude of indebtedness and thankfulness.[31] But what Christ Jesus saved the Saints **to** is far greater than what He saved us from.[32]

We Saints are not to live our Christian lives looking backward but looking forward, as we press toward the prize God has for those who fulfill their high calling as

Saints.[33] Christ Jesus has a calling, membership ministry, purpose, and destiny for every Saint.[34] He has a greater destiny for the corporate body of the Saints called the Church. My purpose is to help all Saints who read this book find their personal ministry and destiny, as well as to prepare them to participate in our corporate destiny.

The First-Century Church Saints: The New Testament describes the early Church Saints as being full of faith, active, and moving powerfully in signs and wonders.[35] From the Day of Pentecost, the believers preached the gospel with boldness and power until the Church had grown from approximately 120 people to thousands who went into the world and turned it upside down for Jesus Christ. When persecution hit Jerusalem the believers suddenly had to flee, leaving behind the apostles who had led them. Acts chapter 8, verses 1 and 4 tell what occurred:

> ...At that time a great persecution arose against the church which was at Jerusalem; and they [the Saints] were all scattered throughout the regions of Judea and Samaria, except the apostles....Therefore those who were scattered [the Saints] went everywhere preaching the word.

Did the Saints shrivel up in their faith because no pastor was there to hold their hands? No! Everywhere the believers scattered they rose up and demonstrated the message of the **gospel of the Kingdom** of God through miracles, signs, and wonders.[36] They confirmed Jesus' words that these signs shall follow those who believe:

> And He said to them, "Go into all the world and preach the gospel to every creature. He who believes

and is baptized will be saved; but he who does not be-lieve will be condemned. And these signs will follow those who believe: In My name they will cast out demons; they will speak with new tongues; they will take up serpents; and if they drink anything deadly, it will by no means hurt them; they will lay hands on the sick, and they will recover." [37]

More Christians but Not Full Believers: Nearly 2,000 years later **the gospel of salvation** through Jesus Christ has gone to every political nation, and efforts are underway to reach almost every ethnic group. Hundreds of millions of people consider themselves Christians. One-third of the world's population identify with some branch of Chris-tianity, whether they ever attend church or read the Bible.[38] Only the Holy Spirit knows for certain, but Church growth experts estimate that approximately one in ten of the world's people has a saving-faith knowledge of Jesus Christ.[39] However, even though the salvation message is being proclaimed, most Christians are not manifesting in their personal lives and ministry what Jesus said they would.

There are two primary types of meetings for the Saints in churches today. Some are based on tradition and ritual where the believers function as an audience. Mem-bers of the congregation are expected to participate where the ritual requires it and otherwise to listen to the minister as if they were attending a lecture. Other meet-ings are led by ministers who flow in various degrees of evangelism, prophecy, healing, and miracles, often with great fervor, excitement, and faith. When Christians in these churches find themselves drawn to the moving of the Spirit and feel an urge to participate, they often seek to go into "the ministry" themselves.

All Saints Will Be Great Ministers: Jesus has more for His Church than just getting more and more people into professional pulpit ministry. Before Jesus' return, His Church will operate in all the fullness that the Scriptures declare. Jesus Christ declared to His followers, "He who believes in Me, the works that I do he will do also; and greater works than these he will do, because I go to My Father."[40] For many years I have prophesied that in the near future, the average Saint will do greater works than the greatest minister today. That time is very near. Thank God for the ministry of men of God like Billy Graham, Oral Roberts, and Benny Hinn. But Jesus said that these signs will follow those **who believe**—not just those who have a well-known ministry, are on television, or stand behind a pulpit. All the believers/Saints are to manifest Christ's life and ministry.[41]

The demonstration of the gospel of the Kingdom of God was not just for the first-century Church. Chapter 7 of the Book of Daniel gives a key Scripture for the coming Day of the Saints:

*"But **the saints** of the Most High shall receive the kingdom, and possess the kingdom forever, even forever and ever." ...Until the Ancient of Days came, and a judgment was made in favor of the saints of the Most High, and the time came for **the saints** to possess the kingdom...." "Then the kingdom and dominion, and the greatness of the kingdoms under the whole heaven, shall be given to the people, **the saints** of the Most*

High. His kingdom is an everlasting kingdom, and all dominions shall serve and obey Him. "[42]

The remaining verses in the chapter reveal all the ministries that take place when the Saints are fully activated. These attributes and manifestations will be expounded upon in Chapter 10.

APOSTLES AND PROPHETS SENSE MAJOR CHANGES

Present-truth ministers are proclaiming that the Church will begin to function in a radically different way in the twenty-first century than it has in the past. The Church coming into the twenty-first century parallels Joshua and the children of Israel getting ready to begin their conquest of the promised Canaan land. Joshua told the people to sanctify themselves and follow the ark of the covenant, "...That you may know the way by which you must go, for you have not passed this way before."[43] Since the first century, the Church has not functioned with all fivefold ministers of apostles, prophets, evangelists, pastors, and teachers fully activated into their ministries and properly related to God and to one another.[44] Neither has it had all of its members activated and functioning in their membership ministries.[45] Other apostles and prophets in the Body of Christ are recognizing this transformation as well. Following is what a few of them are saying.

C. Peter Wagner, a widely-recognized church-growth expert and apostle/statesman in the Body of Christ, says, "The greatest change in the way of doing church since the Protestant Reformation is taking place before our very eyes." He continues:

My hypothesis is that the bride of Christ, the Church, has been maturing through a discernible process during the past few centuries in preparation for completing the task of the Great Commission. My starting point is the Protestant Reformation in which the theological underpinnings were firmly established: the authority of Scripture, justification by faith and the priesthood of all believers. The Wesleyan movement then introduced the demand for personal and corporate holiness.

The Pentecostal movement later profiled the supernatural work of the Holy Spirit in a variety of power ministries. The office of intercessor was restored in the 1970s and the office of prophet was restored in the 1980s. The final piece came into place in the 1990s with the recognition of the gift and office of apostle.

This is not to say that the Church is perfect. It is to say that the infrastructure of the Church, so to speak, may now be complete. The Church is much more prepared to advance the Kingdom with a speed and intensity that has not been possible in previous generations.[46]

In his book, *Shadows of Things to Come*, Rick Joyner looks at Church history to point the Church toward its future. He concludes:

The Lord has had a few Joshuas and Calebs who have been outstanding in their time, full of faith in doing great exploits. But now, at the end of the age, He is raising up a generation with the faith to cross over and possess their inheritance. Sam Jones, Evan Roberts, and William Seymour were great men of faith, but the Lord is about to release ten thousand like them, along with those like William Booth, Hudson Taylor, John Wesley, George Whitfield, Jonathan Edwards, Count Zinzendorf, John Knox, Luther, Peter, and even Paul—*all at the same time!* Together they will ignite a multitude of Nashville, Welsh, and Azusa Street Revivals, multitudes of Great Awakenings, and many Reformations—all together. A generation is arising that will see all of the things that every prophet and righteous man from the beginning longed to see. For those who love God, there has never been a greater day to be alive. The Lord has saved His best wine for last.[47]

Rich Marshall, author of *God@Work*, writes:

A new day is dawning in which the Lord is releasing into the marketplace an army of soldiers who will be used as frontline ministers for the work of the Lord. They are going to usher in a move of God unlike any we have seen....We are about to see a sovereign move of God, not a revival in the traditional sense. It will not be something that takes place in a church or something that can be characterized by a series of meetings. An evangelist or a pastor will not spark this move of God, at least in the traditional understanding....

I don't know how history will record it, and I am not even sure what to call it today. But I know this: God is actively working in the marketplace. We are returning to the Biblical standard where we can expect to see God at work through the lives of business and professional people, CEO's and managers, policemen and nurses, athletes and salespeople.

Yes, God is at work, and He wants to work through you![48]

In subsequent chapters of this book, we will see that the Church has been in the process of restoration for nearly 500 years in preparation for all these things to be fulfilled in the near future. We have not passed this way ever before.

A Blueprint for the Church: Ephesians 3:4-5 NIV declares that apostles and prophets have Christ's anointing for knowing the mysteries of Christ and His times and purposes for His Church: "...The mystery of Christ, which was not made known to men in other generations...has now been revealed by the Spirit to God's holy apostles and prophets." They have the anointing of the "sons of Issachar who had understanding of the times, to know what Israel ought to do."[49] Apostles and prophets have been given the keys for revelation knowledge.[50]

Even among apostles and prophets there are varied and special ministries. A few have the special anointing to receive Christ's blueprint for the Church and to have an overall view and an architectural model of the finished building of the Church. When Jesus made the all-important declaration, "I will build My Church,"[51] He had the blueprint and finished model of the Church in mind. That portion of the mind of Christ has been given to certain apostles and prophets in the Church. This does not make them lesser or greater than other fivefold ministers; it only gives them a greater responsibility to make these things known to Christ's Church.

Making Restoration Truth Known: Christian International has been teaching and training people in the truths of the Prophetic and Apostolic Movements, which are thoroughly covered in some of my other books.[52] The most important truths that were restored in those movements will be discussed in more detail in Chapter 5. These last two movements are bringing the revelation and restoration of prophets and apostles to the Church so that all fivefold ministries will be actively training the Saints for their work of ministry. All that has been restored to the Body of Christ thus far has been to enable each generation to fulfill its destiny and also to make the necessary preparation for activating the next major restoration movement on God's schedule.

The Next Thing on God's Agenda—the Saints Movement: The prophets were restored in the 1980s and the apostles in the 1990s. Now, in this first decade of the twenty-first century Church, it is God's predestined time for the Saints to fully come into their membership ministries. When the fivefold ministers have completed their divine commission of equipping and perfecting the Saints in Christlike character and ministry, then the full manifestation of the Saints can take place. In keeping with other restoration terminology, I have called this Holy Spirit-inspired time of activating God's people the "Saints Movement." It is destined to be a major restoration movement, not just a time of revival or refreshing. It will have the seven major attributes that have been a part of every major restoration movement.[53] Church history reveals that there have been five major restoration movements thus far. The Saints

Movement will be the sixth. We will cover these matters in more detail in coming chapters.

Why Use the Phrase "the Day of the Saints"? For practical purposes, the term the "Saints Movement" is interchangeable with "the Day of the Saints," and we will use both throughout this text. However, I have titled this book *The Day of the Saints* to emphasize some important points. Many Christians are awaiting the "Day of the Lord" or second coming of Jesus Christ. But before Christ returns in glory, He will be glorified in and through His Saints as they demonstrate their likeness to Him and their obedience to His commands.

The term *Day* in this case is not limited to one literal 24-hour day. Like "the day of salvation," it implies a fullness of time or an opportune time.[54] The Day of the Saints will probably last several years before its purpose is complete. Although it will be a genuine restoration movement, this is more than an event that will take place among a few theologians or trendsetters in Christianity. God is giving all His people an opportunity to fulfill all things prophesied about His Church in order to hasten the return of our Lord.[55] We aren't just waiting on Him. He is waiting on us!

ENDNOTES:
1. Daniel 7:18,27; Romans 8:17; Ephesians 1:18-20; 2:19.
2. Matthew 11:11.
3. Ephesians 1:17-19a.
4. John 5:19,30; 8:28; 14:12.
5. Ephesians 2:7.

6. James Strong, *Strong's Concordance* (Iowa Falls, IA: Riverside Book and Bible House, n.d.), **#G40**.

7. Robert Young, *Young's Analytical Concordance to the Bible* (Peabody, MA: Hendrickson Pub., Inc., 1993).

8. Numbers 7:1.

9. Galatians 2:20; Colossians 3:1-3; 1 John 2:15; Romans 14:17; Luke 17:21.

10. John 3:3,5; Romans 8:16; Colossians 1:13; 1 Peter 2:9.

11. Capitalization of the word *Saint* is for emphasis, not a reference to a particular person.

12. 1 Corinthians 3:9; 12:27.

13. Ephesians 2:22.

14. 1 Corinthians 12:7-11.

15. Ephesians 4:11.

16. 1 Corinthians 1:2 KJV.

17. Romans 1:7 KJV.

18. Ephesians 1:1 KJV.

19. Ephesians 2:20; 3:5; 4:11.

20. Philippians 1:1.

21. 2 Timothy 1:2.

22. John 16:13.

23. Bill Hamon, *The Eternal Church* (Santa Rosa Beach, FL: Christian International Publishers, 1981), pp. 175, 177. Much of the historical information on these pages can be found in greater detail in *The Eternal Church*.

24. 1 Corinthians 12:11; Romans 12:4.

25. Bill Hamon, "God's Earth Man," Bachelor of Theology Thesis, 1968, p. 13. Unpublished.

26. 1 Corinthians 12:27.

27. Ephesians 2:20.

28. Bill Hamon, *Prophets and the Prophetic Movement* (Shippensburg, PA: Destiny Image, 1990), p. 11.

29. Ephesians 3:11.

30. Hebrews 8:5 and Exodus 25:40; Matthew 16:18.

31. Isaiah 51:1; *Thompson Chain Reference Bible* study on "thankfulness."

32. Deuteronomy 4:20; John 3:1-3.

33. Philippians 3:14.

34. 1 Corinthians 12:27.

35. Acts 6:8.

36. Acts 8:4-6.

37. Mark 16:15-18.

38. One-third of earth's people call themselves Christians: 17% Roman Catholic, 10% Protestant, 4% Orthodox, and 2% marginal. Figures are approximate. Patrick Johnstone, *Operation World* (Grand Rapids, MI: Zondervan, 1993), pp. 23-24.

39. Ralph D. Winter and Bruce A. Koch, "The State of the World." *Mission Frontiers*, 22, no. 3 (June 2000), p. 22. The 11% of the world's population estimated to be Bible-believing Christians includes segments from each of the Christian groups listed in the previous endnote (as well as a smaller number from other religious groups such as messianic Jews). Also see www.missionfrontiers.org/newslinks/statewe.htm.

40. John 14:12b.

41. 2 Corinthians 5:20; 4:10.

42. Daniel 7:18,22,27.

43. Joshua 3:4b.

44. Ephesians 4:11.

45. 1 Corinthians 12:27.

46. C. Peter Wagner, *Churchquake!* (Ventura, CA: Regal, 1999), pp. 5, 110-111.

47. Rick Joyner, *Shadows of Things to Come* (Nashville, TN: Thomas Nelson, 2001), p. 222.

48. Rich Marshall, *God@Work* (Shippensburg, PA: Destiny Image, 2000), pp. 141-142.

49. 1 Chronicles 12:32a.

50. Luke 11:49-52.

51. Matthew 16:18b.

52. Hamon, *Prophets and the Prophetic Movement*, pp. 59-79.

53. Ibid, pp. 81-121.

54. 2 Corinthians 6:2.

55. 2 Peter 3:9.

CHAPTER 2

PROGRESSING, ARRIVING, AND BECOMING

Saints will not automatically begin manifesting the supernatural works of Jesus by sitting in the pews and doing "business as usual." Some of you reading this book will have the opportunity to make a paradigm shift—a complete change in your way of looking at the Church and the roles of believers. Change can be very uncomfortable. However, you have a choice: You can stay in your comfort zones, or you can become more like Jesus. You may feel that all your friends and relatives are like the 11 disciples sitting in the boat during the storm, but Jesus may be telling you, "Come."[1] Like Peter, you need to arise in faith and courage and get out of the boat to walk on the water of new truth and ministry with Christ Jesus.

REVELATION LEADS TO PROGRESSION

How We Become Who We Are: Every person's **physical** being is determined largely by his genetic heritage. The color of eyes, hair, and skin is determined by that of the parents, grandparents, and genealogical history. Our **soul**—intellect, emotional makeup, and personality—is determined some at birth. However, the way we think and function is mainly determined by our environment, education, experience, and all the things that have influenced us.

The sum total of who we are at the present as physical and soulish persons is determined by all the things just mentioned. Who we are in our **spirit** is determined by our relationship with God, who is a Spirit.[2] Our experiences with Jesus Christ, our salvation, our revelation and experience with His truth and Spirit-life, determine what type of Christian or minister we are in Christ's Church. In reality, a person cannot think or act any differently from what his total being has become over the years, just as a computer cannot perform and respond any differently from what has been programmed into it. Having God's grace and this understanding enables me to have patience with people who do not believe the way I do about God's purpose for His Church.

Revelation Can Make a Difference: The only exception to seeing things differently from the conditioning of past experiences and environment is receiving divine enlightenment. The Holy Spirit can suddenly illuminate our minds to see things never understood before, enabling us to respond differently.[3] The teaching and ministry we receive determines what type of Christian we will be.

Mentors are photographs of our futures. The teaching we receive and the anointing we respect become the beliefs we establish and the type of ministry we exhibit.

The fivefold minister who attracts and enthuses us the most becomes the model for our lives. Normally we will become a reproduction of that person. We can neither choose our biological parents nor decide what set of parents will raise us to adults. Sinners normally do not choose which minister will bring them to a saving knowledge of Jesus Christ. However, Christians can choose which church and minister they want to mentor them, especially if the church where they were "birthed" is not growing them beyond their babyhood Christianity.[4]

As a general rule, a minister will not advance beyond the restoration truth, doctrines, bylaws, and tenets of faith of his denomination. And a congregation will not advance beyond its pastor's degree of restoration truth and Christian maturity. The exception to the rule is when the minister or church member receives advanced teaching and spiritual experiences outside his local church or denomination.

For example, apostle Paul met several disciples who had been mentored by the teaching and ministry of John the Baptist. They had been "Baptist" Christians for quite some time before the following incident took place—20 years after John the Baptist was beheaded and 22 years after the Church was established.[5] They had been faithfully living and practicing their faith as good Baptist believers.

[Apostle Paul] *said to them, "Did you receive the Holy Spirit when you believed?" So they said to him, "We have not so much as heard whether there is a Holy Spirit." And he said to them, "Into what then were you baptized?" So they said, "Into John's baptism." Then Paul said, "John indeed baptized with a baptism of*

47

*repentance, saying to the people that they should be-
lieve on Him who would come after him, that is, on
Christ Jesus." When they heard this, they were baptized
in the name of the Lord Jesus. And when Paul had
laid hands on them, the Holy Spirit came upon them
and they spoke with tongues and prophesied.*[6]

In present-day terms, we would say that Paul, a
Charismatic minister, met some Evangelical Christians
who had never heard about the baptism of the Holy Spirit with the evidence of speaking in other tongues. He enlightened them on the more advanced truth, then prayed
for them to receive the gift of the Holy Spirit. They received and spoke in tongues, an action that updated them
in Christian truth and experience. If these Baptist Christians had never been exposed to the present truth from
the apostle Paul, which was beyond what anyone was
teaching and experiencing in their circle of Christian fellowship, they would have stayed on one level of Christianity for the rest of their lives.

During the Charismatic Renewal millions of Christians in
denominations that were established in past restoration
movements were exposed to the teaching on the gift of
the Holy Spirit with speaking in other tongues. Hundreds
of thousands received the experience and came out of
their denominations in order to fully receive, practice,
and propagate that truth. Many other ministers and Saints
who received the experience stayed and formed Charismatic groups within their denominations. Even now, some
30 or 40 years later, major denominations such as Lutheran, Methodist, and Baptist have 20 or 30 percent of their

ministers who are Charismatic. However, most denominational Charismatics have not advanced beyond the initial experience they received during the Charismatic Renewal. And most of those who started independent Charismatic churches also have not advanced beyond their original Charismatic experiences and teachings.

Many Never Make the Transition: Some people in Christendom have never advanced beyond their first involvement with Christianity. We could say there are Christian groups who have their camps set up all the way from Egypt to within the promised Canaan land. Some families have been camped in the Catholic church for numerous generations and have never, to this day, advanced on to the first restoration truth that was established some 500 years ago. Likewise, some have been historic Protestants for years and have never experienced Evangelical-Holiness Movement truths. In like manner, some Pentecostals have not advanced beyond what was restored in the Pentecostal Movement a hundred years ago. Even many Charismatics have not advanced into the Prophetic/Apostolic Movement truths and spiritual experiences. No doubt many who are now involved in the Prophetic and Apostolic will not move on to be leaders and participants in the Saints Movement.

As for me and my house, I do not want to stop anywhere short of the fullness of restored truth. With the mentors I have had and the exposure to teachings on restoration and revelation concerning God's overall purpose for His Church, I should always be a follower and promoter of restoration truth. Thanks be to God for keeping me open to newly restored truth. My long-term, in-depth study of Church history has made me knowledgable concerning the failures of past movements. We must be open to new truth, but not gullible to false revelations or the reviving of old erroneous teachings and practices.

Like everyone else, I am the sum total of my past. My personal testimony helps to outline the process of progressing, arriving, and becoming.

How the Author Came to Believe and Perceive

Spiritual DNA of the Author: Let me share some personal background so that you can see how I have developed in my concepts of Christ and His Church. I was born in southeastern Oklahoma, July 29, 1934. My father and mother were farmers; my two brothers, two sisters, and I were raised on a farm five miles from the small town of Boswell, Oklahoma. Electricity was not brought to our community until I was 15 years old, and telephone lines were brought in still later. My father's family was Methodist and my mother's family was Baptist. Because one church sprinkled and the other immersed people in water baptism, my parents could not agree on which church to attend. So they attended neither. After I became a minister, my mother revealed to me that she had received a born-again experience when she was nine years old and felt called to preach. My father had never had an experience with God.

First Experience With Church: I had never been inside a church building or been part of a church service until some ministers came to our community and built a brush-arbor about two miles from where we lived. About ten of us young men, including my brother, cousins, and friends, rode our horses to those brush-arbor meetings. Truthfully, most of us went because many young girls were attending. That was my initial motivation also, for I was dating a young lady whose mother had helped to sponsor the brush-arbor meetings. Like me, the young lady had not yet made a commitment to Christ.

Since there was no electricity, the meeting hosts hung kerosene lanterns on the poles that held up the brush covering. The local people who built the brush-arbor played string instruments and sang beautifully and loud. Every night the preacher preached and then gave a long persistent altar call for people to "get saved."

Bible Revelation and Confirmation: After attending a few nights, I noticed that the preacher was preaching out of a book called a Bible. I wanted to check out what the preacher was saying, so I asked my mother if we had one of those books. We had an old Gideon Bible with the back and some of the pages torn off. I took it and, without letting anyone know, began reading. I found that the Bible really did talk about life after death and that people would spend eternity in Heaven or hell. I developed a deep desire to escape that hot place called hell. If it was much hotter and more miserable than Oklahoma in July, I should avoid it by all means!

God Can Use Dreams to Motivate: During this time a dream made me even more desperate. In the dream a person was standing on a platform announcing that this was the train for Heaven; everyone who wanted to go should get aboard. I jumped on. As it began to ascend to Heaven and pass through some clouds, a voice said, "Give your ticket for Heaven now." Suddenly, everyone else went into Heaven and I was back on Earth. What was this ticket to get in and where did you get it? I had never needed a ticket for anything except when we rode our horses to town and paid a dime for a ticket to the weekly movie.

A few nights later I had another dream. The same things happened in this dream, only this time I pulled out a gun to force my entry through the gate to Heaven! But again, everyone else went in and I was back on Earth. Finally, in one of the messages during the brush-arbor meetings, the preacher said, "Jesus is the ticket to Heaven."

A point of contact activated a born-again experience. In the second week of the five-week revival, I began to seek God. Each night I walked my girlfriend home while leading my horse and then rode back to my house. After unbridling and unsaddling my palomino, Smokey, I shucked ten ears of corn for his feed. Then I knelt and lifted my hands as I had seen the Saints doing at the brush-arbor meetings. This continued for two weeks.

Nothing seemed to happen until the night of my sixteenth birthday. At her mother's urging, my girlfriend had gotten me a particular present. She gave it to me in a box that I tied onto the back of my saddle. After arriving at home and going through my regular routine, I opened the box, and there was a new Bible with a beautiful cover and a zipper that closed the cover around it. As I held it in my hands, something started happening within me. I do not remember what I prayed that was any different from what I had prayed for the prior two weeks, but suddenly I felt clean and pure with a glow filling my inner being. I started laughing and crying at the same time. I was kneeling beside my bed and did not realize I was getting louder and louder. My father awoke and threatened to give me a whipping if I did not shut up and go to sleep. I slipped out to the smokehouse and worshiped the Lord for two hours.

Down the Sawdust Trail: The next night, after working in the fields all day cultivating corn with a team of mules, my brothers and friends and I attended the meeting again. The preacher gave the same persistent altar call. Only this time, my girlfriend wanted to go forward and said she would if I would. As I stood up, she and three of her friends stood and we all walked down to the altar, which was no more than a rough 2-by-12 bridge board laid across some blocks of wood set up on the sawdust covered ground. As we started walking forward, all the singers and the preacher started shouting, "Hallelujah!" I wondered why they were getting excited—we were the ones going for the goods.

Receiving the Gift With the Evidence: As we knelt and began praying, I saw a vision of Jesus hanging on the cross speaking to me that He died for me so I might live for Him. As I was viewing this scene, words were pouring out of my mouth. In my natural conscious mind I was expressing thanks to God. A little elderly brother started praying with me. I wasn't conscious of his presence for awhile until I heard him praying loudly, asking God to "send the fire" and "send the rain." He then said, "Let it go, that's it!" I did not know what I was to let go of, so I took my hands off the altar. He then started saying, "That's it, just talk it out!" I thought to myself, *What is he trying to say? I'm talking as fast and loud as I can.*

However, I was surprised at what was coming out of my mouth. It was not my usual Okie English. For the next 30 minutes, a language in some other tongue flowed through me, and great joy filled me. I just kept talking and pounding the altar bench with my hands. I was told later that I had been preaching in the Spirit. All four young people who went to the altar with me received the gift of the Holy Spirit and began to speak in tongues. As I was carrying on at the altar, I could hear my horse-riding buddies laughing and making fun of me. But I did not care. I had something going on that was better than what they thought about me.

After the five-week revival ended, those who had accepted Christ met once a week with a preacher in a little one-room country school house about three miles from my home. These meetings continued for about three months. Then, for the first time, I rode my horse five miles to the town church attended by many of the Saints who had helped in the meetings.

Initial Church Group Involvement: I did not know one church group or denomination from another. These people said they were Pentecostal, and the name on the outside of the church building was Assembly of God. Those old Saints shouted, "danced in the Spirit," and sang with great enthusiasm (they seemed old to me since I was the only teenage young man in the church). They sang some songs such as "Power in the Blood," but the majority of the songs were about leaving this world and going to Heaven— "When I die, Hallelujah, by and by, I'll fly away." I had no intention of dying soon, but I rejoiced along with them about the future glories of Christ's second coming.

The preacher often preached on living separate from the world. Anything to do with sports or entertainment was sinful. A statement that I make sometimes is comical but somewhat realistic: "Everything was a sin but breathing, and that had to be done in church to be sanctified." Since I was hungry to learn all I could about my new faith, I put into practice what I was learning. God's grace kept me faithful to the Lord, though none of my family or former friends were Christians.

Six weeks before I was to graduate from high school, my family moved to Hollis, Oklahoma, to work in the cotton fields, because all of our hogs and some of our cattle had developed a disease and died. Somehow I finished high school and graduated while I was still 16 years old. In the fall we moved across the state line to Wellington, Texas. I lived with my parents until we had finished picking cotton that fall. During this time an experience established within me a truth that would determine the way I trained Saints in prophetic ministry more than 30 years later.

God's Providential Preparation: A brother I had met at church told me that he could pull 1200 pounds of cotton in one day. It didn't sound possible. The most I had ever picked or had seen anyone else pick was less than 400 pounds. This brother challenged me to come and work in the same field with him the following week. He worked with a 14-foot cotton sack while I worked with a 12-foot sack. He took two rows at a time and I took one, working off of one of his rows so that I could stay right with him. We worked over 12 hours that day, from dawn to dark. When he had his sack full and went to the weighing wagon to empty the cotton, I went with him. I stuck with him like Elisha did with Elijah. The first day, Monday, I broke my record by pulling over 400 pounds of cotton. On Tuesday I pulled over 500, over 600 on Wednesday, and 700 on Thursday. On Friday, our last day together, I pulled 818 pounds and my friend finally pulled his 1200. Just by working alongside someone who was a professional in his field and doing everything he did, I more than doubled my greatest ability and production.

This is the way I trained our core prophets who are now national and international prophets and apostles. My father used to say, "The way to train a young mule is to harness him with an old mule who knows how to pull the plow properly." If you are a young untrained Christian who wants to be much more fruitful and successful, then get harnessed with a mature man or woman of God who knows how to be a productive minister.

Making a Transition to New Restoration Truth: In October 1951 at age 17, I moved away from home and got a job in Amarillo, Texas. While I was attending the First Assembly of God, some of my friends started visiting a church that was having a great move of the Holy Spirit. That congregation sang their praises to God instead of shouting them. When the worship became lower in volume, prophecies were given. For an hour or more they would have waves of worship and prophecy. What my friends told me seemed strange compared to the Pentecostal shout and frenzied dance unto the Lord. But after a few weeks I was birthed into that type of worship, and I started attending that church regularly in October 1952.

Their preachers proclaimed a victorious Church with a glorious future. They also emphasized that every Christian has a membership ministry in the Body of Christ. For the first time, I heard teaching on the Church not being a denomination or church building but the many-membered corporate Body of Christ. I had given tongues and interpretation of tongues in my Pentecostal church, so now I began prophesying in the congregation during services.

Progressing to Be an Ordained Preacher: In my heart was a great desire to be a preacher, but I did not know if that was what God wanted. Even if He did, I did not know how to become one. In February 1953 a prophet came to the church and spoke to me my first personal word of prophecy, which gave me hope and encouragement that God was going to call me into the ministry. In late August I drove my 1948 Studebaker to Portland, Oregon, to attend Bible College. In October of that school year I received prophetic presbytery where four ministers prophesied much of my gifts, calling, and destiny. The following February I was ordained and launched into ministry at the age of 19. I evangelized for a month and then took a pastorate in Toppenish, Washington.

After being a single pastor for almost two years, I married Evelyn Hixson on August 13, 1955. During our six years of pastoring we traveled to an annual restoration conference in North Surrey, British Columbia, Canada, where the seeds of Church restoration were planted into my spirit. For the next 25 years, I studied Church history. I researched everything I could find that recorded the revivals and movements that had transpired in the Church since it began.

A Quick Work: Until my sixteenth birthday, I was an "American heathen" who was completely ignorant of spiritual things and committed to living for myself and my own pleasures. Three and one-half years later, I was an ordained pastor who was participating in the present move of the Holy Spirit and begging God to use me to change the world. Of course, God had many years of training and preparation planned for His young, headstrong minister before He could entrust me with His full purpose. But once I was born again, I never looked back. Eventually, I had the privilege of leading both my parents and all my brothers and sisters to the Lord. Today all of my children serve in the ministry with my wife and me, and all of our grandchildren know the Lord and can flow in the gifts of the Spirit.[7]

In the Day of the Saints, the process may be even quicker. Some people who have been lining the pews for years, and even some who have become comfortable in their pulpits, will opt to stay in their present situations. Meanwhile, the Holy Spirit will draw others out of the world's systems, infuse them with present truth through His anointed ministers, and make them into the radical warriors of the Saints Movement. Like young David who dared to fight against Goliath, they won't settle for the status quo, but will take up the weapons of warfare and over-come enemies until they see their families and areas of in-fluence come under the lordship of Christ Jesus.[8]

Eschatological Predictions vs. Prophetic Revelation: In the early years of my ministry, my eschatological view-points were based on the writings of dispensational the-ologians. I was expecting the imminent return of Christ, as I had been taught by my Pentecostal mentors. In fact, they implied that one was not a true believer if one did not expect Christ to return at any moment. Between 1954 and 1963 I taught in the local church I pastored and in churches I visited that the second coming of Christ would have to take place by the end of 1963. I spread Larkin's dispensational charts across the front of my church to show how it was all going to happen. Being a theologian, I had it all figured in my head. But my prophetic anoint-ing also caused me to sense in my spirit that something was going to happen in the early 1960s.

I don't think you need to be told that Christ's second coming did not take place in 1963. But something did happen. The Charismatic Renewal began to sweep through the Church world in 1963. Jesus Himself did not return, but His Holy Spirit did come upon the Church in a much greater way.

Some 25 years later, another dispensational minister predicted that Jesus was going to return in 1988. He even wrote a book giving 88 reasons why it would happen then. The second coming of Jesus did not take place in 1988, and many have since laughed at those predictions. Never-theless, something spiritually significant did happen that year. Another restoration movement took place—the Prophetic Movement. Ever since dispensationalism became popular among Evangelical and Pentecostal Christians four centuries ago, numerous dates have been set for the second coming of Christ.

My experiences and research caused me to reevaluate some of the dispensationalist beliefs I formerly held, and I am now more of a "restoration-reformation" theologian. Now let us look at the difference in the two beliefs and how they affect one's view of God's purpose for His Church.

"Going Up" vs. "Growing Up"

Different Theological Concepts: God has a purpose for His Church. How a person views God's purpose is determined by theological background. This in turn affects expectations about the second coming of Christ and end-time eschatology. Our views of God's purpose affects our beliefs concerning what part the Church will play in the fulfillment of all things. There are basically two major concepts: the dispensational viewpoint and the reformed restoration viewpoint.

The Dispensationalist Viewpoint—"Going Up": The dispensational viewpoint was established during the Evangelical Movement.[9] It is the view that the ministry of apostles and prophets was brought forth to lay the foundation of the Church Age and to write the books of the New Testament. When the foundation was finished and the Bible was completed, the ministry of the apostle and prophet was no longer necessary and was therefore dispensationally deleted from the Church.

Many dispensationalists also believe the same about the miraculous element of the Church. They do not believe that supernatural miracles, healings, demonic deliverance, or speaking in unknown tongues with the baptism of the Holy Spirit are still to be active in the Church today.[10] The only supernatural experience they accept is that of a born-again experience by the sovereign, supernatural work of the Holy Spirit. The main reason they accept that truth/experience is that it had already been restored in the Protestant Movement, when the dispensational viewpoint became popular.

The Dispensationalist Concept of the Church: The only purpose dispensationalists see for the Church is for the Saints to be witnesses of Jesus Christ for the salvation of others. Their view of the end-time Church is a lukewarm "Laodicean church" based on Christ's words to the church in Laodicea in Revelation 3. They believe there will be a remnant holding on in faith until Jesus comes and rescues the Church from total annihilation. They see the rapture— the translation of the Saints—as God's heavenly helicopter coming to evacuate the Saints off the Earth before the antichrist takes over the world and the great tribulation begins. The only purpose for Christ's second coming is to remove the Saints from the Earth so they will not be here when the woes and judgments of God's wrath are poured out upon the wicked of the earth. With this concept, most of them believe in a pre-millennial and pre-tribulation rapture. This means that they believe the next item on God's agenda is the "going up" of the Saints out of this world, which they believe will occur before the great tribulation.[11] Dispensationalists see evil in the world as evidence that Jesus is coming at any moment, and they believe the only thing preventing Him from returning is His grace in giving the unsaved more time to be born again.

The dispensationalist viewpoint is currently held by many Christians who describe themselves as Evangelical or fundamentalist. Even many Pentecostals, who believe the baptism of the Holy Spirit is a valid experience in the Church today, agree with the dispensationalist viewpoint of the end-time purpose of the Church. Some groups emphasize that there will be merely a "remnant" or "chosen few" left in the Church when Jesus returns. Therefore, their primary goal is to keep themselves apart from the corrupt world system until they are rescued to Heaven. Many others emphasize the need to witness to as many people as possible in the short time left before Christ returns. Basically, they believe the purpose of the Church is to win more Christians so more people will be saved from hell. Then God will have a big family of redeemed people whom He can take to Heaven to love on and enjoy throughout eternity. They look forward to going to Heaven to have an eternal vacation and get away from their problems on Earth. This was some of my thinking when I was expecting the second coming of Christ to take place in 1963.

Evangelicals Are Missions-Minded: Because these groups have a greater vision for the "quantity" of the Church than for the full restoration or "quality" of the Church, they have been used of God to introduce many to a saving knowledge of Jesus Christ. Through their preaching of the gospel of salvation, multimillions have been led to the Lord. Some of the largest denominations in the world have grown because of their vision for outreach and missions. Many of these believers read their Bibles regularly, pray, disciple others, and are committed to abstaining from sin. They are faithful to the vision they have received.

Holy Spirit Revelation: However, Jesus has more for His Church and for planet Earth. Many years ago when everything seemed to be going wrong, I was having a major "pity-party" and praying to die, asking God to let me escape the misery of this world. I heard the Lord answer back. He said, "Bill Hamon, isn't it strange that you are wanting to get up and out and I am wanting to get back and down to Earth?" Someday I will meet Him in the air as He is coming back and I am going up. But until that time I want to help Him fulfill what He wants to do down here on planet Earth.

Dennis Peacocke, a speaker and author who likens the Kingdom of God to a godly business enterprise or franchise, had a similar experience. He writes:

> I clearly remember one day in 1987 when I was out jogging, and the Holy Spirit impressed me with the statement: "Dennis, you and I are going in opposite directions. I'm moving more and more to get on the earth, and you're waiting to get off it." I began to weep, for I began to comprehend the problem. God's kids are trying to get off the planet and into the "spirit" while God is moving to get increasingly on

the planet and into the material world through His children, to extend His franchise. All of a sudden Christ's prayer, "Thy kingdom come, thy will be done, on earth as it is in heaven" (Mt. 6:10), took on a whole new level of understanding.[12]

Eternity with Christ—Eternal Vacation or Vocation? God gave me some revelation and insight concerning what the Saints will be doing in Heaven, on God's new Earth, and in the ages to come. Now I seek to give Saints a greater vision of their inheritance in Christ as joint-heirs with Jesus in all that He is going to be and do, both now and throughout eternity.[13] Saints need to know that eternity with Christ is not an eternal vacation, but an eternal *vocation*. We will not be hallelujah hobos, drifting clouds, or wandering stars; nor will the Saints ever become angels, cherubim, or seraphim. We will forever be redeemed mankind, the Saints.

Eternity with Christ is living in a real heavenly world that includes God's government, the work of carrying on God's business, and a social order of Saints relating to one another and ministering to one another with God's love. The Body of Christ is as eternal as its head, Christ Jesus; therefore, membership in that Body is an eternal calling. Saints need to be delivered from the Dark Age concept of Heaven as a mythical, spooky place where people float around in long robes with strange looks on their faces and halos over their heads, doing nothing but praising the Lord continuously as they drift through eternity. God's new Heaven and new Earth will be real places with real people living and working together, doing realistic things.

If we are faithful stewards, we will rule and reign with Christ. That is why it is important for the Saints to operate according to Kingdom principles as business people and leaders. Read Isaiah 65:17-25 to discover some of the things that will take place after God creates new heavens and a new Earth.

The Restoration Viewpoint—"Growing Up": Reformation-restoration theologians teach that the whole New Testament is the blueprint for the building of the Church. Every truth, ministry, and supernatural manifestation found within the Bible is for the Church to receive, believe, and manifest today. According to this viewpoint, the first-century Church was the pattern for the whole age of the mortal Church. But there came a great falling away of the true Church that began around the third century and continued until nearly all the truths and supernatural ministries of the Church were lost. The Church went into a thousand-year period of time called the "Dark Age of the Church" that lasted until the 1500s. At that time the period of the Great Restoration of the Church began.

The restoration of the Church has progressed since that time by "restoration movements." Each restoration movement has restored back into the Church some of the truths and ministries that were lost during the great falling away. Restoration theologians believe that the greatest apostasy of Christ's Church has already taken place. Although the world's cup of iniquity will continue to increase and false voices will go out seeking to deceive even the elect, the progressive Church as a whole will overcome and grow more and more glorious. Restoration

Christians believe that before Christ returns the Church will be fully complete in **maturity** as well as in the **number** of members.

> *To each Saint was given a white robe, and they were told to be patient a little longer until the **number** of their fellow servants and of their brethren, who were to die as they had died should be **complete**.*[14]

The Church will not "go up" until it has "grown up." Part of "growing up" for the Church includes the restoration of all things so that the Church will be conformed to the image of Christ. We do not want to be guilty of the failure of the generation to which Isaiah gave the prophetic indictment, "None saith, Restore!"[15] None of the leaders of that time were believing for or working toward bringing restoration to God's people and the nation of Israel. No one had a vision for restoration. Though none were saying restore, yet God declared, "I will restore."[16] Not only will the gospel of salvation be preached to the entire world, but also the gospel of the Kingdom of God, which includes speaking the words of Jesus and doing all the supernatural works that Jesus did. In this way the Church will truly be the manifested Body of Christ on the earth.

Ten Times More Scriptures on Growing Up: The Bible is clear that Christ Jesus is interested in His Church coming to full maturity. The Scriptures definitely teach there will be "line upon line, precept upon precept," restoration of truth upon restoration of truth until the Church comes to its divinely predestined purpose. There are three Scriptures that talk about the Saints "going up."[17] But there are more than 30 that talk about the Saints "growing up."[18] The Scriptures speak of restoration; growing from faith to faith, strength to strength, glory to glory; and growing in grace and knowledge until we "grow up in all things into Him" and are "conformed to the image of His Son," "a glorious church, not having spot or wrinkle," "like Him," "to a perfect man, to the measure of the stature of the fullness of Christ." God puts ten times more importance on our maturing into Christ's image and ministry than He does on our being raptured to Heaven. Let us major in what God majors in.

GOD'S PROVISION AND PREPARATION FOR RESTORATION

Jesus and His Church are joint-heirs in everything. Ministers who promote the restoration of the Church view the Church (the Saints) as playing a vital role in all God has purposed to do in and through the human race. God has had His special people who have been instrumental in fulfilling His purpose on Earth from the creation of Adam, and He will continue to use such people throughout the history of the human race.

God Himself created the heavens and earth. Planet Earth was created with the substance from which God wanted to create the body of man. God's six days of creation prepared the Earth for man's habitation. God formed man's body from the dust of the Earth and then breathed into him His eternal breath of life. The heavenly Father created for Adam and Eve, His son and daughter, a beautiful, magnificent home called the Garden of Eden, which was to be their headquarters for fulfilling God's purpose. The Creator made them in His own image and likeness and commissioned them to take dominion over everything He had created on Earth, to subdue it, to be fruitful and to reproduce themselves until they filled the whole earth with God's glory.[19]

Throughout history God has used His people to fulfill His purpose on Earth. Noah built the ark to preserve and transition the human race from the old world to the new. **Abraham** was used to start a special chosen race of God's people who became the nation of Israel. God promised Abraham He would bless him and the race that he fathered, and all people on Earth would be blessed through them. **Moses** was used to bring God's people out of their bondage in Egypt and to give them God's law, their pattern for living according to God's ways and not those of the nations around them. He built God's tabernacle, the place designated for God's presence to dwell among them. **Joshua** was instrumental in taking the people of Israel across the Jordan River and destroying by military force the inhabitants of the land. He established Israel as a nation in their "promised land" of Canaan.

Samuel started the school of prophets that launched hundreds of prophets as God's main voice of communication to humankind. He also established the reign of kings over Israel. **King David**, the man "after [God's] own heart," defeated the enemies of Israel and established her as a godly nation chosen to fulfill God's purpose.[20] **Daniel** received a revelation that Jeremiah's prophecy concerning Israel's 70-year captivity was reaching fulfillment and that it was time for full restoration.[21] He began to intercede in prayer for the prophetic fulfillment of Israel's restoration to their homeland.[22] EVER SINCE GOD CREATED MANKIND, HE

HAS DONE NOTHING ON EARTH WITHOUT A PERSON PARTICI-
PATING WITH HIM IN BRINGING IT TO PASS.

God could not find a man who could fulfill His major purpose of bringing redemption and reconciliation of man back to God.[23] Therefore, God sent His own Son to become a mortal man.[24] **Jesus** became the only human to be fathered by God Himself. Adam was created by the hand of God, but Jesus is the only begotten Son of God.[25] God's perfect man, the only sinless man to ever live, became the perfect and only acceptable sacrifice for the redemption of mankind. Through Jesus' death, burial, and resurrection, a new creation of humankind was brought into being. A people that were not a people became the people of God.[26] They became a new race upon the earth called the Church race.

The only way to become a part of this new race is to be born again, not by a natural birth, but by a spiritual birth.[27] By believing in the heart and confessing with the mouth that Jesus Christ died for his sins and rose again, a person receives Christ into his life. He is "born again" and becomes a **new creation** in Christ. Old things pass away and all things are made new.[28] When a person becomes a new creation by being born of God, Almighty God becomes his Father and Jesus Christ becomes his Lord and Savior. He is baptized into a Body of anointed believers called the *Ekklesia* in Greek, or the Church, the new creation race of special called-out Saints.[29]

GOD'S RESTORATION PROCESS IS CONTINUING

Who Are Restoration Christians? Basically, every Protestant is a restoration person—a member of a church denomination that came into existence because of a restoration move-ment. The restoration movement restored certain truths, ministries, and practices—present in the early Church—that were not active in the existing churches at that time. In order to propagate and practice these truths, some be-lievers found it necessary to start a new church group or denomination.

A Key Example Is Martin Luther and the Lutheran Church: God used Luther to restore the truth that one can become a child of God solely by God's grace and faith in Jesus Christ, without the religious tradition and self-works of doing penance as taught and practiced by the Roman Catholic church.[30] Until the 1500s, the Catholic church was the only Christian church in the Western world. Luther himself was a Catholic priest. However, the restora-tion truth that Luther preached caused his denomination to excommunicate him.[31] They declared his teaching to be contrary to church teachings that were sanctioned by the pope. Luther's teachings caused the first restoration movement called the Protestant Movement. Ultimately, he became the founder of the first restoration church or new church denomination (Lutheran) that came into being because of a restored truth that had been lost during the Dark Age of the Church. That was the beginning of the period of the Great Restoration prophesied by apostle Peter in Acts 3:21.[32]

Restoration Churches: Every mainline Protestant church denomination came into being and exists today because of a restoration movement that has taken place during the last 500 years.[33] Every mainline Protestant Christian belongs to a denomination that became established because of a major restoration movement. Therefore, all Protestants are restoration Saints to some degree. Differences lie in how much they want to be restored. As explained, most Saints' vision goes only as far as the restoration of truth that was encompassed in the founding of their denomination. But the Holy Spirit's work of restoring all truth has not ceased after any given restoration movement was brought forth and certain denominations were established. No restoration movement thus far has restored all the truths and spiritual experiences that Christ has predestined for the fully restored Church. But each has restored some of the total truth that God intends for His Church.

So how will we know when the period of the restoration of the Church is completed? There is a statement of truth that is trustworthy for determining whether more restoration movements are coming to the Church: **IF THE LITERAL SECOND COMING OF CHRIST HAS NOT TAKEN PLACE YET, THEN MORE SPIRITUAL RESTORATION IS COMING TO THE CHURCH.**

Acts 3:21 emphatically states that the second coming of Christ cannot take place until all things are restored. Jesus is extremely desirous to return for His Church. As soon as the last thing that the apostles and prophets have prophesied and that is written in the Bible concerning the Church is fulfilled, then immediately Christ will give a great shout, Gabriel will blow his trumpet, and Jesus will return accompanied by the spirits of the departed Saints.[34] The moment the last thing is restored, Jesus Christ will resurrect the bodies of the Saints and reunite them as redeemed spirit-soul-and-body people. During the same moment, He will immortalize the bodies of the Saints still living on Earth, instantly lifting them up in the air to join with the other Saints.[35] By this miraculous act, Christ Jesus will reunite His Church from Heaven and from Earth into one eternal Church to be His Bride and co-reign with Him over Heaven and Earth.

Based on this scriptural truth, if we believe the second coming of Jesus Christ has not taken place yet, then we must believe for more restoration. For if all things were already restored, Christ Jesus would have already returned as sovereign Lord and King over all the Earth. If all things have been restored, we should now be resurrected and translated Saints in the immortal Church. Since we have not received that experience and are not functioning as an immortal Church, then Christ has not returned and all things are not restored and fulfilled in the mortal Church. For this reason, present-day Saints should be working toward and believing for more restoration, rather than just gazing into the heavens hoping for the second coming at any moment.[36]

Preach on the Truths That Produce God's Purpose: We should be preaching more about the Day of the Saints than about the imminent return of Christ. Preach His second coming, but also prepare the way and make ready a people so that Christ can return. We are not waiting on Him; He is waiting on us! While some Christians have been asking for His literal coming, Christ has been coming spiritually again and again to the Church in several major restoration movements.

Evangelicals and Pentecostals have been declaring for hundreds of years that the next thing on God's agenda is the second coming of Christ. As when Noah proclaimed for 100 years that a flood was coming, one of these days the declarations will be right. He will come! Christ's prophesied second coming will soon be history just as the prophesied flood is now history. However, if Noah had preached about the flood, but had not at the same time prepared the ark so he and his family could be the transition generation, they would not have been prepared to make the transition from the old world to the new.[37] Today a transition generation of people are preparing their ark of conformity to the image of Christ so that they can make the transition from the old Earth to the new Earth.[38] We cannot hasten His coming by just longing for it, but we can hurry it along by co-laboring with the Holy Spirit in restoring all things.

JESUS AND HIS CHURCH WILL CO-LABOR FOREVER

God's Home and Headquarters on Earth: While Jesus was on Earth, His natural body was the home and headquarters of God here on Earth. Now the Church, as the corporate Body of Christ, is the home and headquarters for Jesus Christ here on Earth.[39] The personal body of Jesus was used of God to provide all things, overcome all things, and fulfill and accomplish all things necessary for the redemption of mankind. The shedding of His blood paid the price for the purchase of His Church.[40] He authorized it by His resurrection from the dead. He then birthed the

73

Church by His Holy Spirit on the Day of Pentecost.[41] The body of Jesus contained the fullness of God and was used to accomplish all of God's will and purpose for the human race.[42]

God's purpose for the human race was to have a special group of redeemed people to be in relationship with Him and to show forth His glory on the Earth.[43] These special people make up His Church.[44] It was God's purpose for the Church to be the Bride of Christ, thus making the Saints who are part of the Church/Bride heirs of God and joint-heirs with Christ Jesus.[45] This means that the Church is one with Christ and participates with Him in all that He shall ever do or be both now and throughout eternity.[46] Does God have a purpose for the Church? Yes, just as much as He had and has a purpose for Christ Jesus.[47] God has purposed for the Church to be the full expression of Christ Jesus as Jesus is the full expression of His heavenly Father.[48]

Jesus Personally Fulfilled His Part: In His physical body on Earth, Jesus fulfilled every prophecy concerning Himself personally until His second coming. "But those things which God foretold by the mouth of all His prophets, that the Christ would suffer, He has thus fulfilled."[49] When Jesus declared, "It is finished!" and "[Father,] I have finished the work which You have given Me to do," it revealed that Jesus had finished the work that had to be done by Himself personally, alone.[50] That part of Jesus' ministry is over forever. After Jesus had fulfilled all things, He ascended back to His Father who then said to

Him, "Sit at My right hand, till I make Your enemies Your footstool."[51]

Jesus' Main Ministry Now: Jesus now sits at the right hand of God in that heavenly place making intercession for the Saints.[52] He is praying that we may finish all He began and accomplish all that He appropriated for His Church. Never again will He have to do anything alone. Whatever else is to be done, He will do with, in, and through His Saints! Jesus is interceding for His Saints that they will work with His heavenly Father to make all His enemies His footstool, to restore and fulfill all things, to prepare the way and make ready a people for His second coming.

Jesus has eternally joined Himself unto His Church. He united Himself with His Church in its **origination** and did not forsake His Bride during the period of **deterioration**. He has continued to give Himself to His Church time after time in **restoration**, and He will continue until His Church/Bride reaches Her **ultimate destination**. Jesus has delegated His "power of attorney" unto His Church for the performance of His eternal purpose. Just as Jesus declared that the Father had delegated all authority unto Him, so has He now delegated all of His authority unto His Church.[53] This does not take glory from Jesus, just as Christ having all the power of the Father did not distract from God's glory. The authority of Jesus was based upon His doing the will of His Father. In like manner, the authority of the Church Saints is based upon their ministering with the mind of Christ according to God's Word, will, and way.[54]

All things yet to be revealed, restored, or fulfilled will be accomplished in, by, and through Christ's Church. Jesus knows that His Father has decreed that He must be held in heaven "until the restoration of all things, which God has spoken by the mouth of all His holy prophets since the world began."[55] Father God has declared to His Son, "You have paid the extreme price. You have provided all things and have accomplished all things necessary for every purpose of Mine to be fulfilled. You have done it all. Now sit here at My right hand and enjoy watching Your Church, which You purchased with Your own blood and empowered by Your Holy Spirit, subdue all Your enemies and put them under Your feet as Your footstool."[56]

What Is Next on God's Agenda? The next major thing to take place on God's divine timetable is not the second coming of Christ but another major restoration movement. There can be **no second coming until there is a full restoration** of all things spoken by the prophets. This is what apostle Peter was making reference to when he told us to hasten the coming of the Lord![57] We cannot hasten Christ's coming by just preaching that it is going to happen soon. But we can hasten it by preparing the way and making ready a people for His second coming.[58] We prepare the way by receiving prophetic revelation on what needs to be restored and then becoming instruments in the hand of the Holy Spirit.[59] We make ready a people by transforming every Saint into the image and likeness of Jesus so that he or she can manifest Christ's full manhood and ministry.[60]

The Omega Generation: Present-day fivefold ministers and Saints must accept the reality that there are things the last generation of the mortal Church must fulfill and accomplish before Christ can return. In order for the "Omega Generation" Saints to fulfill God's purpose, they must come to the fullness of all the way, truth, and life of Christ.[61] The Saints must come to the unity of the faith until they become one, even as Jesus and His Father are one.[62] Jesus declared that the world would not believe and be won until the Saints are united with one another in Him. The greatest harvest ever recorded in Church history will happen when this unity takes place. Apostle Paul declared by divine revelation that all fivefold ministers must continue ministering to the Saints until every member of the Body of Christ is fully functioning in their membership ministry.[63]

The Saints are Christ's instruments for prophetic fulfillment. The twenty-first century Church has a destiny to fulfill prophetic Scriptures just as Jesus fulfilled prophecies. There are many Old and New Testament prophetic Scriptures yet to be fulfilled by the Church. The mortal Church must fulfill all Scriptures pertaining to God's purpose for the last generation Church before Jesus can return. Therefore, **it is necessary for us to understand those prophetic Scriptures that must be restored and activated into reality before Jesus can be released from Heaven.** When we know the things that must yet be activated, restored, and fulfilled in order for Christ to return, then we can knowingly co-labor with God for their full restoration.[64]

Now we will take a look at the early Saints who established the original Saints Movement, in order to understand the inheritance God is in the process of restoring to us as twenty-first-century Saints.

ENDNOTES:

1. Matthew 14:29b.
2. John 4:24.
3. Ephesians 1:18; 3:3-5.
4. Hebrews 5:12-14.
5. Acts 19:1-6.
6. Acts 19:2-6.
7. For more details on the spiritual multiplication process, please see Dr. Hamon's book *Birthing God's Purposes* (Santa Rosa Beach, FL: Christian International Publications, 2000).
8. Matthew 20:16.
9. The dispensational viewpoint is also known as cessational, which comes from the belief that the apostles and prophets and supernatural manifestations of the Holy Spirit ceased with the completion of the Bible.
10. Bill Hamon, *The Eternal Church* (Santa Rosa Beach, FL: Christian International Publishers, 1981), p. 133.
11. Revelation 7:14.
12. Dennis Peacocke, *Doing Business God's Way* (Santa Rosa, CA: Rebuild, 1995), pp. 5-6.
13. Ephesians 3:10,21; Romans 8:17; Revelation 2:26-27; 1 Corinthians 6:1-3.
14. Revelation 6:11 (Phillips); See also Luke 14:23.
15. Isaiah 42:22b KJV.
16. Joel 2:25a.
17. 1 Thessalonians 4:16-17; 1 Corinthians 15:51-52; Philippians 3:21.
18. Scriptures on progressive growth include Psalm 84:7; 92:12; Proverbs 4:18; Isaiah 28:10; Hosea 6:3; 14:5,7; Malachi 4:2; Mark 4:32; Acts 3:19-21; Romans 1:17; 8:29; 2 Corinthians 3:18; Ephesians 2:21; 4:12-13,15; 5:27; Philippians 3:14; 2 Thessalonians 1:3; Hebrews 2:10; 5:14; 6:1-2; 1 Peter 2:2; 2 Peter 1:5; 3:2; 1 John 3:1-3.
19. Genesis 1:26-27; 2:8.

20. 1 Samuel 13:14.

21. Daniel 9:2.

22. Daniel 9:3-19.

23. Isaiah 59:16.

24. John 3:16.

25. John 1:14.

26. 1 Peter 2:10.

27. John 3:6.

28. 2 Corinthians 5:17.

29. W. E. Vine, *Vine's Expository Dictionary of New Testament Words* (Nashville, TN: Thomas Nelson Publishers, 1940), p. 1308.

30. Hamon, *The Eternal Church*, p. 121.

31. Ibid, pp. 149-156.

32. It is noteworthy that the official day set by historians as marking the end of the Dark Ages and the beginning of the Protestant Movement, the movement most akin to the coming Saints Movement, is October 31, 1517. At that time October 31st was known as the eve of the day designated "All Saints Day."

33. Hamon, *The Eternal Church*, "Restoration of the Church" chart, p. 158.

34. 1 Thessalonians 4:16-17.

35. 1 Corinthians 15:51-52.

36. Acts 1:11.

37. Genesis 6:13-14.

38. 2 Peter 3:13.

39. Ephesians 2:22.

40. Acts 20:28; Ephesians 5:23-32.

41. Romans 1:4; Acts 2:1-4,17-21.

42. John 17:4; 19:30.

43. Ephesians 1:12.

44. 1 Corinthians 12:12-27.

45. Revelation 19:7-8; Romans 8:17.

46. Ephesians 3:21.

47. John 17:18.

48. Hebrews 1:3; 2:10; Romans 8:29.

49. Acts 3:18.

50. John 17:4; 19:30.

51. Hebrews 1:13b.

52. Romans 8:34.
53. Matthew 28:18-19; Luke 10:19.
54. 1 Corinthians 2:16; Bill Hamon, *Prophets and Personal Prophecy* (Shippensburg, PA: Destiny Image, 1987), pp. 87-103.
55. Acts 3:21.
56. Acts 3:21; Hebrews 1:13.
57. 2 Peter 3:12.
58. Luke 1:17.
59. Ephesians 3:5.
60. Romans 8:29; Ephesians 4:11-16.
61. John 14:6; Galatians 2:20; Colossians 3:1-4.
62. John 17:21-23.
63. Ephesians 4:11-13.
64. 1 Corinthians 3:9; 2 Corinthians 6:1.

CHAPTER 3

THE FIRST-CENTURY SAINTS MOVEMENT

The pattern for the coming "Day of the Saints" is the Saints Movement that changed the world in the first century. Our understanding of the first-century Saints Movement comes from the Book of Acts and the New Testament epistles. Since the Holy Spirit is restoring all the truths and practices that were present in the early Church, it is important that we understand them. Before we look at the Saints Movement, we will briefly describe the "movements" that came first—the "Jesus the Messiah" Movement and the Early Church (Apostolic) Movement.

THE "JESUS THE MESSIAH" MOVEMENT

After a 400-year period of silence since the Old Testament prophets spoke, the nation of Israel had been conquered by Rome; many Jews were looking for their prophesied Messiah. At that time, John the Baptist began preaching for men and women to "Repent, for the kingdom of heaven is at hand!"[1] Then he pointed to another, Jesus Christ, of whom he said, "Behold! The Lamb of God who takes away the sin of the world!"[2] This man Jesus began teaching the multitudes about the Kingdom of God. He demonstrated the works of the Kingdom: setting captives free, opening blind eyes, casting out demons, healing the sick, and raising the dead.

Many began to believe that Jesus was the Christ, or Messiah, the Anointed One. His popularity increased and He gained many followers. At the same time the religious establishment set themselves in opposition to Him. The Pharisees, who considered themselves experts in the law of Moses, took the lead in opposing Jesus. They were not looking for a new "move" of God but for a fulfillment of their interpretations of biblical prophecies and the traditions they had developed over time. They expected a political savior for the Jewish nation who would free them from the shackles of bondage to the heathen Roman Empire.

A Supernatural Kingdom: Jesus was not interested in fulfilling the Pharisees' expectations. He had come with a purpose from His heavenly Father. By fulfilling the law and the old covenant, He could usher in a new covenant. He outlined the bylaws of His own Kingdom, one that is not of this Earth. The proofs that made the message of Jesus as the Messiah believable were the miracles, signs, and wonders He performed.[3] The people were astounded both by the supernatural demonstrations of power and by His words of wisdom and authority.[4]

When Jesus kept speaking of a supernatural kingdom, rather than a temporal one, some of His followers became disillusioned. Judas Iscariot was one of them; his disappointment led him to betray Jesus for 30 pieces of silver. Many more of Jesus' followers had their hopes dashed when Jesus was tried and crucified by the religious leaders and the Roman authorities. The movement that proclaimed Jesus as Israel's Messiah and looked to Him for leadership was shaken. Even the disciples who had spent three years with Him were in confusion and despair between His crucifixion and His resurrection.

But the movement took a dramatic turn when Jesus appeared to the 12 apostles and to many of His disciples as having arisen from the dead. Now He was recognized not only as the Messiah, but also as the incarnation of God Himself. From that point on Jesus' followers began proclaiming Him as the Firstborn from the dead, the One who has conquered death, hell, and the grave.[5] Those who put their trust in Him are given the opportunity to receive eternal life, just as Jesus proved that He has eternal life. "For God so loved the world that He gave His only begotten Son, that whoever believes in Him should not perish but have everlasting life."[6]

The Restoration of Humanity to God and the Establishment of the Church: The man Christ Jesus was the person God provided to bring the redemption and restoration of humankind. Jesus came and died on the cross, giving His life's blood to save humanity from sin. But bringing humanity out of sin was not an end in itself. It was a means to an end.

Jesus brings people out of satan's sin-bondage to make them members of His Church. Christ's redemptive purpose was to produce a people who would be the Saints of God called the Church. If you do not understand that God's eternal purposes revolve around Jesus Christ and His Church, then you will never grasp the need and purpose for Church restoration. Each movement builds upon the prior one. Jesus said He came not to destroy the law, but to fulfill it.[7] His coming prepared the way for the apostolic move and the gift of the Holy Spirit. The Holy Spirit guided the early Saints and has since been leading the Church into all truth, including that which was lost and is now being restored.

Jesus had provided all things for the birth, growth, and maturity of His Church.[8] He planned, purchased, produced, and empowered it. He made methods, means, and provisions for its perfection and presentation to Himself as a glorious Bride without spot, wrinkle, or blemish, perfect in purity and maturity. The precious blood of Jesus paid the price for sinful human beings to become Saints of Christ's Church. The message that Jesus preached was, "You must be born again...for I AM the only way, truth, and life...repent...the kingdom of God is at hand."[9] The Church is the spiritual Kingdom of God, the place where King Jesus has His domain. The Church is God's dwelling place and headquarters on Earth: Christ's corporate Body for the physical expression and extension of Himself to humankind.[10]

THE EARLY CHURCH (APOSTOLIC) MOVEMENT

The 12 Apostles: To form the leadership of His new movement, Christ Jesus chose as His disciples 12 men who were involved in trade and business endeavors. They were from the multi-cultural population centers of Galilee, not from the Jewish spiritual center of Jerusalem. Jesus invested three years in them, teaching, imparting, and activating them in the principles of the Kingdom of God. When He ascended back to His Father in Heaven, He commissioned them to wait in Jerusalem for the gift of the Holy Spirit, saying, "You shall receive power when the Holy Spirit has come upon you; and you shall be witnesses to Me in Jerusalem, and in all Judea and Samaria, and to the end of the earth."[11]

After Jesus' resurrection and ascension the believers sought the Lord for a replacement for the apostle Judas, who had committed suicide. Matthias was chosen, and he joined the 11 men appointed by Jesus as one of the apostles. At that time, Jesus' original apostles retained their "apostles of the Lamb" status while becoming Church apostles, establishing Christ's New Testament Church by supernatural miracles and apostolic teaching. These men effectively "gave up" their prior business endeavors to concentrate on teaching and demonstrating what they had personally witnessed during their three years with Jesus. Nevertheless, their prior training and backgrounds would have greatly affected the development of the Church, just as Jesus' experience of growing up in a carpenter's home and taking over the family business prior to His traveling ministry was part of His preparation. The early Church was built upon business people, just as Christ Jesus will use Saints in every field of work in the coming days.

The Book of Acts: The Book of Acts records the birth and ministry of the newborn Church. The full title of Acts that is most popular at present is *The Acts of the Apostles.* However, throughout history this book has been called by a variety of names, including *The Acts of the Holy Spirit* or *The Acts of the Church.* I believe the latter two titles are more accurate because Acts records the ministry of the Church, not just the ministry of the apostles. As we will see in a moment, it records acts by "average" Saints such as those who will be prominent in the Day of the Saints.

The Book of Acts begins with the ascension of Jesus and moves to the outpouring of the Holy Spirit in the year A.D. 30. Acts tells us that 120 Saints gathered together in the Upper Room to pray and await the promised gift of the Holy Spirit. On the Day of Pentecost when the fire of God descended upon the believers, each of them was empowered by the Holy Spirit. This was the birthing of the Church. God sovereignly planned this event to transpire at a time when thousands of Jews from various geographic regions were present in Judea. Apostle Peter took responsibility to prophetically exhort the witnesses and urge them to repentance. Three thousand heeded the message and were added to the Kingdom that very day. The Church Age began at that time and will continue until the literal second coming of Jesus Christ.

Rapid Growth: All of a sudden the number of believers had jumped from about 120 to over 3,100 Saints. That meant that less than four percent of the Church had been present in the Upper Room, and the 12 apostles were less than one-half percent of the Church. The number increased daily.[12] Acts tells us that the Saints met together for meals and fellowship and that they shared with one another to provide for each others' needs. This marks the beginning of the ministry of the believers. With such rapid growth, there is no way the 12 original apostles could have met the spiritual and financial needs of several thousand people. As these "average" Saints were "praising God and having favor with all the people," they were manifesting Christ's life to one another as His Body.[13]

Progressive Revelation: Throughout the Early Church Movement, the apostles were still learning about the nature of the Church. When they received Christ's command to wait for the baptism of the Holy Spirit, they still did not understand Jesus' purpose for His Church, because they asked if He was going to restore the kingdom to Israel at that time.[14] When Saul, who became apostle Paul, was called by Jesus to discontinue his persecution of the young Church movement, he was given great revelation insight into God's blueprint for His Church.[15] He is the one who received the revelation regarding the fivefold ministries, although others were operating in these principles. It was not until a few hundred years later that the Scriptures were canonized to make the New Testament.

Separation From Judaism: The Book of Acts portrays the story of God's leading the Early Church out of bondage to the law of Judaism into the promised land of Kingdom living. The Holy Spirit did a progressive work over time to fully deliver the Church in precept and practice from bondage to the law. Ten years after the origination of the Church the apostles realized that non-Jews could become Christians without becoming Jews first. Thirty years after the birth of the Church, the Jerusalem congregation was still trying to keep the law and promote Christianity too. It was not until the destruction of Jerusalem in A.D. 70 that Judaism and Christianity were recognized by the world as two separate entities.

From that point on, the center for God's operation on Earth was no longer the temple in Jerusalem, but the indwelling presence of the Holy Spirit in each and every believer. Everywhere they went the Saints took the supernatural power of Jesus Christ with them. The Early Church fulfilled Christ's words that, "He who believes in Me, the works that I do he will do also; and greater works than these he will do, because I go to My Father."[16] Before the initial 40 years of the newborn Church had transpired, the first-generation Saints had spread around the world. Though the Church leaders were still having problems making the transition from the Mosaic covenant to the Church covenant, the Good News continued to spread, propagated by the Saints.

MINISTERS DOING BUSINESS

Chapters 6 through 8 of the Book of Acts give the scriptural setting for the first-century Saints Movement. They also reveal the pattern and principles for the twenty-first century Saints Movement. The preparation for the Day of the Saints began in the sixth chapter of Acts, where business people were ordained to do business as representatives of Jesus. Since there will be much emphasis in this book on Saint ministers in the marketplace and public square (government), we need to understand the concept of business, or "king," ministers.

King and Priest Ministers: The Scriptures in Revelation 1:6 and 5:10 discuss Saints being kings and priests. Priest ministers function in the Church as clergy, whereas kings can be portrayed as the ministers in the marketplace. All Saints are members of the Body of Christ and have a membership ministry to manifest. All are called to be the salt of the earth, the light of the world, witnesses for Jesus, and demonstrators of the Kingdom of God. Priestly ministers fulfill their membership ministry mainly inside the local church. Kingly ministers fulfill their membership ministry in their workplace, profession, or home.

The terms *kings* and *priests* are not meant to be exclusive, because many people function to some degree in both areas. For example, someone may be a store owner by primary profession and an anointed, effective Sunday school teacher at the same time. Scripture tells us that we are all a royal priesthood. However, these terms also help us to understand the special functions to which Jesus calls His Saints. In the Old Testament, Israel had both political leaders who saw to the affairs of the nation and priestly leaders who oversaw the functions of the temple.

Christ Jesus is both the great High Priest and the King of kings. But many times we see Him primarily in His "spiritual" role as an itinerant minister. Yet Jesus was raised by a kingly minister. In his book *God@Work*, Rich Marshall states:

> When God sent His Son to live on this earth, He chose to put Him in the home of a businessman. We understand that Mary is the mother of Jesus, and that God is His Father. But we also know that Joseph fulfilled the role of father on the earth. God

entrusted His Son into the hands of Mary and Joseph, a carpenter—a businessman....I am convinced that God does nothing by mistake, and that He wastes no opportunity. Therefore, it could be that Jesus was raised in the home of a businessman as a part of the plan and purpose of God. If God had sent His Son into this society to be born of a woman, I personally believe that He would have placed Him in the home of a business leader like He did with Mary and Joseph....

The Lord reminded me that what He does in the natural realm is intended to speak to us in the spiritual realm. "Yes, I put John the Baptist into the home of a priest, and I put My Son into the home of a businessman. Remember the purpose, My calling on John? He was to announce the arrival of My Son." ...What the Lord whispered into my spirit that day was this: "That is still the purpose for My priests. They are to announce the coming revival. And as it was with My Son, born into the home of a king, a businessman, My purpose for the kings is to bring that revival in. I will use them, the business and professional people, CEO's and employees, to bring in the harvest."[17]

Don't Exclude the Kings: One of the reasons that most of the religious leaders of Jesus' day did not receive Him as their Messiah is the same reason that many Saints have been limited in their ministries today: an overemphasis on activity and position in the religious sphere and an underemphasis on the spiritual significance of "secular" positions. The Pharisees did not expect their Messiah to be a carpenter from Nazareth who put no value in the intricate details of their spiritual traditions. Today many Christians believe that only work done inside the local church is truly building the Kingdom of God.

In the coming Day of the Saints, there will be an understanding of the importance of godly men and women impacting all aspects of society for Kingdom purposes. God is calling His people to superimpose His Kingdom in the business world, politics, the arts and media, athletics, entertainment, medicine, science, and every other area of life. In future chapters we'll be looking at specific ways Saints can impact the marketplace. Now let's look at Acts 6.

The Establishment of Business Saints as Deacons: In Acts 6:1-7 we find that the priestly apostles were being pulled into the business part of the church ministry.

> *Then the twelve summoned the multitude of disciples and said, "It is not desirable that we should leave the word of God and serve tables. Therefore, brethren, seek out from among you seven men of good reputation, full of the Holy Spirit and wisdom, whom we may appoint over this business; but we will give ourselves continually to prayer and to the ministry of the word."* [18]

Like many modern-day ministers, the 12 apostles became overly involved in daily administration. They realized they had to return to "[giving themselves] continually to prayer and to the ministry of the word," if they were to focus on their apostolic ministry and establish the new believers in the foundations of the faith. So they had the Saints select seven men who were full of the Holy Spirit, faith, and wisdom to take care of these special administrative needs. The apostles laid hands on these seven men and ordained them as businessmen. They took a position that many have proclaimed to be the ministry of deacons.[19]

Administrators of Social Services: Most Saints today tend to think of deacons as those who serve in the local church—those who count offerings, help set up the sanctuary, etc. But these first-century ministers were meeting extensive practical needs in the daily lives of the congregation, not just during a weekly service time. The scriptural account makes it clear that hands-on serving, such as waiting tables, was included. But because of the number of people involved in the church at that time, it is also reasonable to conclude that this was a large operation—more like running a large soup kitchen or even administrating a social service program than waiting on a few tables. God's plan for the Church was to act as the "social security" for His people, not to leave that to a secular or heathen bureaucracy. This is the type of enterprise these gifted businessmen were leading.

Ministers in the Marketplace: Because they are more commonly known by the name of *deacon*, we will call Philip, Stephen, and their five associates *deacons*. However, in our present-day terms, these seven could be called "ministers doing business" or ministers in the marketplace. We could call them the kingly ministers who are business people, not pulpit preachers. Ministers in the marketplace are not just called to the natural realm. Just like priestly ministers, they are to manifest the supernatural works of Jesus in their daily lives. Because they are called to spend most of their time outside the local church, the lives of these

Saints will be witnessed by many who are not yet believers. This is exactly what happened to Stephen.

Deacon Stephen began to be mightily used of God for more than natural things. "And Stephen, full of faith and power, did great wonders and signs among the people."[20] This obvious power threatened the old religious order until they falsely accused Stephen. When he was brought before their council and given opportunity to speak, he gave the dynamic, anointed message recorded in the seventh chapter of Acts. It is interesting to note that this message, the longest one recorded in the New Testament, was spoken by a minister in the marketplace, not by one of the apostles. Stephen demonstrated how a Saint can give a testimony for Jesus Christ under the most strenuous situations.

Rich Marshall writes:

> As soon as I mention that Stephen preached, there is an assumption by some that he left the business world and entered the ministry to become a preacher. But that is not the case with Stephen, and it need not be the case today....So why did Stephen preach? He probably didn't set out to preach. He was simply operating in the new anointing that came on him through the laying on of hands. Suddenly he was operating in the miraculous—wonders and signs. In the daily activities of his life, he began to see the power of God in new and awesome ways.

> According to the Scripture, Stephen was simply one of the multitude. Paul Cain has stated on numerous occasions that he believes that the coming revival will be led by a team of "nameless, faceless leaders." That is exactly what Stephen had been....

Even though we may say Stephen was an unknown, it is obvious that the Lord knew him and that he knew the Lord. It is also obvious that when given the opportunity to speak about one of their own, the Church knew him....How many "Stephens" are there in our churches today—just members of the church, just one of the crowd, just a businessperson—that is, until we look closer? On closer examination, we find a group of wise and respected, Spirit-filled individuals just waiting for a release—a release that brings the understanding that you can minister under the anointing of the Holy Spirit in the marketplace.[21]

THE FIRST-CENTURY SAINTS MOVEMENT

Stephen closed his message by declaring that he was seeing a vision of the heavens being opened and Jesus standing at the right hand of God. These remarks inflamed the religious leaders with rage. They stoned Stephen to death and activated great persecution against the Church. However, while the devil meant the persecution to bring the destruction of the Church, God used it to launch the early Church Saints Movement.[22]

> *Now Saul* [the one converted later who then became the apostle Paul] *was consenting to his* [Stephen's] *death. At that time a great persecution arose against the church which was at Jerusalem; and they were all* [the Saints] *scattered throughout the regions of Judea and Samaria, except the apostles.... Therefore those who were scattered* [the Saints] *went everywhere preaching the word.*[23]

This persecution activated the first-century Saints Movement. Stephen's stoning to death for his irresistible presentation of truth released great persecution on the Saints in Jerusalem. The original apostles stayed at Jerusalem, but the Saints went everywhere preaching about Jesus. They not only preached but also did what Jesus said believers would do. They healed the sick and cast out devils. "And they went out and preached everywhere, the Lord working with them and confirming the word through the accompanying signs."[24] Ministers in the marketplace were activated and began manifesting the miraculous—in other words, being the Church. This incited great persecution by the Pharisaical religious leaders, but the persecution did not hinder the spread of Christ's message. When Saul started his intense persecution of the Saints in Jerusalem, the Saints scattered into other regions. Everywhere they went, they preached the gospel and demonstrated the Kingdom of God with supernatural signs and wonders.

Acts chapter 8 shows what the saintly believers did when they became a demonstration of the first-century Day of the Saints. Immediately Philip (not the apostle Philip, but one of the seven deacons):

> ...went down to the city of Samaria and preached Christ to them. And the multitudes with one accord heeded the things spoken by Philip, hearing and seeing the miracles which he did. For unclean spirits, crying with a loud voice, came out of many who were possessed; and many who were paralyzed and lame were healed. And there was great joy in that city.[25]

This is the follow-up proof text to show what the believers did when they went everywhere preaching. Philip at this time was not recognized as a fivefold minister but as one of the Saints. Rich Marshall describes what happened:

As the Church is scattered, we notice that the apostles stay in Jerusalem. So it was the kings whom God raised up to lead the next wave of missionary movement. One of the leaders is another of these Spirit-filled businessmen, Philip. Philip began in Samaria where he likewise experienced the manifestation of the miraculous in his ministry. He is led by an angel to minister to another leader from the "kingly" ranks, a man holding great authority under the queen of Ethiopia, and in charge of her treasury. Suddenly, the potential for widespread revival becomes a reality through only one day in the ministry of one of God's most anointed businessman preachers ever.[26]

Stephen and Philip, examples of the type of Saints who will be in the twenty-first century Saints Movement, were full of the Holy Spirit, had a good reputation, and faithfully did whatever the leadership appointed them to do. These two typical New Testament believers spoke boldly with wisdom and power. They were Holy Spirit-filled, as evidenced by speaking in other tongues. They healed the sick, cast out devils, did mass evangelism and personal evangelism, were transported by the Spirit from one place to another (Philip), and were mighty witnesses for Jesus Christ.

Persecution Expanded the Kingdom: The early Saints did not want persecution or hard times any more than we do today. In fact, when faced with the besiegement of Jerusalem in A.D. 70, the Christians living there at the time heeded Jesus' words, "Then let those who are in

Judea flee to the mountains."[27] Josephus calculated that 1.1 million Jews perished in the city, another 257,660 were killed in surrounding areas, and 97,000 were taken captive.[28] Clarke states, "It is very remarkable that not a single Christian perished in the destruction of Jerusalem, though there were many there when Cestius Gallus approached the city."[29] By obeying the prophecy of Jesus, they escaped the prophesied destruction and were enabled to continue to spread the gospel in the areas where they fled.

In this historical case, many Christians escaped horror by remembering and following Jesus' prophetic word. However, just as Stephen was filled with the Holy Spirit, yet did not escape stoning and martyrdom, not all early Christians were spared from death and destruction. When they faced these trials they rose up in courage, and God used their sacrifices for the good of His Kingdom.

Saints today may face similar circumstances and must be prepared "in season and out of season." The tragic events of September 11, 2001, have brought some examples. You may have heard reports of Saints who heeded the Holy Spirit's warning not to go to the World Trade Center that morning. Others, uncharacteristically, were not feeling well and did not go to work that day. Yet many others, on planes and at the towers, were fulfilling their duties and their call as believers and lost their lives. In our day and culture, living for Christ has come under attack, just as it did during the Roman Empire. The Saints must rise up in boldness and bring the presence of Christ to whatever situation they find themselves in. We will look more at what the Bible says regarding Saints as martyrs and overcomers in Chapter 10.

The Results of the Early Saints Movement: By the year A.D. 100, the Church had been alive and active for 70 years. About the year A.D. 90 the cruel Emperor Domitian began a second imperial persecution of the Christians, and John, the only original apostle still alive at that time, was imprisoned on the isle of Patmos. There John received the Revelation contained in the New Testament. General consensus is that he died at Ephesus about A.D. 100.

By that time, the first-century Saints Movement had spread the gospel to millions. At the close of the first century there were families who had been Christian for three generations. The Church could be found in every land and in almost every city from the Tiber River to the Euphrates; from the Black Sea to north Africa. Some scholars believe it extended as far west as Spain and Britain. Its membership included several million. Over the next 200 years tens of millions more were added, and millions were martyred for the cause of Christ.

The well-known letter of Pliny to the Emperor Trafan, written about A.D. 112, states that in the provinces of Asia Minor bordering the Black Sea the temples of the heathen gods were almost forsaken, and the Christians were everywhere a multitude. The standards of moral character were high and the supernatural power of God was being manifested by many Saints. Although the quality of spiritual life and purity of doctrine was less than it had been in the earlier, apostolic days, the Church, nevertheless, was strong, aggressive, growing, and rising to dominance throughout the world. The apostle Paul declared by the Holy Spirit that the gospel had gone to everyone on Earth.[30]

Church history tells us one of the reasons the Church arose and overcame the intense persecution of its early years is because of the faithful stand of Saints, who functioned as servants and even slaves in Rome. Eventually, by their testimony of living out the teachings and supernatural ministry of Jesus, so many people had been saved that the Christians were in the majority in Caesar's own household. God's people had invaded the public square (government).

WHY HASN'T JESUS COME BACK?

Jesus Will Work Through His Church: The first-century Church Saints thought Christ's return was imminent. They lived with an expectation of His coming. But Jesus had a much greater purpose to accomplish in His Church than they had anticipated. Everything Jesus will ever do from the Day of Pentecost to endless eternity will be done with His Church. He is the Head and the Church is the Body of a single unit. Christ and His corporate Body is God's chosen instrument for executing all of His eternal purposes. Jesus loved the Church and gave Himself for her. Jesus purchased the Church with His own blood. The death of Jesus on the cross paid the redemptive price for every person who would become a member of the Church. The resurrection of Jesus authorized the bringing forth of the Church, and the coming of the Holy Spirit on the Day of Pentecost gave birth to the Church.[31]

God's Provision for the Church: The Saints of the Church have been cleansed by the blood of Jesus and called by the name of Christ (Christ-ian). They have been covered by the robe of righteousness and the garment of praise for their clothing, and the Christian armor for their protection. The Word of God is their sword of the Spirit for warfare in the name of Jesus Christ. The gifts of the Holy Spirit are their weapons of warfare.[32]

The fruit of the Holy Spirit is the preserving ability that makes the Saints the salt of the earth and brings conformity to the image of Jesus Christ. The fivefold ministry of apostles, prophets, evangelists, pastors, and teachers was given by Christ as an extension of His headship ministry to perfect, equip, and mature the members of the Church to Christ's full stature and maturity. All of these provisions and principles were established as the pattern and purpose of God in the beginning of the Church and were ordained to continue throughout the age of the mortal Church.[33]

The Church Is Central to God's Purpose: Christ's death, burial, resurrection, ascension, and sending of the Holy Spirit established the Church as a central part of God's eternal purposes. The Church Age is a dispensation and continuing covenant that God made with the mortal Church. From the typology of the dimensions of the Holy Place in the tabernacle we find that the Church Age is destined to last about 2,000 years.[34] Everything that was established in the Church is to remain functional until the mortal Church is immortalized into the eternal Church. Then Saints of the eternal Church will become co-laborers with God to administer His affairs and execute His eternal purposes as they sit together with Christ Jesus on His Father's throne, ruling and reigning together forever.[35]

God's Appointed Time: A particular principle manifested throughout Scripture and nature reveals that certain events cannot happen until there is a progressive fulfillment of other things that allow, enable, or make it possible for that event to take place. In nature we find that fruitful crops cannot be harvested until the process of planting, growing, and maturing has been fulfilled. A woman cannot become pregnant until conception has taken place. And she cannot give natural birth until the times of development and labor have been fulfilled. This same principle is revealed in the Bible.[36]

We can see it in regard to the first coming of Jesus as Messiah 2,000 years ago and regarding His second coming at the end of the Church Age. Christ was held in Heaven for 4,000 years before He was allowed to come to the Earth as Redeemer of humankind. "But when the fullness of the time had come, God sent forth His Son."[37] Christ Jesus had to wait until the time appointed by the Father. The terms "appointed time" and "fullness of the time" do not mean just an arbitrary date God picked out of nowhere. The "time" is when everything is properly fulfilled and ready for an event to take place.

Prophecies Had to Be Fulfilled Prior to the Coming of the Messiah: Many prophecies concerning nations, peoples, and places had to be fulfilled and placed in proper order for the coming of the Messiah. Prophet Daniel prophesied about four great world empires that would arise; each would rule the world for a period of time and then be replaced by another world empire. The Messiah would come during the reign of the fourth empire and begin to build His own world empire of the Church. The Messiah could not come until the Babylonian Empire had fulfilled its time, then the Medo-Persian Empire, the Grecian Empire, and finally the Roman Empire. Jesus' predestined time to come was during the reign of the Roman Empire. The "fullness of the time" was determined by the fulfillment of God's words spoken by His prophets.[38] More than 35 times throughout the Gospels and the Book of Acts we read that this or that happened, "That it might be fulfilled which was spoken by the prophet."

Prophecies About the Messiah Had to Be Fulfilled: Even when Jesus came to Earth from the Father, there were many prophetic Scriptures that He had to fulfill before He could ascend back to the Father. He had to live out many messianic prophecies about His place of birth, ministry, suffering, death, burial, and resurrection.[39] His greatest enemies could not kill Him until He had fulfilled these Scriptures. The apostle Peter declared, after Christ's ascension back to Heaven, that all those messianic Scriptures in the Old Testament "Christ...hath so fulfilled."[40]

Volumes have been written on the proofs of Jesus as the promised Messiah. In fact, Jesus fulfilled 59 messianic prophecies. And we should note especially that Jesus fulfilled more of these prophecies concerning His life, death, and resurrection in His last few days than He did in all the rest of His life. Likewise, THE SAINTS WILL FULFILL MORE SCRIPTURE IN THE LAST GENERATION OF THE MORTAL

CHURCH THAN HAS BEEN FULFILLED DURING THE LAST 20 CENTURIES.

Prophecies About the Church Must Be Fulfilled: Just as Jesus could not ascend to the Father until He had fulfilled all prophecies concerning His first coming, the same is true concerning the second coming of Christ Jesus. Many things that the prophets and apostles have spoken and written in Scripture must be fulfilled before Christ can return. These things are being revealed by His holy apostles and prophets and restored in the Church through His "times of restoration." When the Church Empire is completed to the fullness that Christ predestined it to be, then:

> ...the God of heaven will set up a kingdom which shall never be destroyed; and the kingdom shall not be left to other people; it shall break in pieces and consume all these kingdoms, and it shall stand forever.[41]

Some Christians have asked, "Since Christ Jesus is Almighty and can do as He pleases, and if it is His will and pleasure to come back, then why doesn't He?" Why didn't His "imminent return" take place in the first or second century of the Church? By that time millions of Christians had been martyred and multimillions were still alive on Earth. The gospel had gone to every creature under the sun. Records indicate that Christian ministers of that time preached in all the known countries of the world. Most biblical historians assume that the gospel went to all the known world at that time. However, the Holy Spirit is not limited to man's knowledge; He knew that the gospel had been preached in all the earth.[42] The Church was demonstrating all the power and principles recorded in the Book of Acts. It was a New Testament apostolic church, with miracles and mighty ministry. The apostles were active and ministering apostolic power, which we are now seeking to see fully restored. So why didn't Christ return at that time?

The Principle of "Until" in Scripture: Christ's greatest desire is to return to Earth so He can resurrect and translate His Church into immortality and oneness with Himself. Yet He cannot do so until certain things are fulfilled to bring His Bride to the fullness of purity and maturity that the Father has predetermined. One word in Scripture reveals this principle more than others—the word *until.* Just as Jesus could not ascend back to the Father in Heaven **until** certain things had been fulfilled, even now He cannot descend from Heaven back to Earth **until** the Church fulfills certain things. Certain prophecies given by the prophets in the Old Testament, by Jesus Himself, and by the apostles and the prophets in the New Testament must be fulfilled before the event called the second coming of Christ can take place.

For example, when Jesus arose from the dead and established the Church, He sat down at the right hand of the Majesty on High. His Father said, "Sit on My right hand, **until** I make Thine enemies Thy footstool."[43] Peter said of Jesus: "Whom the heaven must receive **until** the times of restitution of all things, which God hath spoken by the mouth of all His holy prophets."[44] The fivefold ascension gift ministers must function **until** every Saint is ministering and the Church has become a perfect man, even to the fullness of the maturity of Christ.[45] "Jerusalem shall be trodden down of the Gentiles, **until...**" and "...blindness in part is happened to Israel, **until** the fulness of the Gentiles be come in."[46]

Three Areas Will Dovetail Together in Prophetic Fulfillment: Three areas must come to prophetic fulfillment before the fullness of time will be accomplished. The nations of the world, Israel, and the Church must each come to the place of full quantity, quality, accomplishments, and fulfillment of certain predestinated purposes. The world's cup of iniquity must reach its fullness, even as the sin of the Amorites had to become full before Abraham's descendants could possess Canaan.[47] God's promises that He swore with an oath to Abraham concerning natural Israel and the land of Palestine must also be fulfilled. And finally, all prophecies concerning the Church must come to pass. God has sovereignly planned for these three areas to come to fulfillment simultaneously. However, the key to the other two is the Church. How the Saints respond to God determines the status of natural Israel and of the gentile nations.[48]

THE SUPERNATURAL NATURE OF THE CHURCH

The Church was not birthed in doctrine or church creed. It was birthed by the supernatural and into the supernatural power of God. The first Christians believed and practiced Mark 16:16-20, John 14:12, and Matthew 10:8. When they preached the gospel, they expected the word to be confirmed with signs following. They did not preach a dead sermon, but proclaimed a living Christ who was able to do through them what He did through His personal body: heal the sick, cleanse the lepers, raise the dead, cast out devils, and transform individuals into new creatures as they were washed in the blood and became born of the Spirit.

Prerequisite for Spiritual Manifestations: It is good to know that spiritual manifestations of the supernatural power of God are not dependent upon a person's maturity, doctrinal correctness, or holy character. The only prerequisites for demonstrating the Holy Spirit power that Jesus gave to born-again, Spirit-filled Saints were belief and yieldedness. Then the supernatural gifts would operate. Because of this, the early apostles and Saints were able to preach the gospel and demonstrate the power of God while the Holy Spirit was still establishing the Church doctrinally in the dispensation of grace and truth in Christ Jesus. Peter preached the gospel, healed the sick, and raised the dead for years before he understood the truth that the gentiles could become direct members of the Body of Christ without coming through Judaism.

Acts Is the Pattern for the Church: The Book of Acts does not record all of the performances of the Church Saints, just as the Gospels do not record all of the teaching and miracles of Christ.[49] But what the Holy Spirit did inspire to be recorded is sufficient to give us the teachings, experiences, and ministry of the New Testament Church. The Church is not a man-made institution. It does not exist or operate on natural laws or religious forms. The Church operates according to spiritual laws and functions in the supernatural. The blueprint and pattern recorded in Acts portrays the Church as a supernatural people operating in supernatural principles.

Everything found in the Book of Acts—the truths, principles, gifts, and fruits of the Spirit; the miracles and ministries of the apostle, prophet, evangelist, pastor, and teacher—were intended not only for the first generation Church but for the whole Church Age. If we made a list of beliefs and practices in the Book of Acts and the Epistles, we would find quite a contrast between the early Church and most modern Christian denominations. That is why it is so important that we open ourselves up to the Holy Spirit to allow our traditional mind-sets and comfort zones to be changed. Otherwise we will not come into the fullness of all God has planned for His Saints as manifestations of the Kingdom of God on Earth.

> Take the miracles out of the Book of Acts, and there is little left. However much critics may disparage the evidential value of miracles, the fact remains that God made abundant use of miracles in giving Christianity a start in the world.[50]

The Stumbling Block of Rationalism: What God began in a supernatural way is not to be reduced to natural means of operation. Many theologians have developed arguments as to why the miraculous element is not to be as common in modern times as it was in the early Church. Though many of these men and women are genuinely trying to explain why the experience of many Christians today differs from New Testament times, their conclusions are not scripturally valid. They are influenced by rationalism, the belief that reason or intellectual conception provides the only valid basis for action or belief and that reason is the prime source of knowledge and spiritual truth.[51] This way of thinking causes skepticism and unbelief. Because the supernatural realm cannot be readily understood by reason—that is, in the natural mind—rationalism rejects miracles, prophecy, and other experiences of the spirit realm.

Since rationalism is such a widespread belief in the Western world, many Western Christians and ministers have accepted it as partly or completely valid. The majority of the world's population recognize the validity of the spirit realm, even if they have not been born again by salvation through Jesus Christ. Millions of Hindus, Buddhists, Muslims, and followers of folk religions spend great time, money, and effort seeking to appease spirits in hopes of avoiding danger and living fruitful lives. In the Day of the Saints, when the followers of Jesus Christ go throughout the Earth demonstrating the Lordship of Christ over the supernatural realm, millions upon millions of these non-Christians will come into the Kingdom. They already know and accept the reality of the supernatural world. When they see that Christ Jesus and His Holy Spirit are stronger than every spirit, many of them will eagerly exchange their allegiance to demonic "gods" to follow the true God, just as multitudes did in the first century.

In nations where Saints are flowing in the supernatural, harvest is already taking place. This will be greatly expanded in the Saints Movement. The Church in the West has the challenge of rejecting and renouncing an ungodly dependence upon rationalism and entering into the experiential reality of the Church as described in the New Testament. Otherwise we will continue to wallow in lukewarmness, until we are displeasing to God and lose the degree of power and status we do have.[52]

THE GREATEST HARVEST IS AHEAD

Even if all do not participate, the Kingdom of God will continue to advance. Jesus said:

> *To what shall we liken the kingdom of God? Or with what parable shall we picture it? It is like a mustard seed which, when it is sown on the ground, is smaller than all the seeds on earth; but when it is sown, it grows up and becomes greater than all herbs, and shoots out large branches, so that the birds of the air may nest under its shade.*[53]

The great harvest that will soon take place will not be reaped by just a few great apostles, prophets, and evangelists, but by God's prepared and anointed Saints.

More Members Needed for Christ's Corporate Body: The human body requires a certain quantity of cells and members to be a complete and fully functioning body. Each member of the body contains many cells. The Godhead is the only one who knows how many members are to be in the eternally functioning Body of Christ, the Church. The Church was in the womb of the Old Testament, with all of its members in God's mind, until it was birthed in the New Testament.[54] I believe there is a predestined number that is in God's original blueprint and specifications for His corporate Body.

There are still multimillions of people whom God needs in order to fill all the places at His banquet table for the wedding of His Son. In Jesus' parable, when the ones who had received the wedding invitation made excuses why they could not come, the father (God) became very angry and said to his servants (the Saints), "The wedding is ready, but those who were invited were not worthy. Therefore go into the highways, and as many as you find, invite to the wedding."[55] In Luke's narrative of this wedding supper, the master said:

> "Go out quickly into the streets and lanes of the city, and bring in here the poor and the maimed and the lame and the blind." And the servant said, "Master, it is done as you commanded, and still there is room." Then the master said to the servant, **"Go out into the highways and hedges, and compel them to come in, that My house [Church] may be filled."**[56]

This will be one of the KEY TEXTS in the Day of the Saints.

The Compelling Ministry: How will the Saints compel them to come in? They will use the fundamentals of personal evangelism—giving people an invitation to receive Christ. However, their compelling will be by the supernatural power of God and not just by persuasive words. By being like Jesus, speaking His words and doing His deeds, the Saints will draw all men unto Him.[57] This is what the Prophetic and Apostolic Movements are preparing the Saints to do. A company of Saints will be equipped by fivefold ministers to go forth under the prophetic and apostolic anointing to do what Saint Philip prototyped.

Apostolic and Prophetic Evangelism: The practice of personal evangelism, where a Saint personally witnesses to an unbeliever, was restored during the Evangelical Movement and has taken on new dimensions with each additional move of God. The Prophetic Movement is now adding a new dimension to evangelism—instructing and activating Saints in the supernatural gifts of the Holy Spirit.[58] They are being trained within the Church, but they will not remain there. The goal is to send teams into the highways and byways, and with the supernatural ministry of the Holy Spirit to compel the people to come into the Kingdom of God. Saints will minister like Jesus did to the woman at the well—using divine revelation to open a person's heart to the reality of the need for a Savior.[59] The results will be tremendous, because the Holy Spirit can make the good news of Jesus Christ relevant to each individual far better than an evangelistic formula can. I believe that during the Saints Movement more souls will be saved than have been saved in all the other restoration movements combined.

Equipping the Saints in Evangelism: There has been some confusion in church circles that evangelism is primarily the responsibility of those called as fivefold evangelists. However, this is not true. Evangelism is to be carried out by all Saints. The function of evangelists is to train and equip the Saints to be effective witnesses of Jesus Christ. Evangelists help to impart to believers a heart for the lost. Naturally, those who are fivefold evangelists are particularly gifted in leading others to a saving knowledge of Jesus Christ. Yet equipping the Saints is their primary job description.

The Saints are now being trained in their military bases of international training centers and their local church armories. The goal is to have them taught, equipped, and field trained to be the officers who will lead God's army of prophetic evangelist Saints during the coming Saints Movement. They will minister under the covering and leadership of the fivefold apostolic and prophetic generals who trained them. These Saints will function like God's army prophetically described by the prophet Joel.[60]

The Saints Movement will fully manifest apostolic-prophetic evangelism with God's consuming fire and miraculous power. Evangelism has always been in the heart of God, but in the upcoming Day of the Saints it will be escalated to a level that has not been seen since the first-century Saints Movement.

All Fivefold Ministries Must Be Present: John the Baptist, the prophet, came in the spirit of Elijah to prepare the way for the Messiah. The company of prophets and apostles will equip the Church in the spirit and power of Elijah to prepare the way for the second coming of Jesus as King.[61] **That's why the full restoration of apostles and prophets is so essential.** All fivefold ministers must be alive, active, and unified in fulfilling their divine commission of Ephesians 4:11-16. The full restoration and activation of all fivefold ministers will bring about the teaching, training, activating, mentoring, and maturing of the Saints.

Jesus created fivefold ministers for the Saints to be taught, trained, activated, and fully equipped in their "compelling" tools of the supernatural gifts of the Holy Spirit. Then as every member functions and every joint supplies, the Body of Christ can fulfill its prophesied purpose and destiny. The preparation for the Saints Movement is to activate and mature Saints in the marketplace and public square (government). The Holy Spirit has been commissioned to bring all these things to pass.

Take the Example of the First-Century Saints: God has been working to progressively restore to His Church all the truths and ministries that were present in the first century. The first-century apostles remained in Jerusalem while the Saints went everywhere manifesting that Christ was resurrected and alive by doing in His corporate Body what He did while in His mortal, physical body. As the Saints went everywhere reaping the great harvest, the apostles followed up by getting the new converts filled with the Holy Spirit and established into local churches.[62] Now, in the twenty-first century, apostles have been restored. Today, as the Saints reap the great harvest, the fivefold ministers will then teach, train, activate, mentor, and mature them into Christ's ministry and maturity. These fully equipped and matured ones will become the great army of God who will bring about the restoration of all things in obedience to Christ.

ENDNOTES:
1. Matthew 3:2b.
2. John 1:29b.
3. John 4:48.
4. Matthew 7:28-29.
5. Revelation 1:18.
6. John 3:16.
7. Matthew 5:17.
8. John 17:4; 19:30.

9. See John 3:3; 14:6; Mark 1:15.

10. Ephesians 2:22.

11. Acts 1:8.

12. Acts 2:47.

13. Acts 2:47.

14. Acts 1:6.

15. Ephesians 3:3-5; Colossians 1:25-27.

16. John 14:12.

17. Rich Marshall, *God@Work* (Shippensburg, PA: Destiny Image, 2000), pp. 20-22.

18. Acts 6:2-4.

19. Philippians 1:1; 1 Timothy 3:8-13; Acts 6.

20. Acts 6:8.

21. Marshall, *God@Work*, pp. 35-38.

22. Acts 7:57–8:1.

23. Acts 8:1,4.

24. Mark 16:15-20.

25. Acts 8:5-8.

26. Marshall, *God@Work*, p. 37.

27. Matthew 24:16.

28. Bill Hamon, *The Eternal Church* (Santa Rosa Beach, FL: Christian International Publishers, 1981), p. 78.

29. Adam Clarke, *Clarke's Commentary* (Nashville, TN: Abingdon, 1977), p. 228. For more details, see Hamon, *The Eternal Church*, pp. 75-77.

30. Colossians 1:23.

31. Acts 20:28; Ephesians 2:13-16; 5:25-27; Colossians 1:18-29; 1 Peter 1:18-19.

32. John 1:7; Mark 1:17; Isaiah 61:3,10; Ephesians 6:10-18; 1 Corinthians 12:7-11; 2 Corinthians 10:4-5.

33. Galatians 5:22-26; Romans 8:29; Ephesians 4:11-13.

34. The outer court fence measured 1,500 linear feet—a type of the Dispensation of the Law; the holy place measured 2,000 cubic feet—a type of the Mortal Church Age; the holy of holies measured 1,000 cubic feet—a type of the Millennial Age.

35. Revelation 2:26-27; 3:21; 1 Corinthians 3:9; Psalm 149:6-9.

36. Mark 4:26-29.

37. Galatians 4:4a.

38. Matthew 1:22; 2:15,17; 4:14; 8:17; 13:35; 21:4; John 12:38.

39. Micah 5:2; Isaiah 53:4-12.

40. Acts 3:18b KJV.

41. Daniel 2:44b. See also Daniel 2:30-43.

42. Colossians 1:23.

43. Hebrews 1:13 KJV.

44. Acts 3:21a KJV.

45. Ephesians 4:8-15.

46. Luke 21:24 KJV; Romans 11:25 KJV.

47. Genesis 15:16.

48. Romans 11:31.

49. John 21:25.

50. Henry H. Halley, *Halley's Handbook* (Grand Rapids, MI: Zondervan, 1965), p. 564.

51. *Webster's II New College Dictionary* (New York: Houghton Mifflin Company, 1995), p. 919.

52. Revelation 3:14-22.

53. Mark 4:30b-32.

54. Psalm 139:14-16.

55. Matthew 22:8b-9.

56. Luke 14:21b-23.

57. John 12:32.

58. 1 Corinthians 12:7-11.

59. John 4:7-30.

60. Joel 2:1-11.

61. Malachi 4:5; Matthew 11:7,14.

62. Acts 8:4,14; 10:44.

CHAPTER 4

UNDERSTANDING GOD'S RESTORATION PROCESS

In order to fully participate in the coming Day of the Saints, each believer must have vision. Each of us must have a personal revelation that Jesus has not only called us, but also is equipping and enabling us to manifest His supernatural life and power through our lives and ministries. Vision inspires us to persevere through the preparation process until we are fully equipped to reach our goal or, in this case, our divine calling and purpose. Each of our individual destinies and callings is connected to God's overall purpose for His Church. Understanding God's restoration process will give us the vision we need to fulfill His purposes for us today.

THE AUTHOR'S MINISTRY CALLING

Chapter 1 explained that God has gifted apostles and prophets to sense what He wants to do in His Church. My fivefold calling is that of prophet-apostle. The first 30 years of my ministry I functioned as a prophet while pastoring for six years, traveling in ministry for several years, teaching in a Bible College for five years, and then building Christian International School of Theology into a worldwide distance-education college. For the last 18 years I have functioned equally in my calling and anointing of apostle. I have written four major books on the restoration of prophets and apostles.[1]

Every minister has a special calling to complete, a revelation to reveal, a ministry to fulfill, and a definite part to play in fulfilling a membership ministry in the Body of Christ. It is like the members of the human body where the eye is not more important than the ear, but just has a different function. Heavenly rewards for members of the Body of Christ are not based on which member of the Body they were called to be, but on how faithful they were in fulfilling that membership function.[2] Individual membership ministry is not given just for the member but for the successful function and fulfillment of the whole Body of Christ. Membership ministry is sovereignly given by Christ's grace and not by the works of man. It is not merited or earned, but it is received, acknowledged, activated, and fulfilled by the faith and obedience of the individual. There is no glory to the member, for it all goes to Christ who gave the ministry.

Understanding the Times: For the above reason, I can plainly reveal that the membership ministry I received as a prophet-apostle of God was the ability to know the times and seasons, what the Church ought to do now, and what the Church shall do in the future. God declares that He will do nothing unless He first reveals it to His servants the prophets.[3] Some prophets sense the seasons and times for God's plans and when they are to be implemented. This anointing of the "sons of Issachar who had understanding of the times, to know what Israel ought to do" has been my gifting and divine ability for 48 years of fivefold ministry.[4] The primary field of my educational studies, doctorate degree, and revelation from the Holy Spirit is the past, present, and future of the Church.

The revelation of the restoration and destiny of the Church came in my early twenties and has continued to grow and expand over the years. My greatest passion and vision is for Christ and His Church. Revelation and anointing have been given to me to teach, activate, and mature Church members in their membership ministry in order to see the corporate Church reach its full restoration and fulfill its destiny. Most of my teaching has had to do with educating the Saints concerning the restoration of the Church and doing my part to co-labor with Christ in bringing full restoration to His Church. My goal is to impart to you a greater understanding of Christ's plan for His Church and for your personal destiny within His plan.

Command to Write Out the Vision: I believe I have received a prophetic vision from God concerning His future purposes for His Church. The Old Testament prophet Habakkuk received such a vision and was commanded to:

> *Write the vision and make it plain on tablets, that he may run who reads it. For the vision is yet for an appointed time; but at the end it will speak, and it will*

not lie. Though it tarries, wait for it; because it will surely come, it will not tarry.[5]

Through this book, I am seeking to fulfill a similar vision and command to write the vision and make it plain concerning the coming restoration movement. Then all who have hearing ears and seeing eyes to receive the revelation may make proper preparation for participation.

HISTORY IS PROPHECY FULFILLED

God has always given His people prophecy concerning what they are yet to be and do and what is yet to be fulfilled and recorded as the history of the Church. "...God does nothing, unless He reveals His secret to His servants the prophets."[6] Prophecy is a part of the history of the Church that is yet to be fulfilled and recorded. Church history is simply prophecy fulfilled.

The first major book I wrote, which was originally published in 1981, was titled *The Eternal Church.*[7] Its 400 pages cover the Church in its origination, deterioration, restoration, and ultimate destination. The restoration portion covers all of the "times of restoration" (Acts 3:21) that have brought the Church to its present truths, power, and ministries. We will cover the highlights of that process in the next chapter. Under "Destination" I predicted that a move of the Holy Spirit would come to restore the prophets and apostles back into the Church as Christ had originally ordained. Then all fivefold ministers would be alive and active in one generation to fulfill their divine commission of equipping the Saints for their end-time ministry. Those movements began in the 1980s and 1990s. Now we are predicting a "Day of the Saints" which will one day be history, just as the second coming of Christ will someday be history.

A Few Examples From Biblical History: For over 100 years Noah prophesied that a worldwide flood was coming. The prophecy was unbelievable and unacceptable to his generation, but now it has been history for 4,500 years. Daniel prophesied about four great world empires that would arise one after another over hundreds of years. At the time of his prophecies, Babylon was the reigning empire. Just as God showed him, the Babylonian Empire was overthrown by the Medo-Persian Empire, which was later overthrown by the Grecian Empire. Finally, the Roman Empire conquered the world. Now Daniel's prophecy has been history for hundreds of years.

The Messiah had been prophesied for 4,000 years. During the Roman Empire He finally came. Now this event, the earthly life of Jesus Christ, has been history for 2,000 years. Even secular historians acknowledge that His life had an enormous impact upon world history. In the eighteenth and nineteenth centuries, so-called "enlightened" skeptics began to doubt the historical truth of other biblical events. They tried to say the Bible was a book of myths or fairy tales. However, modern methods of archaeological and linguistic research are continuing to prove biblical events as historic facts.

The Prophesied *Church* Empire: Daniel also prophesied that after these four major world empires became history, "The God of heaven will set up a kingdom which shall never be destroyed...it shall break in pieces and consume all these kingdoms, and it shall stand forever."[8] That kingdom was set up with the birth of the Church, and it will grow until it becomes the manifest Kingdom of God that subdues all things under Christ's feet. It will fulfill the seventh angel's prophecy that, "The kingdoms of this world **have become** the kingdoms of our Lord and of His Christ, and He shall reign forever and ever!"[9] This prophecy is recorded in Heaven as history, but here on Earth it is in the process of being fulfilled. One day in the very near future it will reach complete fulfillment.

Jesus came and birthed the Church. And nothing will stop Him from fulfilling His prophetic declaration, "I will build My Church!" Jesus said that He was greater than Solomon, a statement that reveals that He will build a Church more beautiful and magnificent than Solomon's temple. Everyone who is a member of Christ's Church should get excited about Jesus plans and destiny for us!

"TIMES OF RESTORATION" PROPHESIED BY APOSTLE PETER

The key Scripture for Church restoration comes from apostle Peter's prophetic presentation in Acts 3. Peter and John had healed the lame man at the gate of the temple, causing all the Jewish people to gather around Peter and John at Solomon's Porch. While they were gathered, Peter prophetically preached that their Messiah had already come, but their religious leaders had rejected Jesus and caused Him to be crucified. Nevertheless, this Jesus of Nazareth was indeed the Messiah, and this had been confirmed—both by His resurrection and by Peter and John's healing of the lame man by the name of Jesus and power of the Holy Spirit.

Peter gave his concluding statement concerning Jesus being the promised Messiah with these words in verse 18: "But those things, which God before had showed by the mouth of all His prophets, that Christ should suffer, **He hath so fulfilled**" (KJV). Then he began preaching about the present and prophesying about the future. The King James Version says it this way:

> *Repent ye therefore, and be converted, that your sins may be blotted out, when the **times of refreshing** shall come from the presence of the Lord; and He **shall send Jesus Christ**, which before was preached unto you: **whom the heaven must receive until the times of restitution of all things**, which God hath spoken by the mouth of all His holy prophets since the world began....And it shall come to pass, that every soul, which will not hear that prophet, shall be destroyed from among the people. Yea, and all the prophets from Samuel and those that follow after, as many as have spoken, have likewise foretold of these days. Ye are the children of the prophets, and of the covenant which God made with our fathers, saying unto Abraham, And in thy seed shall all the families of the earth be blessed.*[10]

Note that Peter declared that the "times of refreshing" will come first, before Christ Jesus returns again. Then in verse 21 he prophesied that "Heaven" is the place that received Christ when He arose from the dead, and it is the place where He will stay until all the "times of restitution" (or restoration) have transpired which God has spoken.

Other translations of verse 21 read this way:

Christ must be kept in heaven till the period of the great restoration (Moffatt).

[Christ] *must remain in heaven until the final recovery of all things from sin, as prophesied from ancient times* (Living Bible).

[Christ Jesus,] *Whom heaven must receive [and retain] until the time for the complete restoration of all that God spoke by the mouth of all His holy prophets...* (Amplified).

Understanding Acts 3:21: Of all the numerous commentaries I have researched, I believe the following comments from *Ellicot's Commentary* give the most accurate and balanced exposition of Acts 3:21:

(21) Whom the heaven must receive. The words have a pregnant force; "must receive and keep."

Until the times of restitution of all things. The "times" seem distinguished from the "seasons" as more permanent. This is the only passage in which the word translated "restitution" is found in the New Testament. Etymologically, it conveys the thought of restoration to an earlier and better state, rather than that of simple consummation or completion, which the immediate context seems, in some measure, to suggest. It finds an interesting parallel in the "new heavens and new earth"—involving, as they do, a restoration of all things to their true order—of 2 Peter 3:13. It does not necessarily involve, as some have thought, the final salvation of all men, but it does suggest a state in which "righteousness" and not "sin" shall have dominion over a redeemed and new-created world; and that idea **suggests a wider**

scope as to the possibilities of growth in wisdom and holiness, or even of repentance and conversion, in the unseen world than that which Christendom has too often been content. The corresponding verb is found in the words, "Elias (Elijah) truly shall come first and restore all things."[11]

Prophets and apostles prophesied the Church's period of great restoration. Apostle Paul also spoke, by the Spirit of revelation, that prophetic Scriptures were speaking of Christ's coming as Messiah. Prophets and apostles also applied these prophecies to the Church.[12] Both Peter and Paul spoke of the falling away of the Church and then the "times of restoration" that would follow.[13] These restoration movements will continue until all things are restored back into the Church and it is brought to the maturity that God requires before Christ can return for His Bride.

The prophesied "period of the Great Restoration" began 1500 years later, and it has now been in the process of fulfillment for almost 500 years. There have been five major Church restoration movements: the Protestant Movement in the 1500s; the Holiness Movement from 1600–1800; the Pentecostal Movement during the 1900s–1940s; the Charismatic Movement from the 1950s–1970s; and the Prophetic/Apostolic Movement in the 1980s and 1990s. Now our prophetic expectation is to see the sixth restoration movement being brought forth within the first or second decade of the twenty-first century Church.

The majority of Peter's prophecy about the coming times of restoration has been fulfilled and recorded. That portion is now Church history. Only two or three restoration movements remain to fulfill its time period. Then it will all be history. The "Omega Generation" of Saints will fulfill the final prophecy concerning the mortal Church and write the last chapter of its history in the annals of Heaven. When the Church has fulfilled all she has been called and prophesied to do, the times of restoration will be fulfilled and Jesus will be released from Heaven to receive His Church Bride.

UNDERSTANDING RESTORATION TERMINOLOGY

Since all of you who are reading this may not be fully knowledgable of Church history, restorations, and renewals, I will give some clarity.

Professional Terminology: Medical doctors, lawyers, or computer experts learn terms that they use to explain their function. They become used to using those terms until they forget that those who have not been trained in that field do not grasp what they are saying. Our oldest son, Tim, earned his master's degree in computer science. When he came home, he would start explaining what he was learning and doing. His mom would say, "Hold it, Tim, I don't understand a thing you are saying! Now back up, start all over and put that in 'Mama language' so that I have some idea of what you are saying."

Those of us who have graduated from seminaries and have been in ordained ministry for many years have learned certain ministerial terms and have used them often until they become everyday household words. We have to remember to put our teaching and preaching into "Mama language" because probably 98 percent of the preacher's audience or the author's readers are not theologians.

"Theologian" is an example of one of those terms! Who is a theologian? It is a person who has devoted his life to studying about God and His Church.

Terms Redeem Time and Space: The reason people use long professional terms is that they can convey a thought with one word to those who are familiar with the terms, whereas it takes a sentence or more to convey the same thought to those who do not understand them. I saw an illustration of this while grading college students' tests, especially the essays. Those with a college education conveyed their thoughts and covered the subject in one page, but those with only a high school education took two or three pages to say the same thing. For this reason, a section entitled "Definitions and Explanations of Terms" in the back of this book will help those who are not familiar with the terms and phraseology that have developed during the last three restoration movements.

Don't Fall Behind: In her teaching, my wife says, "If I had gone to college with my son and received the teaching and experiences he received, I could understand his advanced terms and speak his computer language." She uses this illustration to make the point that she never wants to stop her education in God and the restoration of His Church. She doesn't want to come to the place where Saints and ministers are talking about things of God that she does not understand because she has not advanced on with God's recent restoration movements.

Restored Truth, Not New Truth: It is important to be clear that when we are talking about restoration of truth and "present truth," we are *not* talking about something being added to the Bible. All restoration movements are based on Holy Spirit enlightenment to understand truths that were given by God when the Books of the Bible were written, but have not clearly been understood by subsequent generations. Embracing restoration truth means receiving divine revelation of truths already in the Bible that we did not see before.

If you have been a Christian for some time, you have probably read and heard a verse of Scripture many times and thought you understood it. Then one day the Holy Spirit enlightens that verse to you by revelation and suddenly you see something that you did not see before. You say, "Aha! Now I get it! I never saw that before!" When that happens, you have the challenge of walking in obedience to the "new" truth.

Restoration times are when this type of experience happens to the Church corporately. Some who receive the restored truth eagerly appropriate it for themselves and walk in their newfound blessing and revelation. Others do not participate. Some don't because they never hear the truth taught in order to receive the revelation of it. Others' mind-sets cause them to shut off the new light of revelation. Some harden their hearts against the new truth after they have received it or let others' opinions and criticisms choke it out.[14]

What Is Your Heart's Cry? I hope the heart cry of all who read this book is to be established in the present truth. We want to have the testimony of Enoch that he "walked with God." Walking with God is twofold. One, it is walking in relationship with Jesus in His righteousness and love. Two, it is walking in the light of restorational revelation as Christ Jesus continues the step-by-step process of restoring and building His Church. "But if we walk in the light as He is in the light, we have fellowship with one another...."[15]

A Holy Spirit Renewal vs. a Restorational Move of God

The Day of the Saints will contain many of the elements of other restoration movements and renewals. The Holy Spirit will probably use the same pattern He has used in bringing about other restoration movements. Most of the restoration movements were preceded by a Holy Spirit sovereign move of revival and renewal. A few examples are the Welsh Revival that took place just before the Pentecostal Movement; the Charismatic Renewal, which happened before the Prophetic Movement; and the "Toronto Blessing" or refreshing that occurred just before the Apostolic Movement. Therefore, we expect there will also be a sweeping sovereign refreshing move of the Holy Spirit to prepare the way for the activating of the Saints Movement. Every movement is preceded by intensified praying and is birthed by intercessory prayer.

There is a difference between a Holy Spirit renewal and a restorational move of God. Both are divine visitations of God, but each accomplishes a different purpose. They are both born of Heaven and are not in competition with each other but work together to fulfill Christ's ultimate plan for His Church.

A restoration movement is when God sovereignly chooses to restore certain major truths, ministries, and spiritual experiences that have not been active since the early years of the Church. There have been five of these major restoration movements since the 1500s, which was when the Holy Spirit activated the prophesied time period of the restoration of the Church. The restoration of the Church will make it possible for the rest of Peter's prophecy to be fulfilled concerning the restoration of all things. My research has shown that there are seven things that are a part of every restoration movement: divine enlightenment and revelation knowledge of the truth; a significant company participating, not just an occasional Saint; new anointing and authority for establishing the truth; a small beginning in an insignificant place; power to reproduce by teaching, training, activating, and maturing the Saints; practicing and publicizing until it becomes contested and controversial; and new songs and music portraying the restoration message.[16]

Times of refreshing, renewal, and revival come just before major restorations. Notice in Acts 3:19-20 that "times of refreshing" come to bring a fresh presence of the Lord. The purpose is to break up the fallow ground of the Church in preparation for the seed of new restoration truth to be planted. These times bring refreshing spiritual rain to prepare God's people for the next restorational move of God. *Refreshing, renewal,* and *revival* are terms used to describe the sovereign move of the Holy Spirit to awaken God's people, shake up church tradition, and win souls to Christ by the supernatural presence of God. *Times of refreshing* cultivate the soil of the Saints to take out "weed seed" attitudes, root problems, and rocks of offense so that the ground of the Church is properly prepared for planting the new truths and ministries needed for the continual building of the Church. The rivers of refreshing flow into the next move of God. The refreshing river of the 1990s is flowing into the Prophetic-Apostolic Movement.

Among most local churches the term *revival* is used to describe a time designated to have special preaching campaigns for the purpose of winning the lost. However, to the corporate Church, revival is a time when the Holy Spirit comes to revive the Saints and renew them to their first love. The result is that the Saints win many people to the Lord. A *renewal* typically does much of the same things. However, in the Charismatic Renewal the Holy Spirit added a whole new dimension. As far as I can determine, there was never a visitation like it in the history of the Church.

The Charismatic Renewal: What made the Charismatic Renewal unique? The Charismatic Renewal was used of God to give every person in Christendom an opportunity to catch up with all the Holy Spirit had restored to the Church since the restoration of the Church began. It invaded every area of Christianity, reaching Catholics, historic Protestants, Evangelicals, Holiness believers, and Pentecostals. The Charismatic Renewal began sweeping throughout the Church world in 1963 and grew in momentum until the mid-1970s.[17]

The main emphasis brought to the non-Pentecostal church world was the gift of the Holy Spirit with the evidence of speaking in other tongues. Historic Protestant ministers did not want to use the Pentecostal terms for the experience of the Holy Spirit, so they used the Greek words *charisma*, which means "gift or divine endowment," and *glossa*, which means "tongues." Because they talked so much about the "charisma" of the Holy Spirit, those who were making reports of what was happening started calling them "Charismatic" and thus the trend became known as the Charismatic Renewal.

The Charismatic Movement: The Charismatic Renewal alone did not fulfill the seven requirements for a true restoration movement. When the Charismatic Renewal is combined with two other smaller movements, together they qualify as a major movement. Therefore, when "Charismatic Movement" is used in relation to a restoration movement, it covers three visitations of God:

1. The Latter Rain Movement
2. The Charismatic Renewal
3. The Faith Movement

With all three of these visitations there was more than enough to categorize them as one major restoration movement called the Charismatic Movement. Standing alone, however, the Charismatic move of the Holy Spirit was only a renewal and a time of updating into all presently restored truth for whosoever would participate. I have taken the space to explain this because you will find references to the Charismatic Movement throughout this book.

PROPHETIC TIMING

In the 1960s all Christians were given a chance to update and be prepared to participate in the next restoration of the Church. Prophetic expectations are that within 40 to 50 years from that time—in other words, about now—there will be another divine opportunity for Christians to be renewed, revived, equipped, and then activated into the Saints Movement.

God's Favorite Time Periods: God seems to work in periods of 40, 50, and 70 years. He sentenced Israel to 70 years' captivity in Babylon. After that, they were given the opportunity to return and rebuild the walls of Jerusalem and the temple.[18] God commanded Israel to have a year of jubilee every 50 years for a time of restoration.[19] He caused it to rain 40 days and nights to flood the Earth.[20] Moses tried to fulfill his ministry as deliverer of Israel when he was 40 years old. When he didn't succeed, he was in the desert for another 40 years, at which time God renewed his call to be a deliverer. Moses was on Mount Sinai with God for 40 days.[21] The ten Israeli spies searched out the land for 40 days.[22] When the children of Israel refused to exercise their faith to go in and possess their promised land, they were sentenced to 40 years of wandering in the wilderness before they were given another opportunity.[23] After Jesus had fasted 40 days He was launched into His mighty messiahship ministry.[24]

Recent movements also fit this pattern. The Pentecostal Movement covered between 40 and 50 years, from 1901 till 1947. The Charismatic Movement includes all the things that God did in the 40-year period from 1948 till

1988. The Prophetic-Apostolic Movement has been underway from 1988 until the present time. The coming Saints Movement will be the third of the five major restoration movements scheduled to take place during what I have termed "The Third and Final Apostolic Reformation."[25]

What Is Next? As mentioned, I believe there will be another renewal similar to the Charismatic Renewal just before the Saints Movement. It will give everyone a chance to update and be prepared to participate. According to God's pattern of doing things in the Bible, it will be about the right time for a renewal. I believe God is going to give the general population of Christians another opportunity to get equipped to participate in the Saints Movement. My hopeful anticipation is that the Day of the Saints will be activated around 2008. There can be no particular year set for it to happen, for its time of activation is not set in Heaven. The timing will depend on how soon Christ's fivefold ministers get the Saints ready to participate and *be* the Saints manifested on the earth. The generals and captains in this great army of Saints will be the ones who have been in training for many years, learning to equip the Saints. The latecomers will be the soldiers.

The Decade of the Saints: As we said in Chapter 1, the Day of the Saints will not be just one literal, 24-hour day. Over the last five decades of the twentieth century, while the Holy Spirit was working in God's people during the Charismatic Movement, He has also been bringing each of the fivefold ministers into their proper calling and ministry. One fivefold office was emphasized in each decade: the evangelist in the 1950s, pastor in the 1960s, teacher in the 1970s, prophet in the 1980s, and apostle in the 1990s. Each of the fivefold ministers was activated in one decade and brought to full ministry and maturity in the next decade. Now, I believe **the first decade of the twenty-first century is the Holy Spirit's designated time for the Saints to come into their proper calling and membership ministry in the Body of Christ.** The Saints will be activated in this decade and then brought to full maturity and ministry in the next decade. The result will be the mighty manifestation of the mature ministry of the Saints.

No More One-Man Shows: The end-time harvest of souls will not be reaped by just a few great apostles, prophets, and evangelists. The day of the one-man ministry is quickly coming to a close. During this coming movement the Saints will demonstrate greater works than today's greatest fivefold minister. No longer will people say, "What a mighty apostle, prophet, or evangelist," or, "What a mighty man or woman." Both the world and Christians will be saying, "What a mighty Church!"

The days of the fulfillment of Isaiah 40:3-5 are upon us now. Verse 3 talks of the coming of the great company of prophets that will begin to cry out in the wilderness of the Church to "prepare the way of the Lord; make straight in the desert a highway for our God." That Scripture began to be fulfilled in a corporate way when the Prophetic Movement launched the company of prophets in the Elijah anointing that was manifested and personally fulfilled in the prophet John the Baptist.[26] Now we are entering into the next phase of the prophecy in verses 4 and 5:

...The crooked places shall be made straight and the rough places smooth; the glory of the Lord shall be revealed, and all flesh shall see it together; for the mouth of the Lord has spoken.

The prophet Isaiah also said of this time, "The loftiness [pride] of man shall be bowed down, and the haughtiness of men shall be brought low; the Lord alone will be exalted in that day."[27] Everyone will be bragging on the Lord Jesus and not on themselves or on one another.[28]

What About the Function of Fivefold Ministers? In my latest major book, *Apostles, Prophets and the Coming Moves of God,* I gave this same projection that after the Prophetic-Apostolic Movement had completed its mission, there would then come a great Saints Movement.[29] I have been preaching this throughout the nations for the last five years. I have heard reports that some who have heard about the Saints Movement have started running in their own immaturity and proclaiming things that are not founded in Scripture. Some started teaching that the days of the fivefold ministers are over, and the Saints are now free to minister as they please since local church structure is no longer needed. Let me say with all apostolic authority that such thoughts are not from God and are absolutely wrong!

The Church will be unified and brought to the same level in Christ so that the Lord alone may be exalted. But this does not imply that the Saints will become a law unto themselves, as God's people did in the Book of Judges where "[the people] did what was right in [their] own eyes."[30] Christ will not have His Saints running around recklessly trying to fulfill their ministry independently of mature prophetic directives, apostolic covering, and pastoral care. God will always have His structure and government in His Church.[31]

The fivefold headship ministries will still provide governmental oversight for the Saints, much as generals and captains give oversight to the soldiers in their army. Prophets will still give direction, apostles will still give covering and accountability, pastors will give pastoral care, teachers will provide sound foundational instruction in the principles of the Word of God, and evangelists will train and equip the Saints for the harvest. God's true fivefold ministers will have a passion for bringing the Saints forth and activating them in their ministries. We must remember that God does things in divine chronological order. He restored the fivefold headship ministries of Christ prior to the coming of the Saints Movement.

THE NEED FOR SOUND BIBLICAL TEACHING IN RESTORED TRUTHS

Having been a Church historian, theologian, and apostle-prophet for decades, I know well the following reality. When God brings a new restoration of truth into the Church by a sovereign move of His Holy Spirit, then good, scriptural, balanced teaching must be made available immediately so that the Saints can be established in the present truth. If this is not done, then spiritually immature, scripturally ignorant and presumptuous, wrongly-motivated ministers, who have more zeal than wisdom, will turn the truth into a tragedy. They will lead some people in the movement off God's path. Their negative example will discourage others from desiring to enter into the reality of the truth God is restoring and may even cause them to oppose it.

During the last 500 years of Church restoration, the movements that did not immediately provide sound teaching from the pulpit and in magazines and books dissipated within a few years. Every denomination today needs to go back to the teaching of their founding fathers and see if they are still teaching and practicing the truth as God originally restored it.

Wisdom From Personal Experience: I was an eyewitness to this very thing happening in a major restoration movement. I became a participant of the Latter Rain Movement in 1952 when the movement was just four years old. During its first ten years of existence, not one major book was written about what God was doing. Only a few booklets were produced, which mainly gave someone's testimony of how they were affected by the movement. No one wrote books giving sound doctrine and scriptural proofs with guidelines for properly establishing and maintaining the truth in wisdom and balance. Within 15 years, most of the hundreds of churches that had been established throughout the United States and the nations of the world during the Latter Rain Movement had disappeared.

About 15 churches on the West Coast of the United States were among the few continuing to teach these truths. Ministers from these churches attended an annual conference taught by Apostle Reg Layzell, who established them in balanced teaching concerning the restoration movement. I was privileged to attend this annual conference from 1954 till 1962, while I was pastoring in

Washington state, and to receive a solid foundation in Latter Rain restoration truths and principles. Sadly, many others who originally received these truths did not hold onto them.

Thank God, though man fails, God does not. Many of the things that were restored in the Latter Rain Movement, but later forgotten by many churches, were brought forth in the Charismatic Movement.

Improper Practices Cause Rejection of Truth: Many major Pentecostal denominations have a problem with personal prophecy and the idea of prophets and apostles because they saw the extremes that took place by some of the propagators of the Latter Rain Movement. Many of the Assembly of God churches lost people to the churches that were started by this movement. Assembly pastors saw many lives ruined because of lack of proper guidelines for personal prophecy. For example, people received unsound prophecies about marriages that eventually contributed to divorces. Some people made unwise geographical moves based on prophecy. I saw the good, the bad, and the ugly. The group I was in fellowship with was led by men of integrity and wisdom. But sadly, that was not true concerning other parts of the movement.

"Baby" Truth vs. Dirty "Bath Water": Most of the Pentecostal denominations "threw the baby out with the bath water." There was plenty of dirty bath water, but there was also a live baby of restoration truth in that water. Today many Pentecostal leaders are reacting negatively to the present-day Prophetic/Apostolic Movement because of their bad experience with the extremes in the Latter

Rain Movement. Nonetheless, the basic problem was the fact that no leaders took time to write the truth and vision in books, so that those who read and participated could run with the vision in scriptural soundness, integrity, and wisdom.

Apostolic-Prophetic Foundation Stones: When I prophetically perceived that there was going to be a Prophetic Movement, I began immediately writing books that gave scriptural teaching and guidelines for the proper ministry of prophets and personal prophecy. My goal was to facilitate the sound establishment of God's truths while helping to prevent the type of hurt and abuses I had witnessed in the Latter Rain Movement. Of course, where there is a "baby" there will always be some dirty bath water, but Church leaders should help the Saints participate with wisdom. The first book, *Prophets and Personal Prophecy*, completed and printed in 1987, has been translated into ten different languages, with copies reaching nearly every nation of the world.[32] It has become a biblical standard on the prophetic for those who believe in prophets and prophetic ministry.

In October 1988 the Prophetic Movement was birthed. I immediately began writing a second book on the prophetic. Titled *Prophets and the Prophetic Movement* and published in 1990, it gives a sound scriptural basis for the truths the Holy Spirit was restoring, an explanation of how the Prophetic Movement aligned with other restoration movements, criteria for determining true and false prophets, and guidelines for knowing the difference between the true ministry of Christian prophets and prophetic people versus the false ministry of psychics, new-agers, and occult practitioners. One of the most important chapters goes into detail on the "Seven Principles of a True Restoration Movement" that we touched on earlier.[33]

I then wrote the third book, *Prophets, Pitfalls, and Principles,* which was published in 1991. It covers numerous pitfalls we are to avoid and the proper prophetic principles we are to practice. Using both my years of biblical study and the experiences of constant involvement in prophetic ministry since 1952, I sought to give wisdom, warnings, and guidelines for prophetic ministers and those who participate in the prophetic. Teaching manuals and workbooks were developed for each book and have been taught to thousands of Saints and church leaders.

Properly Understanding Principles Can Prevent Misuse: Many who are not involved in the prophetic have written, and continue to write, articles on the need for more teaching and accountability in the Prophetic Movement. Nearly all of these authors' fears and areas of concern could be dispelled simply by reading my books or those written by other leaders in the Prophetic Movement. I cannot speak for all who are participating in the prophetic, but as for me and my house (Christian International Ministries Network), we are doing everything possible to make sure the prophetic and apostolic is established on biblical principles and propagated according to God's divine order and purpose. I am just as dedicated to doing the same for the coming Saints Movement. This is one of the major reasons I am writing this book now, although the full birthing of the Day of the Saints may not occur for another two to ten years or more in the future.

PROPHETIC REVELATION ON THE NEED FOR A SAINTS MOVEMENT

After a long 14-hour day working at my computer on this section of the book, I retired about midnight and prayed awhile. I told the Holy Spirit that I needed Father God to give me more of His Spirit of wisdom and revelation so I could know and reveal more of why He planned a Saints Movement. Just before I turned the light out, I asked the Lord, "Why do we need a Saints Movement?" I dozed off for a few minutes, and then suddenly I was wide awake. Scriptural thoughts and divine enlightenment were flooding my mind. I picked up pen and pad and wrote as quickly and continuously as I could. Following is the revelation flow the way it came to me. May you receive the same divine inspiration and revelation that was upon me as I was receiving it. I pray that the prayer in Ephesians 1:15-23 will be fulfilled in you as you read this inspired answer as to the need for a Saints Movement.

Jesus wants every Saint to be mature and activated in membership ministry in the Body of Christ.[34] Though every professing Christian will not go on to maturity, the Holy Spirit has been commissioned to keep working until Christ has a sufficient number to make up a corporate Body of believers—Saints capable of fulfilling His end-time purpose for the Church.[35]

God has a divine purpose for the Omega Generation of the Church to fulfill. There has never been a generation

like them before, and neither will there be one after-
wards.[36] These Saints will be called upon to face and overcome an enemy that no other generation has succeeded
in overcoming.[37] In order to do this they must be conformed to the image of Jesus Christ, dead to sin and self
with their lives hid with Christ in God, not living their own
life but living the divine life of Christ within.[38] They will
function like God's army described by the prophet Joel.[39]
They will have and demonstrate power like the two witnesses described by the apostle John.[40]

They must be knowledgable of and know how to use
their weapons of warfare—the Word of God, the life-blood
and name of Jesus, and the gifts of the Holy Spirit.[41] They
must be suited up in their Christian armor along with the
garment of praise and robe of righteousness.[42] The Saints
must be trained and enabled to wield the sword of the
Lord fearlessly.[43] They must come to the unity of the faith,
knowledge of the Son of God, unto a perfect man, which
is one who has reached the measure of the stature of the
fullness of Christ Himself.[44] Saints must continue growing
until they grow up into the fullness of the way, the truth,
and the life of Christ—who is Head of the Church and
Commander in Chief of His army of Saints.[45]

For the time will soon come for the Ancient of Days
to make a judgment in favor of the Saints.[46] At that time all
the power and authority that Christ obtained for the
Church will be given to the Saints to take the Kingdom.[47]
God's Kingdom of Saints will go forth conquering and to
conquer until they subdue all other kingdoms.[48] The rule
of the Kingdom of God shall be over all the earth and the
Saints shall reign with Christ as kings and priests.[49]

The next progressive step towards all of this taking place is the Saints Movement. Fivefold ministers must intensify their ministry of teaching, training, activating, and maturing the Saints in their membership ministries and weapons of war.[50] The Holy Spirit has been given a schedule and time frame in which to complete the equipping of the Saints. He will work with those who work with Him, and He will leave to themselves those who will not.[51] The pastors must transform their nursing home and retirement center churches into armories and military training camps. It is time to fulfill Joel's prophetic charge to the end-time Church:

> Blow the trumpet in Zion, and sound an alarm in My holy mountain!...Proclaim this among the nations: "Prepare for war! Wake up the mighty men, let all the men of war draw near, let them come up. Beat your plowshares into swords and your pruning hooks into spears; let the weak say, 'I am strong.'"[52]

Take your praise that you have used just to receive a blessing and turn it into **warfare praise**.[53] Take your prayers that you have prayed to meet your own needs and turn them into aggressive, **intercessory warfare prayer**.[54] Let the songs you have sung just for a melodious feeling be turned into **songs of deliverance**—for there is to be deliverance in Zion![55] Let your shout be more than a charismatic ritual. Let it become a **shout of faith** that collapses the walls of the strongholds of the enemy, so that the Saints may possess their promised possessions and fulfill their prophetic destiny.[56] Arise, oh sleeping giant of the Church! Put on your **full armor**, take out your sharpened sword and all your **weapons of war**, and begin marching throughout the world, conquering and subduing all things unto Christ Jesus, your Savior and conquering King.[57]

I am sharing with you what the Lord shared with me concerning some of those things that Christ Jesus has prepared and planned for His mortal Church. Selected Scriptures prove each thought presented. There will be even more glorious things revealed and activated for the ministry and life of Christ's immortal Church in the ages to come. The revelation thoughts recorded here are expanded with more insight and detail in other chapters. This gives just a glimpse of why the Saints need to be taught, trained, and activated in order to fulfill God's purpose for the "Omega"—or last-days—Generation that will be brought to the forefront in the Saints Movement.

In the last chapter we looked at the "Alpha Generation"—the first-century Saints. We will address the Omega Generation more specifically in Chapter 11. First we want to outline more of what the Holy Spirit has been doing in the 1,972 years since the Church was birthed. We can fully appropriate all the wisdom and revelation that will empower us to fulfill the will of God for our generation. Then we will look at more "how to's" to gain practical understanding of taking up our weapons as this coming army of the Lord.

Step-by-Step to the Final Step: Like every restorational movement of the past that has taken the Church a step further, the Saints Movement will take the Church within one or two steps of its final destiny and ultimate fulfillment. There is nothing more important for a Saint than to start preparing now and continue on until... " 'Eye has not seen, nor ear heard...the things which God has prepared for those who love Him.' But God has revealed them to us through His Spirit."[58] The Holy Spirit will bring new truth and grace from the Word of God, enabling the Saints to appropriate the full power and authority that Christ Jesus appropriated for us. May the spirit of wisdom and revelation be given so that the eyes of the Saints may be enlightened to know their full inheritance in Christ and the exceeding greatness of His power within which is available when the Saints believe.[59] Christ will be glorified in His Church throughout the endless ages. "To Him be glory in the church by Christ Jesus to all generations, forever and ever. Amen."[60]

ENDNOTES:

1. *Prophets and Personal Prophecy*; *Prophets and the Prophetic Movement*; *Prophets, Pitfalls, and Principles*; *Apostles, Prophets and the Coming Moves of God*. See the back of this book for ordering information.

2. Matthew 25:21.

3. Amos 3:7.

4. 1 Chronicles 12:32a; see also Revelation 10:7.

5. Habakkuk 2:2b-3.

6. Amos 3:7.

7. Bill Hamon, *The Eternal Church* (Santa Rosa Beach, FL: Christian International Publishers, 1981). See the back of this book for ordering information.

8. Daniel 2:44b.

9. Revelation 11:15b.

10. Acts 3:19-21,23-25 KJV.

11. Charles John Ellicot, gen. ed., *Ellicot's Commentary on the Whole Bible* (Grand Rapids, MI: Zondervan, 1954), vol. 7,

"The Acts of the Apostles," E. H. Plumtree, p. 19. Emphasis added.

12. Ephesians 1:17-23; 3:1-11.

13. Acts 3:21; 2 Thessalonians 2:3.

14. Mark 4:3-9.

15. 1 John 1:7a.

16. For more details on these seven principles, see Bill Hamon, *Prophets and the Prophetic Movement* (Shippensburg, PA: Destiny Image Publishers, Inc., 1990), pp. 81-122.

17. Hamon, *The Eternal Church*, pp. 238-241.

18. Jeremiah 25:11-12; 29:10.

19. Leviticus 25:11.

20. Genesis 7:4.

21. Exodus 24:18.

22. Numbers 14:34.

23. Numbers 32:13; Joshua 1:2.

24. Matthew 4:1,17.

25. I am currently writing a book by this title. C. Peter Wagner and others term this the "New Apostolic Reformation." See Dr. Wagner's book *The New Apostolic Churches* (Ventura, CA: Regal, 1998) for more information.

26. Bill Hamon, *Prophets and Personal Prophecy* (Shippensburg, PA: Destiny Image Publishers, Inc., 1987), pp. 24-28.

27. Isaiah 2:17.

28. 1 Corinthians 1:31; 2 Corinthians 10:17-18.

29. Bill Hamon, *Apostles, Prophets and the Coming Moves of God* (Shippensburg, PA: Destiny Image Publishers, Inc., 1997), p. 244.

30. Judges 17:6; 21:25.

31. Isaiah 9:6-7; Daniel 2:44.

32. Languages include Spanish, Mandarin Chinese, Japanese, Dutch, Korean, German, Indonesian, Latvian, and Italian.

33. Hamon, *Prophets and the Prophetic Movement*, pp. 81-121.

34. Ephesians 4:12; 1 Corinthians 12:1-27.

35. Ephesians 3:10; Revelation 17:17.

36. Psalm 102:18.

37. 1 Corinthians 15:26.

38. Romans 8:29; 6:11-16; Galatians 2:20; Colossians 1:27.
39. Joel 2:1-12.
40. Revelation 11:1-5.
41. Corinthians 10:4; Ephesians 6:17; Revelation 12:11; Ephesians 1:21-23; Mark 16:17-20; 1 Corinthians 12:8-11.
42. Ephesians 6:10-18.
43. Ephesians 6:17.
44. Ephesians 4:12-16.
45. John 14:6; Revelation 19:11-16.
46. Daniel 7:22,27.
47. Matthew 28:18-20; Luke 10:19.
48. Genesis 1:26-27.
49. Revelation 11:15; 1:6; 5:10.
50. Ephesians 4:11; 2 Timothy 2:2.
51. Joshua 24:20.
52. Joel 2:1; 3:9-10.
53. Psalm 149:5-9.
54. 2 Timothy 2:4; 2 Corinthians 10:3-4.
55. Psalm 32:7; Joel 2:32.
56. Joshua 6:20.
57. Ephesians 6:11,13.
58. 1 Corinthians 2:9b-10a.
59. Ephesians 1:18-21.
60. Ephesians 3:21.

CHAPTER 5

A BRIEF HISTORY
OF CHURCH RESTORATION

If you are a child of God by faith in Jesus Christ and you are reading this book with mortal eyes, then Christ still has not returned. What is this time, called the "Period of the Restoration" in Acts 3:21, supposed to produce before it fulfills its predestined purpose? Since we are still in the time period of restoration, we need to have a thorough understanding of its process, methods, principles, and purpose. This understanding will greatly enhance the Saints with the knowledge they need to co-labor with Christ in fulfilling His destiny for His Church and planet Earth.

"Restoration Movement" Defined: The phrase *restoration movement* is used by Church historians and theologians to describe a time when the Holy Spirit acts sovereignly within the Church to restore a biblical truth or ministry back to its proper order and function. As we saw in the last chapter, God commissions the Holy Spirit to restore more truths and ministries back into His Church in alignment with the "times of restoration" prophesied by Peter in Acts 3:21. Over 500 years of recorded Church history of restoration movements have provided the historical reality and factual truth of "Church restoration." God the Father has certain methods that He has directed the Holy Spirit to use in restoring Christ's Church to the place of its purity and maturity for presentation as a proper Bride to Jesus Christ the Bridegroom.

THE CHURCH AGE

Acts is the pattern for the New Testament Church Age. The coming Day of the Saints will have everything found in the first-century Church. All the truths, ministries, doctrines, and supernatural manifestations that were in the Early Church as portrayed in the Book of Acts were to continue throughout the Church Age. This was the new covenant that God made with the Church, similar to the covenant of circumcision God made with Abraham.[1] The law and the tabernacle provided God's covenant for proper relationship with Him from the time Moses received the law of God on Mount Sinai until the time of Jesus on the cross. By His death, burial, and resurrection, Jesus fulfilled the law and the old covenant. He also ushered in a new covenant, which is identified as the New Testament in the Holy Bible.[2] No additional covenants or adjustments to Christ's covenant with the Church have happened since the New Testament was written. Religious theologians have added their interpretations to it and deleted the relevance of its accuracy and application, but

God has not tampered with it. All that is written is just as workable now as it was when it was written.[3]

Dispensations Defined: An explanation of the notion of "times" may be helpful here. Christian theologians and historians have divided human existence on Earth into different periods of time called "dispensations," "covenants," or "ages." These are normally synonymous terms. A dispensation is a period of time during which God works with humankind according to a set of divine rules and principles, which humankind must follow in order to have fellowship with God and to fulfill His will. The pattern of God's plan and purpose for that generation is established at the beginning of the dispensation and continues to be God's will and way for humanity until He changes the pattern, after which another dispensation, covenant, or age is established.[4] In this context, "dispensation" is different from the dispensationalism that we discussed in Chapter 2. What we covered in dispensationalism were the doctrines that developed which deleted from the Church most of its New Testament truths, power, and ministries.

The chart on the next page gives the most commonly accepted designations for the various dispensations, covenants, and the periods of time that they cover.

The Four Major Phases of the Church Age: Within each of these ages are shorter periods of time referred to as times, seasons, years, and last days, as well as times of revival or renewal and restoration movements. We are currently in the age of the mortal Church. It includes all the following: The early days of the Church; the great falling away during the Dark Ages; the times of the restoration

movements; and the last days or end times until the resurrection and translation of the Saints at Christ's second
coming. These four major phases can be identified by
four words: **origination**, **deterioration**, **restoration**, and
destination.[5]

DISPENSATION	COVENANT	PERIOD OF TIME (Approximate)
Innocence	Edenic	From the creation to the fall of humankind (eternity past)
Conscience	Adamic	From the fall of humankind to Noah's flood (1500 years)
Human Government	Noahic	From the flood to the call of Abraham (500 years)
Promise	Abrahamic	From Abraham to the law at Mount Sinai (500 years)
Law	Mosaic	From Mount Sinai to the coming of Christ as Messiah (1500 years)
Grace	Church	From Pentecost to Christ's second coming (2000 years)
Millennial	Kingdom	From the beginning to the end of the Millennium (1000 years)
Universal	Everlasting	From the end of the Millennium into eternity (eternity future)

The **origination** covers the time when the Church was birthed on the Day of Pentecost in A.D. 30, established fully as a separate entity from Judaism in A.D. 70 with the fall of Jerusalem, and expanded as the gospel was taken to the ends of the earth by the third and fourth centuries. The **deterioration** of the Church covers the period of the great falling away into an apostate condition from the fourth century to the fifteenth century A.D. The **restoration** of the Church officially began with the Protestant Movement and has progressed through 500 years of restorational moves of God. The **destination** of the Church covers the future and final ministry of the mortal Church and then its resurrection/translation into its immortal reign with Christ during the endless ages to come: "To Him be glory **in the church** by Christ Jesus to all generations, forever and ever. Amen."[6] This section of the book will reveal how the restoration movements up to the present have prepared the way for the coming Saints Movement.

Denominations Came From Periods of Church Restoration: Hundreds of Christian denominations, organizations, and independent church groups exist within mainline Christendom. Based on their involvement in Church restoration and their doctrines and practices, they can be divided into six major categories: (1) Catholic/Orthodox, (2) Historic Protestant, (3) Holiness-Evangelical, (4) Classical Pentecostal, (5) Latter Rain-Charismatic, and (6) Prophetic/Apostolic. Most of the following historical summary of these groups comes from my study of Church history entitled *The Eternal Church.*[7]

Catholic and Orthodox Churches: The Roman Catholic and Eastern Orthodox churches maintained the Christian faith during the time period of the Church's deterioration. Not only did religious traditions of men cause the vibrancy of the Early Church to be dimmed during the Dark Ages, but other threats came from outside the Church. Pagan tribes, commonly called the barbarians, and the warrior followers of Mohammed's fanatical religion, Islam, sought to conquer the Christian world. Even while many church leaders fell into apostasy, some monks, devout priests, nuns, and godly believers helped to preserve the faith. But these groups were not a part of the great restoration of the Church. The Protestant Movement formed the beginning of Church Restoration.

THE FIVE RESTORATION MOVEMENTS SUMMARIZED

Church historians have designated the year A.D. 1517 as the official beginning of the period of Church restoration. There have been five major movements since that time:

1. The Protestant Movement
2. The Holiness Movement
3. The Pentecostal Movement
4. The Charismatic Movement
5. The Prophetic-Apostolic Movement

Five Major Movements: All Christians who have received God's present truth accept these last five groups as restoration movements that were ordained of God. They are called major movements because each one restored back into the Church truths and ministries that were lost during the Dark Age of the Church. All Protestant Christians find their roots and present affiliation and function in one of these five groups. You need to ask yourself, "Why am I in this particular group?" And, "Am I receiving and experiencing all truth that has been restored to the Church?" If the answer is yes, then you are fulfilling apostle Peter's command for the Saints to "[be] established in the present truth."[8]

Progressive Restoration of Truth: Categorizing these individual movements according to the particular century and decade when each truth and ministry were restored gives more specific insight to actual dates and denominations that developed from that particular truth restoration. The Holiness Movement actually covers all the truths restored during the 300-year period from 1600 to 1900.[9] The Charismatic Movement covers all the truth restored from 1950 to 1980, including three distinct truths that were restored by different movements within the Charismatic Renewal.[10] The Prophetic-Apostolic Movement covers the last two decades of the twentieth century through probably the first decade of the twenty-first century. (See chart on following pages.)

The Historic Protestant Movement: Historically, the Protestant churches came into existence because Martin Luther, John Knox, Thomas Cranmer, and numerous other ministers broke away from the Catholic church, fighting for and establishing the right to be churches separate from Catholicism. **Spiritually,** the movement came into existence because a man of God received a revelation of truth that made it impossible for him to continue in the religious system that he believed was contrary to the Word of God. Luther would have had to deny his knowledge of the Word of God, his conscience, and his newly received spiritual experience in order to remain a priest who promoted the doctrines and practices of the Catholic church.

YEAR	MOVEMENT	MAJOR TRUTHS RESTORED	DENOMINATIONS FOUNDED
1500	Protestant Movement	Salvation by grace through faith (Eph. 2:8-9).	Lutheran, Episcopalian, Presbyterian, Congregational
1600	Evangelical Movement	Water baptism, separation of church and state.	Mennonite, Baptist, All Fundamental-Evangelical churches
1700	Holiness Movement	Sanctification, the Church set apart from the world.	Methodist, Nazarene, Church of God, all Holiness churches
1800	Faith Healing Movement	Divine physical healing in the atonement.	Christian Missionary Alliance, Church of God
1900	Pentecostal Movement	Holy Spirit baptism with unknown tongues.	Assembly of God, United Pentecostal, Foursquare, Church of God in Christ
1950	Latter Rain Movement	Prophetic presbytery, singing praises, and Body of Christ membership ministries.	Non-denominational churches
1950	Deliverance Evangelism	**Evangelist** ministry and mass evangelism reactivated with miraculous healings.	Independent churches and ministerial fellowships

1960	Charismatic Movement	Renewal of all restored truth to all past movement churches. **Pastors** were restored to being sovereign head of their local churches.	Charismatic churches and Charismatic groups within denominational churches
1970	Faith Movement	Faith confessions, prosperity, and victorious attitude and life. **Teacher** ministry reestablished as a fivefold minister.	Faith and Word churches
1980	Prophetic Movement	Personal prophecy, activating gifts, warfare praise, prophets to nations. **Prophet** ministry was restored and a company of prophets brought forth.	Prophetic churches and networks
1990	Apostolic Movement	Apostolic leadership, release of miracles, networking, great harvest. **Apostle** ministry restored to bring divine order, finalize restoration of fivefold ministers for full equipping of the Saints.	Apostolic churches and networks
20??	Saints	Saints demonstrating the gospel of the Kingdom and reaping the harvest!	

Restorationally, Protestantism came into existence because the Holy Spirit initiated the period of the restoration of the Church. The Protestant churches brought back into the Church the revelation, proper application, and re-establishment of the first doctrine of Christ—repentance from dead works.[11] Europe was the place of the movement's birth and growth; the priests and people who came out of the Catholic church were the ones who propagated the movement. The printing press, a new product of that time, was used to publicize its restorational truths. Three national church denominations were established in the Protestant Movement: the Lutheran in Germany, the Presbyterian in Scotland, and the Anglican in England (called Episcopalian in America).

God used Martin Luther to proclaim the message that one is justified by the mercy and grace of Jesus Christ through faith and not through works. The teaching of the priesthood of the believer was revolutionary. The reformers preached the Word, inspiring faith in God. The result was that the corporate Body of Christ, His Church, awakened from her lethargy and apostasy and took the first of many restorational steps toward the coming Saints Movement, which will take the Church one step closer to the second coming of Christ.

The Holiness-Evangelical Movement: This movement's purpose was to restore the Saints on the second foundation stone of the Church called the doctrine of "faith toward God."[12] The movement was conceived in Europe, but America became the place of its birth and growth to maturity. The men God used were numerous, but John Wesley is perhaps the man most noted for promoting holiness.

The people who participated and the ministers who prop-agated the truth came primarily from Protestant Move-ment churches.

The message was threefold: believer's baptism by im-mersion, sanctification, and divine healing. The preach-ing of the Word was accompanied by special singers, great conviction, blessing, emotional manifestations, and physi-cal healings. New modes of transportation, the steamship and trains, carried the message to the ends of the earth. The result was that the eternal Church crossed the "Red Sea" of water baptism, became sanctified and separated from the world, and then journeyed on to receive Christ's redemptive work of divine healing at the "waters of Marah." Thus, the second giant step had been taken by the Church in the restorational walk to its "Canaan" of full maturity in Christ Jesus.

The Classical Pentecostal Movement: The Pentecostal Movement's purpose was to restore the Holy Spirit to His powerful performance in the Church. By gifting the indi-vidual believer with "other tongues" in the baptism of the Holy Spirit and by releasing the gifts of the Spirit to the Church, Jesus restored the third doctrine of Christ to the Church—**the doctrine of baptisms.**[13] The place of its birth was the United States, after which it spread to the world, with the greatest percentage of growth among Christians in Latin America.

The Pentecostal Movement claims no single person as its founder; however, Charles F. Parham and W. H. Seymour come as close as any of those involved to qualifying for the role. The people who participated and the ministers who propagated the Pentecostal truth came mainly from the Holiness Movement churches. The message was the baptism of the Holy Spirit evidenced by speaking in "other tongues." The ministry was the preaching of the Word accompanied by healings, miracles, speaking in other tongues, and gifts of the Holy Spirit. All types of musical instruments and singing were used to promote the gospel and to worship God. "Dancing in the spirit" became accepted as a Spirit-directed expression of praise. New methods of commuting and communicating this restorational truth to the ends of the earth included the automobile and the radio.

Thus the Church advanced in its restorational journey through the wilderness to its "water from the Rock" experience. The result was more powerful performance in ministry, greater evangelism, and "rivers of living water" flowing out of the Saints' innermost beings in other tongues. The Pentecostal Movement was another progressive step in the walk of the Saints toward their prophesied destiny.

If all that was needed was to restore the Saints back to a proper relationship with God through justification by faith, water baptism by immersion, sanctification, and empowerment of the Holy Spirit, then the coming of the Lord could have taken place anytime during the last 100 years. But Jesus has not returned yet! Several restoration movements took place during the twentieth century after the Pentecostal Movement.

The Latter Rain-Charismatic Movement: God's purpose for the Latter Rain Movement was to restore to the

Church the fourth doctrine of Christ—**the laying on of hands**.[14] The place of its birth was Canada. It then spread throughout the United States and around the world.

The Latter Rain Movement has never recognized any individual or group as head of the movement, but certain men were notable in making known and maintaining the doctrine of laying on of hands. Oral Roberts taught the laying on of hands for healing. A key leader who propagated the laying on of hands with personal prophecy by the presbytery (called a "prophetic presbytery") was Reginald Layzell. The laying on of hands with prophesying, healings, and miracles was taught by William Branham. The majority of the people who participated and the ministers who propagated deliverance evangelism and Latter Rain truths came mostly from the Pentecostal Movement churches.

We discussed the difference between the Charismatic Renewal and the Charismatic Movement in Chapter 4. Key men who were originally instrumental in activating and spreading the Charismatic Renewal were Dennis Bennett, David du Plessis, and Demos Shakarian. Derek Prince helped make historic Saints conscious of the reality of the spirit world of demon activity. Kenneth Hagin became known as the father of the faith message for prosperity and health.

Those who originally were called Charismatic were ministers and members of historic Protestant denominations. Later those who participated from the Catholic and Orthodox, Holiness, Evangelical, and Fundamentalist churches were called by the same term. Finally, many Pentecostal and Latter Rain leaders reluctantly accepted the word *Charismatic* to identify those who were Holy Spirit-filled, tongues-talking, God-praising, present-truth Christians for that day and hour.

The Message of the Charismatic Movement: The message of the Latter Rain-Charismatic Movement was threefold:

1. The laying on of hands for healing, Holy Spirit baptism, deliverance, Body of Christ membership ministry, and activation of three more gifts of the Holy Spirit.

2. The proclamation of all the Pentecostal and Latter Rain Movement truths to denominational Christians. This was done mainly by denominational ministers who were newly baptized in the Holy Spirit.

3. The proclamation by present-truth and faith ministers concerning the maturing of the Body of Christ and of Christians living victoriously—spiritually, physically, and financially.

The ministry of the preaching of the Word was accompanied by healings, prophecy, and revelation gifts. This caused many souls to be saved, extensive spiritual growth in individual Christians, the numerical growth of churches, and the prosperity of the Saints.

Time to Move On: The result was that the Church/Saints reached their Mount Sinai experience and remained there until divine order was established so that all Christendom had an opportunity to move to the front line of present truth. The Church was encamped at that mountain of truth (Charismatic Movement) for 40 years (1948–1988). I believe that in 1988 the angel of the Church in Heaven started trumpeting a message in Heaven which began to be echoed on Earth by the emerging company of apostles and prophets. It declared, "Church, we have been here long enough. It is time for another restoration movement!"[15]

The Prophetic-Apostolic Movement: God's purpose in this movement was to bring full restoration and activation of the fivefold ministry of prophets and apostles. Several other truths and ministries were restored during this time. Not only was the fivefold office of prophet restored, but a whole company of prophets was brought forth to corporately fulfill the prophecies concerning the Elijah who was to come and prepare the way and make ready a people for the coming of the Lord. This company of prophets and apostles with that "Elijah" anointing will fulfill those Scriptures for Christ's second coming, just as John the Baptist fulfilled them for Christ's first coming.[16]

The Prophetic Movement brought the revelation of how to activate Saints into their spiritual gifts of prophecy, word of knowledge, and word of wisdom. The Apostolic Movement is doing the same for the Saints in the power gifts of healings, faith, and working of miracles. In correlating the progressive journey of Israel from Egypt into Canaan, the Prophetic-Apostolic Movement crossed the Church over Jordan to begin the warfare of possessing their promised Canaan land. The Canaan land of the Church and of the Saints individually is conformity to Christ's image with no "-ites" of selfishness and sin left. God's purpose for the Saints is for them to keep fighting and subduing the enemy and driving out all the "-ites" of everything contrary to the character of Jesus until the kingdoms of this world become the kingdoms of our Lord Jesus and His Church.[17] That is the reason prophetic leaders taught and demonstrated warfare praise and prophetic-apostolic intercessory prayer.

Activation: Another key message and ministry that had not been restored in the Charismatic Movement is revealed by the word the prophetic ministers chose to describe it, *activation*. The core teaching on activation was that all Saints can be prophetic in that they can hear the voice of God and minister the mind of Christ to others. Saints can be activated into the gifts of the Spirit just like a sinner can be activated into the gift of eternal life or a born-again Christian can be activated into the gift of the Holy Spirit. All three of these experiences are sovereignly given by God, received by grace, and manifested by faith. The passion of the leaders of the movement was to teach, train, activate, mentor, and mature the Saints into their membership ministry in the Body of Christ. Emphasis was given to the Scriptures which state: "You can all prophesy one by one"; "Desire spiritual gifts"; "Desire earnestly to prophesy"; and "Prophesy [by the Spirit] in proportion to [one's] faith," not by physical sensations or emotions of the soul.[18] We will look at this in greater detail in Chapter 9.

Some of the Other Major Teachings: The Prophetic-Apostolic Movement restored the understanding of the Holy Spirit sending apostles and prophets to the nations, usually to minister to the heads of those nations. Prophetic ministers believed that the Prophetic Movement brought with it the baptism of fire for intensified purifying of the Saints.[19] The apostolic portion gave more emphasis to God's divine order for building the Church, unity of the Body of Christ, world harvest, miracles, and deliverance. However, the major purpose of God for restoring the prophets and apostles was to complete His fivefold ministers. Instead of just three being recognized, all five must be active, so that they can fulfill their commission of equipping the Saints to participate in the Days of the Saints.

The movement was birthed in the United States of America and then spread around the world. Along with Paul Cain and others, I have had the privilege of being one of the pioneers and leaders of the Prophetic Movement.[20] The apostolic in the late 1990s was championed and propagated by John Eckhardt, C. Peter Wagner, and hundreds of others around the world. No one person received great recognition, because one of the key points of the movement was "team ministry" and networking together for the corporate good of God's purpose. The new products of commuting and communication that helped spread the message of the movement were jet planes, computers, books, the Internet, and all the new and advanced technologies.

The Apostolic-Prophetic "Joshua Generation": Much teaching was given on the "Joshua Generation" and the transitions that took place when the Church crossed over its Jordan and began possessing its promised Canaan land.[21] The Joshua Generation is leading forth, and the priestly pastors have carried the ark of God's restorational presence across Jordan. The journey of the Charismatic

Movement has fulfilled its purpose of bringing the Church to its Jordan River. The cloud by day and the fire by night that covered and led God's people have been replaced by the fiery prophets and covering apostles.[22] The apostles and prophets have arisen to provide protection, direction, and timing for the forward move of the Church. The manna has ceased, and now it is time to eat the corn of Canaan, drink the milk, and be energized by the honey to destroy the wicked enemies and drive them out of the promised land of the Church.

Receiving a revelation and vision of Christ's restorational purpose and the things that the Church is to accomplish before Jesus returns stirs up the Saints' faith and their zeal for the Lord. Seeing Jesus as the Restorer and the Mighty Man of War develops a militant spirit. It increases the desire to complete the wilderness journey, cross over Jordan, and drive out all of the "-ites" from the promised land that God has promised the Church. The Church has as great a commission and predestined purpose as Israel had to possess, take dominion, and occupy till Jesus comes.[23]

This term *occupy* implies more than a passive resistance. It refers to a militant occupying force enforcing the rule of their conquering king. Saints ministering with prophetic-apostolic anointing will do evangelism, which will reveal the secrets of human hearts and cause people to fall down and worship God and testify of His mighty works.[24] The Church will start walking with those conquering feet as the "Joshua Generation." And just as the promise was given to Joshua, so will it be with the Saints

Movement generation: "Every place that the sole of your foot will tread upon I have given you...."[25]

What Is Next on God's Agenda?

The next restoration movement on the Holy Spirit's schedule after the Prophetic-Apostolic Movement has accomplished its purpose is the Saints Movement or Day of the Saints. This next time of restoration is ordained of God to accomplish certain things. The Saints Movement will progress the mortal Church one step closer to fulfilling its ultimate destination, as other movements have done. Christ sent the Holy Spirit of Truth to take the things of Christ and declare them unto us, to show us things to come and guide us into all truth.[26] Part of the truth that He is guiding the Church into is that which is to be revealed, restored, and manifest by the Saints.

The "Snowball" Principle of Restoration: The fully restored Church will be the stone that the prophet Daniel saw hewn out of the mountain. It will progress like a rolling snowball gaining momentum as it reaches the bottom of the mountain. If you make a hard snowball and roll it down the steep, smooth slope of a snow-covered mountainside, it begins to get bigger and go faster. That is the same way Church restoration works. The Protestant Movement made the snowball at the top of the mountain. With each restoration movement the snowballing Church has become greater and the movements have begun happening faster. The Dark Ages lasted 1,000 years, until Church Restoration began in 1500. Three hundred years later, in 1800, the Holiness Movement came. Then 100 years later, in 1900, the Pentecostal Movement appeared. Fifty years later the Latter

Rain-Charismatic Movement was born. And now, since 1950, there has been a new restorational move or spiritual renewal every decade.

A Gigantic, Final Tidal Wave of Restoration Is Coming: Five major waves of restoration have taken place during the last 500 years, with smaller waves of restoration and renewal between each of those. Several of these smaller waves of restoration and spiritual renewal of various truths and ministries have taken place from 1948 to 1998. And now in this twenty-first century of the Church, several more are on God's refreshing and restoration schedule. The prophets and apostles are seeing on the horizon of God's purpose for His Church a restorational wave of such incomprehensibly gigantic proportions—like a thousand-foot tidal wave—that it staggers the imagination and faith of both those who have prophetically seen it and those who have heard of it. The Day of the Saints will activate the great swelling of the wave and the two movements following it will be greater than all previous restoration movements combined.

Jesus grew in maturity for 30 years, then He spent three years demonstrating and preaching the gospel of the Kingdom of God full-time. The Church has spent nearly 2,000 years growing in maturity and being restored. There is shortly coming a period of time where we actively demonstrate the Kingdom of God to the world.

The Final Restoration Movements: The present revelation and hopeful expectation is that the seventh and final major restoration movement will take place before the year 2030. No one but God knows what it will be called, but prophetic revelation makes us know what it shall be and do. It will activate the Saints into the mighty conquering army of the Lord to establish God's Kingdom throughout the Earth until the kingdoms of this world have become the kingdoms of our Lord Jesus and His anointed Saints (the Church).[27] I will call that future time of restoration the "Army of the Lord/Kingdom Establishing Movement." However, that is in the future beyond the Saints Movement.

A Time Unlike Any Before: As the prophet Joel declared, there has never been a time like this before, and there never will be again.[28] As the prophets and apostles continue to reveal the mysteries of God and echo on Earth what the angels are sounding in Heaven, it will be the time of Revelation 10:7 (KJV): "But in the days of the voice of the seventh angel, when he shall begin to sound, the mystery of God should be finished, as He hath declared to His servants the prophets." The last of the three coming moves of God will bring about the activation of Revelation 11:15 (KJV):

> *And the seventh angel sounded; and there were great voices in heaven, saying, The kingdoms of this world are become the kingdoms of our Lord, and of His Christ, and He shall reign for ever and ever.*

Acts 3:19-25 will be fulfilled concerning the restoration of all things which God has spoken by the mouth of all His holy prophets since the world began. This time will thus fulfill all things necessary for the release of Jesus from Heaven. The tidal wave of restoration headed by Christ Jesus will have such a force and height that it will sweep all evil principalities from Earth and out of the heavenlies. All the kingdoms of this world will be subdued under the lordship of Jesus Christ. The Kingdom of our Lord Jesus and His Christ/anointed Church will be established in the heavenlies and over all the Earth.

ENDNOTES:

1. Genesis 17:10-11.
2. Romans 10:4.
3. Hebrews 13:8.
4. Bill Hamon, *The Eternal Church* (Santa Rosa Beach, FL: Christian International Publishers, 1981), p. 19.
5. Ibid, pp. 47, 85, 115, 307.
6. Ephesians 3:21.
7. Hamon, *The Eternal Church*, pp. 169-305.
8. 2 Peter 1:12b.
9. Hamon, *The Eternal Church*, pp. 187-208.
10. Ibid, pp. 269-305.
11. Hebrews 6:1-2.
12. Hebrews 6:1-2.
13. Hebrews 6:2.
14. Hamon, *The Eternal Church*, pp. 242-248.
15. Deuteronomy 2:3.
16. Malachi 4:5, cf. Matthew 11:9-14; Isaiah 40:3-5, cf. Luke 1:16-17; Matthew 17:11, cf. Acts 3:21.
17. Romans 8:29; Revelation 11:15.
18. 1 Corinthians 14:1,31,39; Romans 12:6.
19. Malachi 3:1-5; 1 Corinthians 3:13.
20. *Charisma* Magazine, September 1989.
21. Bill Hamon, *Apostles, Prophets and the Coming Moves of God* (Shippensburg, PA: Destiny Image, 1997), pp. 108-122.
22. Exodus 13:21-22.
23. Luke 19:13 KJV; Exodus 15:3.
24. 1 Corinthians 14:24-25.
25. Joshua 1:3.
26. John 16:13-15.
27. Revelation 11:15.
28. Joel 2:2.

CHAPTER 6

EQUIPPING
THE SAINTS

In the last chapter we saw that the Holy Spirit is in the process of restoring the full function of apostles and prophets to Christ's Church in preparation for the coming Day of the Saints. In this chapter we will look at each of the five ascension gift ministries of Christ and the importance of every Saint's being equipped by each of these ministries. These offices are the ones Christ has called and commissioned to activate the Saints into the supernatural works of the believer. In addition, the teaching, impartation, and instruction of godly leaders is vital for Saints to grow into maturity in their character to be conformed inwardly to the image of Christ. Even Jesus Himself had to grow in wisdom and stature with God and man.[1]

The Fivefold Ascension Gifts: Apostle Paul revealed that the ones Christ Jesus has commissioned to equip His Saints are those He gifted as apostles, prophets, evangelists, pastors, and teachers. When Elijah ascended to Heaven in a whirl-wind, he left his whole mantle to Elisha.[2] When Jesus ascended to Heaven, He also gave His mantle. But He did not give all of it to any one person. He divided it into five different pieces of gifted abilities, which are His headship ministry given to the Church. Therefore, we call these the "fivefold" ministry gifts. Jesus is the Apostle of the Church, the Prophet, Evangelist, Pastor, and Teacher. Christ was all five of those ministries manifested in one human body. The Scripture declares that the fullness of God's ministry to the world and the Church dwelt in the personal body of Jesus.[3] When the body of Jesus was resurrected and ascended back to the Father, those ministries were then given to certain members of the corporate Body of Christ.

> *When* [Christ] *ascended on high, He led captivity captive, and gave gifts to men....And He Himself gave some to be apostles, some prophets, some evangelists, and some pastors and teachers, for the equipping of the saints for the work of ministry, for the edifying of the body of Christ.*[4]

Fivefold ascension gift ministers are divinely enabled to equip the Saints for their membership ministries in the Body of Christ. Then every member will be able to contribute his part in causing the whole Body to be built to a perfect man, even to the measure of the stature of the fullness of Christ. Every Saint has a ministry of Christ to the corporate Body of Christ and to the world.[5]

The Saints Movement could not be fulfilled until the twenty-first century. Prior to the twenty-first century, the ministry of the Saints could not have been fully implemented since all fivefold ministers were not restored and positioned to fulfill their commission. Now all things are ready for intensified teaching, activating, and equipping of the Saints. During the last half of the twentieth century the Holy Spirit brought all five gifted ministries to the place where they could fulfill this purpose.[6] First we'll look briefly at why the recognition of fivefold ministers, which was present in the Early Church, was lost. Then we'll look at the restoration of each office and why every Saint needs to be properly related with each of these ministries.

THE NEED TO RESTORE THE FIVEFOLD MINISTRIES

Why did the fivefold ministries need to be restored? All five ministries need to be fully active in the twenty-first century Church, especially for the purpose of equipping the Saints to be participants in the coming Day of the Saints. Teaching and books on the biblical validity of apostles and prophets in the Church are needed to negate the erroneous teaching that developed concerning apostles and prophets during the Evangelical-Holiness Movement. At that time some people started teaching that apostles and prophets are not a valid ministry in the present Church. In the past, dispensational theologians took a Scripture Paul wrote to the Ephesians about apostles and prophets and interpreted it in a way that neither Paul nor the Holy Spirit ever intended.

Local Churches Built on the Foundation of Apostles and Prophets: Paul told the Ephesians that they had been brought into the Church and were built upon the foundation of the apostle and prophet, with Jesus Christ Himself being the Chief Cornerstone from which the whole building of the Church is aligned.[7] This was prototyped when apostle Paul and prophet Silas went to Ephesus and won many to Christ. They stayed there and established the Saints into the first New Testament church built upon the foundation of the apostle and prophet. They exalted Christ Jesus as the sovereign Head of the Church, and its Chief Cornerstone.[8] Apostles and prophets are a continuing ministry in the Church, just as Christ continues to be the Chief Cornerstone.

Improper Interpretation Causes Error: Some theologians, however, improperly interpreted this Scripture to say that the Church and its whole age of activity were built upon the ministry of the original apostles and prophets. So they reasoned that as soon as the Church, as a whole, was established (sometime within the first century), then the ministries of the apostle and prophet were no longer needed. Therefore, these theologians dispensationally deleted those ministries after that time. In this view the Bible then became the foundation of the Church as the complete revealed will of God, thereby eliminating the founding and revealing ministry of the apostle and prophet.

This position is difficult to maintain because of the lack of scriptural support and historical proof. The Bible was not canonized and brought together as one book until the third century. In addition, not one Scripture in the Bible indicates that apostles and prophets were ever to be taken out of the Church. God set them in the Church: "And God hath set some in the church, first apostles, secondarily prophets...."[9] God set them in, and He is the only one who can take them out. No Scripture implies that God has taken them out and none indicates that He ever will. The teaching of the theologians and the tradition they developed concerning apostles and prophets could not remove them. Nevertheless, their doctrinal traditions did cause Christians to doubt their right to exist, to be recognized, and to function in the Church.

Two Things That Hinder: The Bible talks about two major things that keep Christ and His Word from being effective and accomplishing its purpose. The first is **unbelief**—not believing the truth of God's Word, that God's Word means what it says and says what it means. The second is **religious tradition**. In Matthew 15:1-9, ministers from the denomination of the Pharisees were criticizing Jesus for allowing His disciples to break Jewish tradition by not washing their hands before they ate. Jesus came right back at the Pharisees, showing how they had developed tradition contrary to the true meaning of the commandment of God. He then said, "Thus you have made the commandment of God of no effect by your tradition...'and in vain [you] worship Me, teaching as doctrines the commandments of men.' "[10] The teaching that apostles and prophets are no longer a valid ministry in the Church is a key example of the traditional teaching of man. This tradition made the Scriptures concerning the ministry of apostles and prophets in the Church of "no effect" in the Church.

This tradition carried over into the Pentecostal Movement and remained the thinking of the Protestant church world until 1948. At that time, the Latter Rain Movement started teaching that apostles and prophets are still to be active ministers in the present-day Church. But it was 40 to 50 years later, in the 1980s and 1990s, when they were fully restored, recognized, and repositioned within segments of the Church. Now among present-truth restoration churches they are accepted, and people are allowed to be called by the name of apostle and prophet, just as evangelists, pastors, and teachers are called by those terms in Evangelical and Pentecostal churches. But, sadly, most Pentecostal and Evangelical ministers are still bound by tradition and would rather believe the commandments of men concerning apostles and prophets than the work of the Holy Spirit.

Study the Scriptures: If you are not completely convinced, then read all the New Testament word-for-word to find out what the Word of God has to say about apostles and prophets. Do not read with a mind-set of what tradition says the Scriptures mean, but be open to what the Scriptures actually say. As Romans 3:4 declares, "Indeed, let God be true but every man a liar…. 'That You may be justified in Your words, and may overcome when You are judged.'" We are going to be judged by whether we believe the Word of God or the traditions of men. The only way we can properly overcome is to believe the unchangeable, pure Word of God.

Why Apostles and Prophets Were Not Fully Restored During the Latter Rain Movement: The restorational Latter Rain Movement teaching concerning apostles and prophets never affected much of the Church world because those called to these offices were never given, nor did they accept, the titles of apostle and prophet. Unlike

176

the first-century Church, public acknowledgment was not granted to those who had the gifted ministry of apostle or prophet. Therefore, the full restoration of apostles and prophets could not be fulfilled at that time. Thank God that during the last half of the twentieth century they were restored and are now being recognized and activated into the Church.

FIFTY YEARS OF FIVEFOLD MINISTRY RESTORATION

In each of the last five decades of the twentieth-century Church, one of the fivefold ministries has been re-emphasized or restored, and certain biblical truths and ways of worship have been reactivated into the Church by the Holy Spirit.

DECADE	FIVEFOLD MINISTRY	MOVEMENT
1950s	Evangelist	Deliverance Evangelism
1960s	Pastor	Charismatic Renewal
1970s	Teacher	Faith Teaching Movement
1980s	Prophet	Prophetic Movement
1990s	Apostle	Apostolic Movement

Description of the Last Five Decades: I believe it was the mind of Christ to first re-emphasize the three offices which have been accepted and somewhat understood (evangelist, pastor, teacher) and then to fully clarify, amplify, and magnify those two which have not been understood, accepted, and recognized—apostles and prophets.

The Decade of the Evangelist: In the 1950s the gifted ministry of the hour was that of the evangelist. Evangelists such as Oral Roberts held great tent meetings. A dual ministry of preaching salvation from sin and deliverance from disease and demons provided the focus. The most prominent ministries were laying on of hands for healing and mass evangelism.

During the decade of the 1950s, the ministry of the evangelist was re-emphasized and amplified. However, within a decade the hundreds of evangelists and their large tent meetings had subsided. The great wave of restoration of the evangelist with gifts of healing and miracles reached the shoreline of fulfillment in the '50s, before receding into the ocean of the last-days' Church ministry. Now these types of ministries are some of the many ways the Holy Spirit moves in the Church.

The Decade of the Pastor: The 1960s was the decade when the ministry of the pastor was emphasized and brought to proper perspective. Two restorational moves of the Holy Spirit brought this into reality. The first, in 1948, emphasized proper divine order for the local church. Understanding came that the local church is to be self-governing and indigenous, with Christ being the sovereign Head and the local pastor serving under the direct headship of Christ.

Churches also came to realize that the pastor is appointed by God and not elected by a board of elders or deacons or by a congregation. A man or woman called by God to the office of pastor needs to submit to God's preparation process until a divinely-directed time of commissioning. The pastor then stands in Christ's stead, and his position is not determined by the vote of those to whom he ministers, any more than the angels and 24 elders in Heaven vote every millennium to determine whether God remains head of the universe for the next millennium. The pastor must have the freedom and authority to fulfill the vision God has given for building the local church.

The second wave that contributed to the magnification of the pastoral ministry was the Charismatic renewal that shook the whole denominational part of Christendom. Millions of denominational people were baptized with the Holy Spirit, and thousands came out of their denominations in order to walk in the fullness of present truth. In the 1960s and 1970s, churches started by Charismatic, restoration, and faith ministers grew to be congregations of thousands within three or four years. Thus pastors became the prominent ministry of the 1960s. In this way, the ministry of the pastor was restored to its rightful place and magnified by the Holy Spirit to its due honor and authority.

The Decade of the Teacher: The 1970s was the decade for proper recognition, acceptance, and magnifying of Christ's ministry of the teacher. The Catholic Charismatic and historic Protestant Charismatic ministers who moved into present truth were not strong evangelistic preachers like the Holiness and Pentecostal brethren. Many of them came from backgrounds in the corporate world and academics where seminars, lectures, and classes are common. The leading ministers in the Charismatic and Faith Movements presented their truths more by teaching than by preaching.

During this time thousands of people drove hundreds of miles to sit by the hour listening to one teacher after another. Cassette tapes were made and distributed in endless numbers. An abundance of books and teaching materials were printed. The office of the teacher was restored to its rightful place of respect and authority and was properly positioned as a Christ-given ministry to the Body of Christ.

The Decade of the Prophet: Prophet Glenn Foster has noted that a powerful prophetic minister came through his church in the 1950s who prophesied that the day would come when the prophets would arise and prophetic ministry would come into prominence. The prophecy also said that the prophetic movement was still 30 years away.[11] Many of us who had been in prophetic ministry for many years had heard the same thing from God, and we looked forward to the 1980s as the decade of the prophet. We were not disappointed. In the 1980s the Holy Spirit began to restore Christ's ascension-gift ministry of the prophet to its proper recognition, acceptance, and authority in the Church.

The vocal and revelation gifts of the Holy Spirit were magnified by the office of the prophet in the 1980s. Thus the company of prophets are a corporate body fulfilling the prophecy of Malachi 4 for Christ's second coming, just as John the Baptist was the single prophet preparing the way for the Lord's first coming.[12] The prophets also brought forth revelation, restoration, and preparation for the full magnification of the God-ordained office of the apostle.[13] The prophets will be the ones to reveal the last restorational truth that shall bring the Church to maturity and finalize the preparation of the Church-Bride for the return of her Bridegroom, Jesus.[14]

The Decade of the Apostle: The full restoration of the apostle began in the 1990s. Apostles are in the process of bringing a restoration of full apostolic authority with signs and wonders, the gift of faith, and the working of miracles. The Christ-ordained office and ministry of the apostle are now being recognized, accepted, and magnified mightily throughout the Christian world.

The discipleship/shepherding movement saw a glimpse of this truth in the 1970s and tried to restore it. However, lack of balance and maturity produced many abuses. Nevertheless, the time for the apostle's full authority and function in the fivefold ministry came forth in the 1990s, and the end result will be unity in the Church. The reverential fear of God and His righteousness will be re-established in the Church as judgment begins at the house of God. Man-made religious kingdoms and the Babylonian system will be shaken as God's judgments are executed by the last-day prophetic and apostolic ministries.[15]

Pioneering Ministers: The last half of the twentieth century was an exciting time of restoration in the Church. Probably no other 50-year period in history has activated so many new biblical truths and ministries back into the Church. It is amazing how many of the pioneering men and women who spanned this time are still alive and active in their ministries. The Holy Spirit will now begin to put pressure on all fivefold ministers to teach, activate, train, mentor, and mature the Saints in their ministries in preparation for the Day of the Saints preaching the gospel, demonstrating the Kingdom, and manifesting God's glory throughout the Earth.

How the Fivefold Ministers Equip the Saints

Every Saint needs to be connected with all of the fivefold ministries. As we grow up in Christ, we need to receive from every aspect of Him. Those truly called and gifted of God to be fivefold ministers will do the same things Christ Jesus would do for His Saints if He were here in a natural human body. Jesus' fivefold nature and anointing is here in His apostles, prophets, evangelists, pastors, and teachers. All are commissioned to equip the Saints to fulfill their membership ministry. However, each has a special portion of the ministry of Christ. Working together they fulfill Christ's commission of building His Church. Now that all five are restored, they can prepare the Saints for their day of manifestation.

Leaders Serving Those Under Them: The fivefold ministers are the drill sergeants and officers of the army of the Lord to train the Saints to be warriors and then lead them in the battle to victory. They are also like fathers and mothers and older family members who raise up the younger generation. These godly relationships provide nurturing, discipline, instruction, and a place of belonging and identity.

The **apostles**, in particular, are like fathers and mothers who impart to the Saints and raise them up as sons and daughters in the faith. The **prophets** bring supernatural revelation and insight concerning the calling and ministry of the Saints. They give vision and reveal the times and seasons of God so the Saints know what to do.

The **teachers** teach the Word of God with simplicity and wisdom as a mother feeds a growing child. The **pastors** nurture the Saints with counseling, clothing them with their Christlike armor and garments. They help the Saints become a family of God meeting in local churches. The **evangelists** impart zeal for souls to be saved and equip the Saints with wisdom and anointing in winning the lost.

How Apostles Equip the Saints: Apostles specialize in supernatural signs and wonders. They give building strategy and lay foundations, along with the prophet, in the lives of people and the local church. The prophet receives the blueprint for the building of the Church, but the apostle is the master builder. Biblical examples of apostles' ministry to the Saints reveal that they help found and ground the Saints in foundations of the faith and present truth. Apostles' miraculous signs and wonders enable Saints to be delivered from evil spirits, disease, and strongholds in their lives. Some apostles not only demonstrate the supernatural but are able to activate the Saints in their power gifts of the Holy Spirit.

As part of the foundation of the Church, apostles are often sent to establish new works and then to support those works. Apostle Paul founded many of the local churches in the New Testament. Apostles in the marketplace may be those who launch a business or who form a network to accomplish certain purposes. As initiators and those who help provide structure and leadership, apostles make a place for the Saints. They provide platforms where others can serve God through their unique giftings. The apostles have a special ability to be master builders of the

Saints in their calling and ministry. Apostles will be key in helping transform Saints from pew-sitters to active participants in the Day of the Saints.

How Prophets Equip the Saints: The prophets help bring vision, spiritual insight, revelations, impartation, and activation of the Saints' supernatural gifts and calling. They do this best with their prophesying and revelation knowledge. All fivefold ministers are to minister the Logos Word to the Saints, but the prophets have a special ability to minister a Rhema word that personally enlightens and activates faith in the Saints.[16] Prophets help bring God's direction and vision to the Church at large, to local churches, to business, cities, and nations, as well as to individual Saints. Some prophets use their gifts of discernment to bring warnings about the plans of the enemy or of potential pitfalls to be avoided. The value of hearing their revelation from God is beyond measure.

Since Christian International has been a forerunner in the Prophetic Movement, we have seen thousands of lives transformed by personal prophecy. All people have a natural desire to know what God has to say to them personally. God created mankind to need vision.[17] When God's word is declared over a matter, it puts a creative force into being to help accomplish His will in that situation. When combined with faith and spiritual warfare, this allows divine purposes to come into being that could never have occurred in the natural realm alone. Prophets are part of Christ's gift of Himself to His Saints for direction and vision and to equip them to hear God for themselves.

How Evangelists Equip the Saints: Evangelists have a special anointing to stir up the zeal of the Lord in the Saints.[18] They have an anointing and passion for winning the lost and making them active members of the Body of Christ and Saints of the Most High God.[19] As well as helping to gather the Saints, evangelists help keep them focused outwardly on the need for bringing the Kingdom of God to the entire Earth. Without their enthusiasm for tearing down the works of darkness and building up the Kingdom of God, churches would be in danger of becoming "bless me clubs" that are so inwardly focused they become stagnant. Evangelists impart to the Saints the need to take the blessing we have received and use it to be a blessing to others, including those who are not yet part of the Church.[20] Their ability to train others in soul winning is vital to growing the Church. Testifying to others about Jesus Christ strengthens our own faith.

How Pastors Equip the Saints: Those truly gifted as pastors have the ability to nurture, stabilize, grow, and mature the Saints. They specialize in building character, faithfulness, and family relationship in the local church family. No matter how many prophecies you have received about mighty ministry, you will never fully reach your destiny without maturity. This is best developed by being submitted to godly leadership, and being allowed to develop little by little, just as a child learns and grows little by little. Even those who have reached spiritual adulthood need to remain in committed relationship with those who have been charged to keep guard over their souls.[21] We tell all those who receive prophetic words through the ministry of Christian International to write out their prophecies and submit them to their pastoral covering.

In the Body of Christ today, many leaders are called "pastors" who actually function in the office of apostle, prophet, teacher, or even evangelist. Some who are not actually called as fivefold ministers may be trying to serve as leaders of churches. When the teaching that apostles and prophets were no longer valid ministries in the Church became popular, terms such as *minister, preacher,* and *pastor* were substituted and continue to be used widely. Many senior pastors of large churches actually function as apostles. Some are teachers who have drawn large numbers of Saints because of their insightful revelation into the Word of God and their ability to express these truths in a meaningful way. As the Holy Spirit has restored the offices of prophet and apostle in the last two decades, less attention has been paid to the fivefold office of pastor.

However, pastors are still vitally important to the Body. Pastoral care exemplifies Christ Jesus' acceptance and love for His Saints.[22] In large churches, many fivefold pastors may be functioning as cell group leaders.[23] They provide the close relationships and family connection for those under their care that senior ministers in megachurches cannot feasibly give to their entire congregations. Other fivefold pastors may be serving as counselors, youth or children's workers, or head of a specific ministry such as the women's or men's fellowship, seniors' or singles' group. They strengthen and encourage those they touch. This aspect of the fivefold ministry must not be overlooked. Pastors' ability to help Saints feel accepted and valued in the Body is a prerequisite for the Saints' growth in maturity and in their giftings. They demonstrate Christ's devotion to His Church.

How Teachers Equip the Saints: Teachers help prepare the Saints in the milk and meat of the Word of God.[24] A true teacher, who is an extension of Christ the Master Teacher, has the special ability to teach the truths of God with simplicity and revelation, enlightening and enabling the Saints in the Word of God. A wise teacher brings out of his treasure both old, foundational truths and newly-restored present truth.[25] We are all to study the Bible for ourselves. And we can all offer something to bless others. [26] But we can also benefit greatly from the years of study, revelation, and gift of expression that teachers have been given by Christ. James 3:1 states that teachers will receive a stricter judgment. Therefore, it is important for them to know and rightly divide the Word of truth. The Saints can be blessed by the wisdom teachers have gained as they have developed to a point of commissioning.

The fivefold ministers are the full expression of the one Christ. Each has a portion of the ministry and character of Christ Jesus to impart and activate within the Saints. God's desire is that every Saint be presented to Himself perfect in the fullness of Christ.[27] Every Saint will fulfill his own special membership ministry but will manifest more of one of the fivefold natures of Christ. This is especially true in local churches. If the senior minister who is the vision holder is a prophet, the Saints under his ministry will be more prophetic. At CI's home campus church, the senior ministers, Tom and Jane Hamon, are strong prophets. Ninety-five percent of the congregation prophesies and most serve on prophetic teams. The apostolic leader will produce apostolic Saints, and the teacher, pastor, and evangelist will reproduce after their calling and anointing. This reveals one of the reasons a congregation needs the ministry of all five expressions of Christ to be a balanced and mature congregation of Saints.

Supernatural Impartation: As fivefold ministers focus on their specific role toward the Saints, they must remember that all fivefold ministers are to equip the Saints to do the work of the ministry. In order to minister the works of Jesus, they must be effective wielders of the supernatural gifts of the Holy Spirit. Jesus never said that the gifts of the Spirit were optional—they are not only for those believers who could not be effective in their own strength. Since fivefold ministers are commanded to equip the Saints, they must be prepared to train them in the supernatural as well as in zeal and instruction.

After a meeting where I had preached on the fivefold ministry, a pastor approached me. He said that as a pastor he did not move in the miraculous manifestations that apostles and prophets do. He saw himself as burying the dead, marrying the living, and being a comforting hand to his people as they went through life. His vision was that only apostles and prophets operate in the revelation and power gifts, not pastors. Because of his mind-set, I asked him, "If pastors don't operate in the supernatural, then why not quit being a pastor and just be a regular believer? Because the Bible says, 'These signs will follow them that *believe!*'" Since the Scripture is clear that all Saints are to manifest the works of Christ, then all fivefold leaders especially need to have a working experience of these things in their lives and ministries.

IMPORTANT INSIGHTS REGARDING FIVEFOLD MINISTERS

In Paul's writings to Timothy and Titus, he gave directives concerning qualifications and standards for bishops, elders, and deacons.[28] These are general instructions and requirements for those who will be in leadership within Christ's Church. But there are no statements in the New Testament that make a distinction between fivefold ministers in relation to qualifying standards of character or supernatural experiences, nor are any distinctions or directives given concerning what positions can be held within the structure of the Church.

Five important insights must be understood concerning fivefold ministers:

1. They are all headship ministries. That is, they are an extension of the headship ministry of Jesus Christ, the Head of the Church. They are not "Body" ministries such as the gifts and ministries that the Holy Spirit gives to members of Christ's corporate Body. Technically speaking, they are not gifts of the Holy Spirit, but ascension gifts of Jesus Christ Himself.[29]

2. All fivefold ministers are called to govern, guide, gather, guard, and ground God's people. However, each has been given special grace and gifted ability in one area more than the others. These one-word explanations should not be seen as limitations

on each minister's activities, but rather as a one-word description of each one's major anointing and divinely given ability. They are like the point of a spear, not the whole head and shaft of the spear.

3. It is unscriptural and unwise to put an apostle, prophet, evangelist, pastor, or teacher into a box of limited anointings and activities. No Scriptures suggest that fivefold ministers are limited to certain ministerial activities or leadership positions. The fivefold ascension gifts of Christ overlap and integrate just as the nine gifts of the Holy Spirit do. Fivefold ministers are not independent ministries but are vitally related to each other in Christ. They are five parts of one whole. It takes all five working together to minister the fullness of Christ's ministry to the Body of Christ. None are inferior or superior, but all are anointed and appointed of God for a specific purpose.

4. It is detrimental to the function of the fivefold ministers to categorize them based on details concerning personalities, performances, and positions. The Holy Spirit is also grieved when people formulate methods for evaluating and determining a fivefold ministry office by a psychoanalysis technique or personality profile. God will not allow anything to take His place in this area.

5. Each fivefold minister knows best his or her own calling and ministry. It is not the

prerogative of the prophet to give guidelines, directions, and restrictions on the
ministry of the apostle. Likewise, the apostle has not been granted authority from Father God to be daddy and director over the
prophet. Only a prophet really knows the
ministry and function of a prophet. And
even one prophet should not try to box another prophet into his prophetic role, personality, or performance. However, we all
must receive from one another and be subject to correction and adjustment in
methodology and interrelationships.

THE MIGHTY HAND OF GOD

The fivefold ministry can be illustrated by the human
hand. Some insight into the interaction between fivefold
ministers and the other members of Christ's Body can be
gained by looking at the natural example of the human
hand and the human body. The Saints are members of the
Body of Christ. They desperately need the hand of God to
minister to them. Most members of the human body are
stationary and limited in their function to the rest of the
body. However, the hand can minister to all members
from the head to the toe. Most of the hand ministries travel and minister to the Saints throughout the worldwide,
corporate Body of Christ. The fully-restored hand of God
of fivefold ministers is now ministering to the Saints,
preparing them for the coming Saints Movement when
Christ will be fully glorified in His Saints.

The Apostle = The Thumb: The thumb more properly represents the ministry of the apostle. Notice that the thumb can touch and minister to all four of the fingers. As the hand functions, sometimes it is flat and all fingers are side-by-side. When taking hold of something, the thumb goes to one side of the object and the fingers encircle from the opposite side. This motion of coming from opposite directions gives power to the hand. The thumb is not in opposition or over the fingers but is designed to complete the hand for its full function and power.

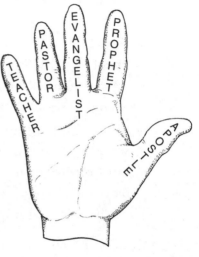

The hand of God of the fivefold ministry has been greatly restricted in its powerful purposes. It has had to function with only four fingers. The power and function is limited greatly by the lack of a thumb. Since all elements of the hand of God are being restored fully, the hand of God will be extended in full power and demonstration.

The Prophet = Forefinger: The forefinger is referred to as the one that points. The prophet has the ministry of revelation and anointing that points the way for the Body of Christ. The forefinger is also the one most closely related to the thumb. Though they approach their grip on something from opposite directions, it is this opposite approach that gives the hand the power to take a powerful grip on things. The prophet and apostle have the closest working relationship in their hand ministry to the Body of Christ.

The Evangelist = Middle Finger: The middle finger extends the farthest on the hand. It is the outreach ministry extended to the evangelization of the world. It is in the middle of all activity of the hand. It is usually the largest of the fingers. The evangelist usually has the largest meetings in evangelistic campaigns. The evangelist is a vital part of the ministry of the hand.

The Pastor = Ring Finger: This is the finger that the wedding ring goes on. The pastor is married to the Saints. He is with them 24 hours a day. Prophets and evangelists come and go, but the pastor is bound to the local Saints by the ring of their shepherding relationship.

The Teacher = Little Finger: Though the little finger is the smallest, it provides balance to the hand. The teaching of the Word of God line upon line, precept upon precept, is desperately needed within the Church. The teacher is a vital member of the hand ministry of Christ to His Church.

The hand is the only outward member of the body that can minister to all parts of the body from back to front and from head to toe. First Peter 5:5-6 says the Saints are to humble themselves under the mighty hand of God and they will be exalted in due time. The fivefold ministry represents the hand of God. It is almost impossible for individuals to humble themselves under God without humbling themselves in submission and relationship to Christ's delegated representatives of Himself to His Church.

TEAM MINISTRY

No matter how powerful a Saint is in individual ministry, every Saint still needs to be connected to a particular expression of God's corporate Body. Iron sharpens iron.[30] Just as the Day of the Saints is about "average" believers rather than big-name ministers, it is also about team ministry, not operating in isolation. Giftings and anointings are given by God and activated by faith. But maturity comes from years of submission to the processes of God which are worked out in us by our interactions with other people. God created mankind to need relationship and we will never be fully functional until we are properly relating to others. Jesus said, "By this all will know that you are My disciples, if you have love for one another."[31] Committed, accountable relationship with Christ's fivefold ministers provides the Saints with accountability, mentoring, opportunities to minister and to exercise flexibility, forgiveness, and love.

The greatest mark of a mature minister or Saint is not the ability to prophesy powerfully or do miracles; it's the ability to get along well and work well with others. The Church is both an army and a family, and it is eternal.

Don't think you will be able to go to Heaven to sit on your cloud, play your harp, and get away from other people. You will have to get along with your brothers and sisters in Christ *forever*! Nor will you be your own boss in Heaven. You will have people over you *forever*! The Saints who resist the changes God is trying to bring into their character now will have to go through the same process in eternity. You might as well get properly positioned and let God adjust you now, so you can be fully usable for His purposes on the Earth today.

No One Person Except Jesus Is All Five: Never allow your faith to become a presumptuous belief that you can have the calling and abilities of all fivefold ministers. Only Jesus had the fullness of all five ministries in one human body.[32] No other human can have the fullness of all five—not even the pope, an apostle over hundreds of ministers, or a pastor of a congregation of thousands. Christ never did, and never will, give all five gifts and anointings to any one person. But when He ascended on high, He did give His ministry to men and women.[33] He took His whole ministry mantle and distributed it into five parts, dividing His wisdom, ability, and performance into five categories. He designated them with certain titles that reveal these special gifts and ministries that He gave to His corporate Body. To some He gave His apostle ministry, to others His prophet mantle, to others His pastoral anointing, to others His evangelistic zeal, and to still others His master teaching ability. Jesus made it so that no one person could succeed as a law unto themselves. We must be dependent upon other members of the Body.

Seeds reproduce after their own kind. The seed principle in Genesis is that every seed is to reproduce after its kind. Based on this principle, all fivefold ministers who are ministering to people should reproduce like kind, not just one or two but many. As an example, one grain of corn seed will reproduce from 1,000 to 2,000 kernels of corn on one corncob. Wouldn't it be wonderful if all great evangelists and successful pastors, who have been in the ministry for several years, had reproduced thousands of ministers who could do the same work and ministry that they are doing? As we get closer to the Day of the Saints, more and more fivefold ministers will begin equipping the Saints with all the resources the Holy Spirit has given them.

The pastor cannot do it all alone. I have seen some pastors who rarely have outside speakers in, as though they assume that they can perfect and properly equip the Saints all by themselves. There is no way a local congregation can reach proper Biblical maturity and ministry without receiving mature ministry from the other fivefold ministers. No Scriptures even suggest that one senior shepherd of a local flock has been given all the truth and ministry needed to perfect his Saints. A pastor may conform his congregation to his doctrines, ways, and ministries—but not into Christ's fullness. The Scripture emphatically declares that it takes all five to do the job.

Commit to Relationship: It is important for all Saints to commit to relationship with fivefold ministers in God's Church, especially in the areas of their calling and anointing. Remember the example I gave in Chapter 2 of doubling my cotton-pulling output by working alongside a master in the field? We learn by serving with those who are operating in what we are called to.

Throughout my ministry I have seen a pattern repeated over and over. Certain Saints and ministers who seem destined for greatness never arrive at their potential because they do not continue in submission to fivefold leaders. At the same time, I have seen Saints who may not have seemed like they would amount to much to the natural eye. Some of them have been broken or hurting or have seemed like failures in man's viewpoint. But they kept being faithful in the place where God had called them, and God began to use them. According to the principle that he who is faithful in little will be given much, soon they were walking in greater anointing and responsibility in their ministry.[34] And their prophecies began to reflect the greater potential they had developed. Some are wandering around as lone rangers, using small flaws they see in others as excuses to keep themselves apart. Meanwhile, others are rising up and flowing in the areas that these ones have left vacant while they waited for something "better."

Even those of us who are heads of ministries need godly accountability and relationships with peers. It's the banana that gets separated from the bunch that gets peeled and eaten! I predict these principles will become even more crucial in the Saints Movement.

If you are not in a place where you are related to fivefold ministers, you need to seek the Lord for how to get properly positioned. If you know that you are at the right church, it may be a matter of joining a cell group, participating in a prayer group led by a prophet/intercessor, or volunteering to help a Bible school teacher with printing or copying. Perhaps you need to attend a training seminar where your gifts can be activated by apostles and prophets, such as those we sponsor several times each year, or join a network of present-truth ministers and Saints.

PASTORS AND PEOPLE MUST CHOOSE

Jesus is in Heaven interceding for the Saints. He is still the Head, but His earthly ministry is being carried out by others.[35] As we have seen, all fivefold ministers have been commissioned to equip the Saints in their member-ship ministries. If local pastors do not respond to this commissioning by providing time and place for this train-ing, then the Holy Spirit will cause one of three things to happen.

1. If the pastor has a vision to fulfill this com-mission but the congregation will not re-spond, then the Holy Spirit will give the pastor a "new generation" congregation by moving out the old passive generation. Or He may move the pastor to a new pastorate or to start a new church.

2. If the congregation wants this commission but the pastor doesn't, God will remove the passive pastor or send the congregation to a pastor who will train and equip them.

3. If God cannot find an existing pastor or congregation who will receive the vision and run with it in a geographic location, God will cause a new prophetic-apostolic church to be established in that area.

Wilderness Wanderers or Canaan Conquerors: For the pastor and his congregation who will not fulfill Christ's commission of equipping the Saints, God may not write "Ichabod" over their door, but He will decree that they will not cross over their Jordan and possess their promised possession or fulfill God's intended destiny.[36] They will stay on the level they are on with less anointing while they wander in the wilderness until they die or Jesus returns.

Two specific illustrations in the Old Testament reveal how God will deal with His people when they are disobedient and refuse to fulfill His purpose in and through them. **First**, the generation of the children of Israel that came out of Egypt refused to fulfill God's prophesied purpose for them of destroying all of the Canaanites and the other nations out of the land that God wanted Israel to possess. Therefore, they were sentenced to wander in the wilderness until their generation died.[37] Despite their disobedience, God did not forsake them. He supernaturally fed them with manna from Heaven for 40 years while raising up a new generation that would fulfill His will.[38]

Second, Saul twice failed to fulfill the commission that God had prophesied to him through the prophet Samuel. God did not kill Saul, but He did cancel his kingship posterity and transfer it to David.[39] Saul was left in his position of king (pastor) over Israel (his congregational or international ministry), but the anointing was removed from him in his second year.[40] However, he continued his ministry for 38 more years. He even expanded the territory of Israel, won many battles, and built many new things. But he did things he should not have done and failed to do some things he was commanded to do, actions that caused God to cancel his prophetic destiny and that of his descendants.[41]

Those who choose not to move on will be like King Saul, who failed to properly and fully obey God. Many heads of ministries will stay active in their ministry, but their churches or organizations will become "old order, the glory has departed," Saul ministries.[42] They will also be like the children of Israel who refused to move out of their comfort zone, to make the transition to become warriors and to drive out the tribes who were squatters on their promised land. God canceled their personal prophecy and destiny of possessing and living in Canaan.[43] God may be supernaturally supplying our needs and helping us in our ministry, but that is only meaningful if we are doing God's will and not our own.

Perfect vs. Permissive Will of God: Some have said, "I may not be doing God's perfect will, but I am in His permissive will." The "permissive will of God" is a contradictory statement. It is really not God's will at all, but merely God allowing us to continue to live and function in our ministry even though we refused to do His will His way. The scriptural statement, "That you may prove what is that good and acceptable and perfect will of God" is not three different categories or levels of God's will. It is three terms describing what His will is: His will is good, it is acceptable, and it is perfect.[44] There is God's one good, acceptable, and perfect will, and there is our bad, unacceptable, and imperfect will. There are not two wills of God. If you are in God's "permissive will," then you are in the same status as Saul and the older generation of children of Israel, who refused to do God's will His way.

We must not allow anything to keep us from going all the way with God, regardless of the cost, changes, and challenges. *Lord, do not let us become "old order Sauls" or "wandering wilderness walkers," but soldiers going forth as "Canaan-conquering warriors." Help us to diligently obey Your voice according to Your specifically revealed Word, will, and way. Let us pray with the intensity and sincerity that Jesus prayed in the Garden of Gethsemane, "Father...not My will, but Thine, be done."* [45]

A Serious and High Priority of God: Jesus is very serious about His Saints being supernaturally equipped and matured to the level of Christ's ministry and maturity. Christ Jesus is going to deal very severely with fivefold ministers who are not willing to fulfill His original purpose for calling and commissioning them. Resources and know-how are now available for equipping the Saints. Heads of churches and ministries will stand without an acceptable excuse when Jesus asks, "Why didn't you equip My Saints for My Body's sake and prepare them to be reapers in the great harvest by activating them in their supernatural gifts and ministries?"

Give Weapons to Those in Armor: Ministers of Christ's Church have worked for hundreds of years to make sure the Saints have on their righteous garments, protective and preserving armor, and the fruit of the Spirit. [46] But now it is just as essential that they be equipped in their supernatural gifts of the Holy Spirit, which are their weapons of warfare. [47] The front-line, present-truth division of the Church has crossed their Jordan River and entered their Canaan by making the transition into offensive warfare.[48] They have come out of their forts of protectionism and defensiveness and have entered their inheritance in Canaan. They are moving into aggressive warfare to destroy all the "-ites" and "-isms" out of their promised land.

You who are reading this book have now been exposed to the heart and mind of God in His divine purpose. How you respond to this truth could affect the fulfillment of your personal prophecies and your ultimate destiny in ministry. How Saul responded to the challenge of truth that Samuel gave him affected the fulfillment of his personal prophecies and destiny. Do not be fearful, passive, or unbelieving, but be stirred and challenged to be one of God's overcomers and receive the rewards of being an overcomer.[49] Read about the overcomers' rewards in Revelation chapters 2 and 3 and become bold, faithful, and courageous warriors like the Joshua Generation.[50]

ENDNOTES:
1. Luke 2:52.
2. 1 Kings 19:19; 2 Kings 2:8,13-14.
3. Colossians 2:9.
4. Ephesians 4:8b;11-12.
5. 1 Corinthians 12:27.
6. Ephesians 4:7-16; Colossians 2:9; Luke 14:17.
7. Ephesians 2:20-21.
8. 1 Peter 2:6; Ephesians 1:23.
9. 1 Corinthians 12:28 KJV.
10. Matthew 15:6b,9.
11. Glenn Foster, *The Purpose and Use of Prophecy* (Glendale, AZ: Sweetwater Publications, 1988), p. 16.

12. Malachi 4:5; cf Matthew 11:9-14; Isaiah 40:3-5; cf Luke 1:16-17; Revelation 10:7; cf 11:15; Matthew 17:11; cf Acts 3:21.
13. Ephesians 4:11; 1 Corinthians 12:28.
14. Amos 3:7.
15. 1 Peter 4:7; Acts 5:1-13; Revelation 11:3-10.
16. 1 Corinthians 14:3; Romans 10:17.
17. Proverbs 29:18 KJV.
18. Isaiah 9:7.
19. Acts 8:4-8.
20. Genesis 12:3; Luke 10:1.
21. Acts 20:28.
22. John 17:12,23; Revelation 7:17.
23. 1 Peter 5:2-4.
24. 1 Peter 1:12; 2:2; 2 Timothy 2:2.
25. Matthew 13:52.
26. 1 Corinthians 14:26.
27. Colossians 1:26-28.
28. 1 Timothy 3:1-13; Titus 1:5-9.
29. 1 Corinthians 12:7-11; Ephesians 4:11.
30. Proverbs 27:17.
31. John 13:35.
32. Colossians 2:9.
33. Ephesians 4:8.
34. Matthew 25:21.
35. Romans 8:34.
36. 1 Samuel 4:21; Joshua 1:1-5.
37. Numbers 32:13
38. Exodus 16:35.
39. 1 Samuel 15:26.
40. 1 Samuel 13:1.
41. 1 Samuel 13,15.
42. 1 Samuel 4:21.
43. Numbers 14:22-23.
44. Romans 12:1-3.
45. Luke 22:42b KJV.
46. Ephesians 6:10-18; Isaiah 61:1-3; Galatians 5:22-23.
47. 1 Corinthians 12:7-11.

48. Bill Hamon, *Prophets and the Prophetic Movement* (Shippensburg, PA: Destiny Image, 1990), pp. 55-58.

49. Revelation 2–3; 12:11.

50. Joshua 1.

CHAPTER 7

SAINTS AS KINGS AND PRIESTS

The Bible declares in Revelation 5:9-10 that Jesus has redeemed us to God by His blood out of every tribe, language, people, and nation. He has made us kings and priests unto our God and we are to reign on the Earth. These verses have several applications. One is that Christians are to rule and reign with Christ as kings and minister unto God and to His people as priests of the Most High God.[1] I believe the Holy Spirit also gave another application of this verse that relates to Saints in the marketplace and public square. This places all Christians in one of two categories: either the "kingly" ministry or "priestly" ministry.

"PRIEST" AND "KING" MINISTERS

The Ministry of "Priests": Saints in this category are those who function like the priests of the tabernacle of Moses—who fulfilled their ministry inside the walls of the house of

God by doing spiritual service. Priestly Christians are preachers and all those who minister the spiritual things of God inside the local church. This group includes not only pastors but also traveling evangelists, prophets, apostles, youth ministers, church staff people, and all other types of church-related ministries. These functions have been accepted as ministers and ministries in the Church/Body of Christ for centuries. They are members of the Body of Christ who have been gifted by Christ to function in that calling and position.

The **"priests"** usually earn their income from the nonprofit organizations established to minister to God's people, particularly in Western nations. Most of them function within the walls of a local church. Others work for a ministry such as the Gideons, Campus Crusade for Christ, or many others. God has established Church structure with apostles, prophets, pastors, evangelists, and teachers. Local church structure is normally established with a senior pastor having a pastoral staff of elders and then deacons. God ordained fivefold ministers and Church structure and no new revelation from God will do away with that, but revelation may bring new alignments that are more scriptural and workable.

Who Is a Minister? In the first-century Church, the word *minister* was not the title of a position, but a service rendered and the ministry of Christ manifested. Every child of God is to minister the things of God and manifest the life of Christ to the world. That is why Christ declares that Christians are the light of the world.[2] There are no directives limiting where Saints are to allow their membership ministries to shine. The Scriptures do not say for us to go to the church building and let our light shine. It is in the world of darkness that we are to let our light shine the most brightly. God is bringing forth Saints in the marketplace and public square who are as dedicated to manifesting and ministering the life of Christ outside the walls of the local church as pastors are inside the local church.

With the restoration of apostles and prophets back into the Church, there is coming revelation for New Testament apostolic order. Along with this restoration is coming a paradigm shift in the way we do Church business. When most people think of church, they think of a building where Christians meet or a church denomination. Christ's Church is not a building or a denomination, but a living corporate Body consisting of lively members of redeemed people.[3] Body of Christ members are gifted to function in all areas of their lives and professions. God can enable a member to function as a fivefold minister outside the walls of the local church, just as He enables ministers to function inside the local church.

This is especially true for the prophet. More than 90 percent of the prophets in the Old Testament never functioned inside the walls of the temple. They never earned their income from "church" ministry. Most were business people or government officials. Daniel was a government official in the Babylonian Empire. Deborah was a judge in Israel. Prophets Nathan and Gad served on King David's staff. In fact, the Scriptures say that David himself, who was a shepherd, warrior, psalmist, and king, was a prophet.

A major shift is coming in the way we think of ministers and ministries in the Body of Christ.

The Ministry of "Kings": Those in this category represent all Christians who earn their income and fulfill their membership ministry mainly outside the local church, in what is commonly termed the secular world. The more prominent kings will be entrepreneurial business and professional people who build their lives and work according to biblical principles of the Kingdom of God. Those called to this ministry need to be educated, trained, equipped, and activated into God's standards for business people. The Holy Spirit has emphasized that the main ingredient Christian business people have lacked is the supernatural working of spiritual gifts. This is the reason why we, at Christian International, call them God's *prophetic* business people, because prophetic people are those who operate in the supernatural gifts of the Holy Spirit.

The pulpit and platform of a Christian who is called to the "kings" ministry may be an executive's desk, a contractor's pickup, a farmer's tractor, a doctor's operating room, or a lawyer's courtroom. It may be a politician's platform or a salesperson's briefcase. It is wherever a Christian lives and functions. The biblical truth that makes this so real is that every Christian is a member of the Body of Christ.[4] Every member has been given divine grace, talents, and gifts.[5] These are not on loan, but are given to each member as part of their divine enabling and function.[6] These supernatural enablements are not just activated when members walk inside the walls of a local church and then deactivated when they walk out. The special skills and gifts God gives are there for use 24 hours a day, whether at home, church, or work. They are given for Christians to be the salt of the earth, the light of the world, and a witness of the reality of Jesus Christ, and to be successful in their life and work.[7]

As we come closer to the activation of the Saints Movement, these believers will no longer see themselves spending most of their time in the "secular" realm. They will no longer believe that the only time they are ministering is when they are contributing to local church activities on evenings or weekends. More and more Saints who have been gifted and anointed as kings are realizing that they are already full-time ministers in their occupations. Ed Silvoso, a leader in the Argentine revival, writes, "In the Scriptures the anointing was always for full-time consecration. Kings, priests, prophets and places were set aside *in toto* for divine service. Part-time anointing, or anointing for part-time ministry *is not found in the Bible.*"[8]

Spiritual vs. Secular: Does God have a secular business people and a spiritual church people? No! He has one people. Christ has one Church with multimillions of members. Every person who has been cleansed by the blood of Jesus, born of His Spirit, and baptized into His corporate Body is a member.[9] Membership ministries are as variable as the members of the human body, such as the eye, hand, heart, backbone, and feet. All members in the Body of Christ, like all members of the human body, are endowed with special qualities and functions to enable them to fulfill their purpose. Some of their abilities may look like natural talent or learned skills, but they were planned and given according to Christ's purpose and function for that person. Just as the physical attributes of a person are determined by their DNA at conception, so every person who is born of God receives a divine DNA of the calling, gifts, and divine enablements needed to fulfill their membership ministry and destiny. These callings and gifts have to be discovered, understood, activated, and matured for successful ministry.

Today there are millions of men and women called to ministry whose destiny is in the marketplace...They need to know that they are not perpetual privates in God's army but full-fledged generals whose ministry is in the heart of the city instead of inside a religious building. In fact, they need to realize that not only is it *okay* to do ministry in the marketplace, but that God has deliberately *called* them and *anointed* them for it. By anointed I mean that they have been chosen and empowered by the Holy Spirit for a divinely sanctioned assignment...

When we study the Scriptures without the distortion of human traditions we soon discover that *percentage-wise* God has called more people to do ministry in the marketplace than in religious settings. By ministry I mean that they did more than just witnessing, they brought transformation to cities...

When Christians in the marketplace are reduced to second-class status, the Church is automatically deprived of its most strategically placed soldiers because they are the ones closest to Satan's command and control centers. If properly equipped, they can do lethal damage to the systems by which the devil holds people captive in our cities. This is why he allocates so much of his resources to make them feel unqualified and inferior in spiritual matters.[10]

God's Criteria for Success: In order for Christians to have a proper sense of success and fulfillment, they must have a clear understanding of how God views success, prosperity, and fulfillment of destiny. Success according to the world's standard is the accumulation of wealth, honor, position, prestige, power, and material things, regardless of the cost to personal life, family, and spiritual life. Success according to God's standard is not based upon the world's ideas of success, but upon whether a person is fulfilling his calling and ministry regardless of what or where it is. THE MOST SUCCESSFUL CHRISTIANS ARE THOSE WHO COME TO KNOW THEIR CALLING, UNDERSTAND THEIR SPECIAL GIFTING, AND FAITHFULLY STAY WITH THAT CALLING UNTIL THEY FULFILL THEIR MEMBERSHIP MINISTRY.

God's only criterion for reward is, "Well done, good and faithful servant." Every Christian wants to hear those words from the mouth of God. Scripture tells us that those words are said to those who are faithful to use what they are given by reproducing more and prospering. A successful and prosperous person according to God's standard is one who is committed to God, has found his calling, and is progressively fulfilling it in alignment with God's Word, will, and way.[11]

An Example: In my position as Bishop and Chairman over the ministries of Christian International, I am accountable to a Board of Governors made up of approximately 40 men and women of God. Most of these board members are "priests" who have been in pulpit or traveling ministry for many years. However, several are "kings" who have proven themselves in the business world. One of these, Dr. Sanford Kulkin, relates the testimony of how he was extremely successful as a consultant to major corporations, yet he had a heart to serve God in ministry. Sandy was raised by Jewish parents. In his early twenties he became a born-again, Spirit-filled Christian. He started a Bible study that had hundreds attending. Several Christians told him that he should become a pastor. He occasionally preached in churches, but he did not have a prophetic directive to go into full-time pastoring. He went through several "Joseph experiences" and eventually became a consultant to major businesses. However, there was always that unanswered question, "Am I a preacher or a businessman?"

In 1989 I invited Sandy to speak at our Christian International Business Network conference. While he was there, I prophesied to him. He had been recommended by some of my ministers as a speaker for our conference, but I personally knew very little about him at the time. Part of the word of the Lord to Sandy was that he had wondered whether he was a businessman or a preacher. The Lord told him, "You are both. You are a minister in the marketplace. You are a prophet of God with an anointing and ministry like Daniel and Joseph." Sandy has since testified, "For years I wondered whether I was a minister doing business or a businessman doing ministry. Nine years ago, as a result of my relationship with Christian International Business Network, the anointing came when I finally realized that I was a businessman called to be a minister in the marketplace." Since the business arena is his primary place of calling and anointing, it is where he is most successful as God's minister.

Where are the Saints? Much research and evaluation have determined that only two percent of Christians earn their living and fulfill their ministry working inside the local church or non-profit ministries, while 98 percent of the Saints work and fulfill their ministry outside the local church. In other words, two percent are pastors and church staff. This figure would be even less if you counted only those on staff who do the priestly ministry in the church. Ninety-eight percent of Saints earn their income, do their work, and fulfill their profession outside the walls of the local church. The Church has provided training and equipping by teaching and enabling those who are called to minister in the pulpit. But we have not adequately taught and enabled those who are called to minister in the marketplace and public square. This is an urgent need to prepare the Church for the Day of the Saints.

GOD'S PURPOSE FOR LOCAL CHURCHES

For centuries Christian colleges and seminaries have functioned to train those with a pulpit calling and ministry. They teach, train, equip, and activate men and women into their pulpit ministry. Now the same must be done for members of the Body of Christ whose calling is to fulfill their ministry in the workaday world.

One of the main ministries of the local church should be to provide the training and equipping of the Saints in the marketplace. This does not just mean kings should attend training opportunities offered by churches that are geared toward priests. If a pastor only has a vision for making priests, he or she will not be able to equip the kings for their spiritual service. Kings must have more than hearing preaching from the pulpit. They need specialized teaching, training, activating, and maturing to minister in the marketplace.

All Saints need the same spiritual foundation. What does a minister in the pulpit need that a minister in the marketplace does not need? If a Christian is really called to a certain profession in the same manner as a preacher is called to fill a pulpit, then does one of them need more of the things of God than the other? We could compare it to different human bodies which contain the same 15 chemical elements.[12] All members of the physical body have the same life-giving blood flowing through them. Yet each member receiving that same blood accomplishes a different task and special performance for the successful functioning of the whole body. Likewise, every ministering member of the Body of Christ, whether functioning in the marketplace or the pulpit, needs the same things to fulfill their membership ministry.

Both the kingly and priestly ministers need to be cleansed by the blood of Jesus and have the life of Christ within. Both need to know the Word of God and be filled with the Holy Spirit. Both need to know the biblical principles to practice to be successful in their personal life, family, and profession. Both need to be trained to know the voice of God and the guidelines for fulfilling that directive word from the Lord. What does the preacher need to fulfill his membership ministry that the Christian businessperson does not need? Nothing! They both need the same foundation to fulfill their different membership ministries.

Run on All Cylinders: As we will see in a moment, all Saints are created with a spirit, soul, and body. Therefore, it is important that Saints are trained and equipped in each of these areas. We have tended to view priests as those who operate in the spirit realm and kings as those who concern themselves with the physical and mental arenas. For example, those involved in trades requiring heavy physical labor or skilled dexterity have to carefully develop their physical capacities. Those involved in the sciences, mathematics, teaching, accounting, and many other fields need to have disciplined and trained their minds to understand the complexities of their positions. But all Saints need to be good stewards of each of the mental, physical, and spiritual areas. Priests need to eat right and buffet their bodies.[13] And kingly Saints need to be activated to operate in the spiritual gifts seven days a week, not just when they are in church. In the next chapter we will look more at specific training especially designed to activate Saints in the marketplace.

This will be revolutionary thinking for most Christians and pastors. When we think "Church," we should think of people, not buildings. When we think of "local church," we should think of the place where the Saints are to faithfully gather weekly for the many beneficial reasons for which God established the local church.[14] This revelation in no wise lessens the importance of the local church, but makes it more vital and meaningful.

Places of Launching: I am the apostolic overseer of hundreds of local churches as Bishop of the Christian International

Network of Churches. I am a strong advocate of the local church with its structure and ministry. However, the local church is not to be a place of limitation. It should be the place of launching members into their membership ministry. It is not just a place for social gatherings. It is to bless the Saints and also build them into mighty men and women of God. The local church should be an armory and military base for training soldiers of the cross.

Too many local churches function more as nursing homes whose main ministry is just to keep the people alive and as comfortable as possible until they die. Too many Christians like to attend a church that functions as a hospital where they are nurtured and taken care of by others. And too many pastors are willing to have it so as long as the members pay their tithes and fill the pews of their local church every Sunday. Churches should have "hospitals" of counseling, healing, deliverance, and restoration to help the wounded, but only for the purpose of getting them healthy enough to get back on the front line of Christian service. Local churches are to be armories for training and equipping soldiers, not just an auditorium for an audience. Saints are to be participators, not spectators, in the game of Christian living and warfare.

A Successful Local Church: In their seminary training, most pastors received the impression that their main ministry was to get people saved and make them faithful church members. This view determines a pastor's success by the number of people he accumulates. Those with mega-churches of 5,000 or more are considered very successful pastors. Numbers do indicate that the pastors are doing some things to draw people and to keep enough of their members so that the church can grow to greater numbers. But Christ Jesus never put importance upon numbers as much as He did upon quality. He sought to reproduce Himself in those God had given Him, so that they might do the works that He did and even greater works.[15] During Christ's three and one-half years of ministry, He spent 70 to 80 percent of His time with His 12 disciples and 20 to 30 percent of His time ministering to the multitudes.

The local pastor and apostle should have the same attitude as Christ toward the local church. Firstly, it is to be a training center; secondly, it is to seek to reach the multitudes; thirdly, it functions as a hospital and restoration center, along with other lesser purposes and functions. Pastors and heads of local churches should have a vision to raise up an army, not just an audience. The goal should be to get a greater number and quality of Saint ministers out in the world demonstrating the Kingdom of Christ, not a greater number sitting in the pews. Saints are given to a pastor and the pastor to the Saints that they may be clothed with their Christian armor and equipped in their weapons of warfare.

Local Church and Para-Church: We must keep in mind that the corporate Church is wherever Saints live and function. The local church is where these Saints gather to derive all the benefits of local church ministry. The ministry of the corporate Body of Christ, the Church, is not limited to the four walls of the local church. Too many pastors have conveyed the idea that the only thing that is "church activity" is what is done inside the local church and directed by the pastor of a local church. Some have propagated the idea that any ministry that was not started by and under the control and direction of the local church and pastor is a "para-church" ministry. This includes all groups such as the Billy Graham Evangelistic Association, Oral Roberts' ministry, Christian television networks like Trinity Broadcasting Network, Full Gospel Business Men's Fellowship International, and any ministry organization that was not birthed in a local church nor under its directorship. Most Charismatic, prophetic, faith, and apostolic leaders now accept these types of ministries and their leaders as being valid "Church" ministers and ministries.

We must not allow the Internal Revenue Service and government of the United States, or that of any other nation, to limit our view of the Church. These official groups view church as merely a building where clergy minister the sacraments to the church members, such as water baptism, communion, marriage, or a funeral, and where sermons are preached. Those things do happen at a local church, but that is not the whole ministry of "the Church." The true Church of Jesus Christ has multimillions of members functioning in every area of life around the world.

When Is the Church Functioning? Having a church service requires several Saints to be gathered together in one place. However, the Church is people, not a meeting. So wherever a Saint is, there is the Church. Each Saint is not the entire Church, of course, but is a member who can manifest God's glory and minister Christ to those around, regardless of the environment or circumstances. Jesus was the Church at work when He ministered to one woman at a well. Philip was the Church ministering when he ministered to an Ethiopian official in his chariot. Paul and Silas were the Church ministering when they sang praises in a jail and ministered salvation to the jailer. Church is not just in a building, but wherever Saints are letting their light shine and are being true witnesses of Jesus Christ. We must incorporate this biblical principle into our way of thinking, without despising or doing away with God's divine order, structure, purpose for, and ministry of the local church.

JESUS IS IN THE CHURCH-BUILDING BUSINESS

Apostle Paul gave the revelation that after Jesus had ascended back to the Father, He sent the Holy Spirit to birth His Church, which He had purchased with His own blood.[16] Jesus had declared while He was on earth, "I will build My Church." He had the master blueprint and picture of the finished Church in His mind when He made that statement. Jesus spent 15 years (ages 15–30) as a carpenter and general contractor building homes and furnishings. Jesus knew He would need some sub-contractors to build His Church according to His master plan. He divided His Church-building ability into five special gifts. He gave these gifts to certain members of His Church to be an extension of Himself to build His Church.[17] The Saints would be the lively stones the builders would use to build God's Church.[18] Each of the five gifted sub-contractors would have their own area of specialty in building Christ's structure.

How It Happened:

"When [Christ] *ascended on high...* [He] *gave gifts to men."...And He Himself gave some to be apostles,*

some prophets, some evangelists, and some pastors and teachers, for the equipping of the saints for [their] *work of ministry...*[so that the Body of Christ may be continually built] *till we all come to the unity of the faith and of the knowledge of the Son of God, to a perfect man, to the measure of the stature of the fullness of Christ; that we...may grow up in all things into Him who is the head—Christ—from whom the whole body, joined and knit together by what every joint supplies, according to the effective working by which every part does its share, causes growth of the body for the* [building up] *of itself in love.*[19]

An entire book could be written on the full implications of each of the words and statements made in these verses. But for our purpose in this book we just need to look at the general picture. Please notice that Christ gave gifts to redeemed mankind to equip the Saints who are members of the corporate Body of Christ. It does not say these gifted ministers were given to local churches. Nor does this Scripture or any other say that they were only to function inside a local church.

General Contractor and Sub-contractors: Apostles, prophets, evangelists, pastors, and teachers are the sub-contractors working with Jesus Christ, the General Contractor and Architect of the building, the Church. According to Ephesians 2:20, the apostles and prophets have the gifted ability to not only lay the foundation of the building, but to actually be the foundation of the Church. The Church is built upon the foundation stones of apostles and prophets. The Saints are the lively stones with which the whole building is built. We must remember that the Church that Jesus said He would build is being built with redeemed humankind. The living bodies of the Saints are temples of the Holy Spirit and the building blocks of the Church.[20]

Biblical Illustration of Stones: A good example concerning the foundation and the stones for the building is found in the way the temple of Solomon was built. The stones for the temple were cut at the quarry for each and every part of the building. Once the foundation was completed, the stones were put in place in the construction of the temple.[21] The Holy Spirit has been preparing people to be lively stones in Christ's eternal Church for centuries.[22]

Prophets and apostles have the gifted ability from Christ to receive the revelation of the blueprint of the building.[23] Apostle Moses received the blueprint for the tabernacle and prophet David received by revelation the blueprint for the temple.[24] It is necessary for the present-day apostles and prophets to have the full revelation of the overall blueprint, for the size and height of the building is determined by the foundation. God wants His Church to be all that He has designed it to be.

All Five Must Work Together and Do Their Part: As apostles and prophets receive their revelation of the blueprint, they then share it with the evangelists, pastors, and teachers so that they know more of their job description as subcontractors. By wisdom and prophetic revelation, apostles and prophets bring the other fivefold ministers and the Saints confirmation, revelation, clarity, and activation of their calling and ministry. All fivefold ascension-gift ministers have an equal part to play in equipping the Saints for their membership ministry in the Body of Christ. Their ministries are not greater or lesser, just different. Each fivefold minister is one-fifth of the total expression and ministry of the one Christ. Like members of the body, all are needed and play a definite part. But some are more essential for the continuing life of the body. The human body can continue without a hand or an eye, but not without a heart or lungs.

Prophets and Apostles Must Be Restored First: The Church cannot come to the fullness of Christ's life and purpose without the full restoration of prophets and apostles. My burden, passion, divine enablement, and commission from Christ Jesus is to equip the Saints in their membership ministries. For the last 25 years of my 48 years of ministry, I have been fulfilling my divine commission to help bring about the full restoration and activation of the members of the Body of Christ who are called to be prophets and apostles. As we have seen, the gifting and ministry of all fivefold ministers are required to equip the Saints for their membership works of service. That is the reason the Holy Spirit activated a Prophetic Movement in the 1980s and an Apostolic Movement in the 1990s, to restore Christ's gifts of prophet and apostle. Evangelists, pastors, and teachers have been recognized and functioning for centuries in the Church, but it has only been during the last 20 years that prophets and apostles have begun to be recognized, accepted, and allowed to take their rightful places of ministry in the Body of Christ.

Updating the Foundation: Evangelical pastors, theologians, and Christian authors who did not have apostolic and prophetic revelation of the complete blueprint of the Church laid a limited foundation in earlier restoration movements. It was as if they projected Christ building a ten-story Church, so they laid a foundation for a ten-story building. But with today's revelation we realize God's blueprint is far more like a Church/building of 100 stories. Apostles and prophets will now lay the full foundation for the "100-story" building of the Church. It will then be able to house all of God's glory, thereby being enabled to fulfill all of God's purposes. One of God's present-day purposes is for fivefold ministers to prepare the Saints for the coming Saints Movement. Apostles and prophets are here to stay until all of God's purposes for His Church are completed.

Some have asked why apostles and prophets are being restored last if they are the foundation of the Church. This is a reasonable question, which I have also asked God. There are several reasons, but let me reveal one reason here with an Old Testament example to portray this truth.

The First Pattern: The original apostles of the first-century Church laid the proper foundation. However, by the fifth century the Church had fallen away from its foundational truths. Nearly the only part of the foundation left was the Apostles' Creed. The major reformers, such as Martin Luther and John Wesley, were apostles and prophets. They laid more of the foundation and gathered more Saints, which are the building material of the Church. It might be more accurate to say they cleared a portion of the original foundation laid by the first-century Church prophets and apostles. This could be likened to the days when Nehemiah and Ezra directed the rebuilding of the temple. We could say that the apostles and prophets who received the revelation that activated each restoration movement cleared another portion of the foundation. The present-day apostles and prophets will clear the last foundation truth needed to fulfill all things. Though the Church-world did not recognize and understand apostles and prophets, nevertheless, I believe all those who were used to bring forth major movements were prophets and apostles.

Finalizing the Foundation: Most of these prophets and apostles did not have the revelation that what they were doing was progressively adding to God's overall pattern and ultimate purposes for His perfected Church. It was not necessary at that time. Today's apostles and prophets are bringing finalization to the foundation. Therefore, it is essential that they have an overall view of the full dimensions of the foundation so that the building of the Church will be all that Christ originally had in mind when He declared, "I will build My Church!" The Church does not just exist in time; while its members are mortal, it is an eternal Body designed to function forever.[25] The Saints in Heaven are still members of Christ's corporate Body, the Church. God, who sits on His timeless and spaceless throne, sees one Church made up of Saints from ages past, present, and future in Heaven and on Earth.

Analogies Are Limited: Before we close with the building analogy, a word of caution is in order. One must understand the principle of Old Testament types and natural things used to illustrate spiritual truths. They bring great revelation and insight, yet you cannot make every part of the typology of the step-by-step process in constructing and building, or of any other analogy, apply literally. For instance, Jesus is called the "Lamb" of God and the "Lion" of Judah, but we cannot make the shape, size, parts, and every function of a lamb or lion literally apply to Jesus.[26] We must not become so literally-minded that we cannot grasp the spiritual truths from biblical analogies and types. We cannot take the illustration of the Church as a building and make it apply to the Church's growth and function in all the same sequences as building a natural building. When the Bible speaks of the Church as a building, a body, or a bride, it is revealing keys to our relationship with Christ. It is also describing how the corporate Body is a whole unit with individual members. These analogies are not perfect representations, but they do help us to grasp important aspects that Christ wants us to understand.

SAINTS ARE SPIRIT, SOUL, AND BODY BEINGS

One of the reasons there has been a wrong perception of the local church is that many Saints, consciously or unconsciously, believe that God is concerned with the spirit realm but not with the natural realm. Scripture does tell us to put our trust and hope in God and not in natural things.[27] However, Scripture also teaches that ultimately all things will be restored. Many Saints look forward to Heaven as an eternal vacation. They have a "spooky spiritual" idea that Heaven is a place where we will be spirit beings who do nothing but float around on a cloud and listen to harp music. They do not realize that the biblical

225

business principles and practices that apply here on Earth also pertain to the Kingdom of God. In order to understand how relevant Kingdom issues are, we need to look at some basics about God and man.

Theologians' View of the Future: Most theologians believe that the future, eternal, heavenly home of Christians is new Earth surrounded by Heaven. **"Pre-millennialist"** theologians believe first there will be a "rapture" and resurrection of the Saints.[28] The Saints will be taken to Heaven for seven years before returning with Christ to set up God's Kingdom over all the Earth for 1,000 years.[29]

At the end of the millennial (1,000 year) reign of Christ and His Church, the devil and his hordes of demons will be released from the pit where they have been bound for a thousand years. They will incite much of humanity to rebel against God. There will be a great battle between good and evil, God and the devil, Satan's army of wicked men and evil angels and God's army of righteous men and holy angels. The devil and all his followers will lose the war and will be cast into the lake of fire. The general resurrection of all the dead will take place, and they will stand before the great white throne of judgment. They will be judged to determine whether they spend eternity with Jesus Christ in His heavenly places or with the devil in the lake of eternal fire and torment.[30]

The Lord will then renovate and cleanse the Earth and its atmosphere with His heavenly fire, making everything on Earth purified, alive, and more brilliant and beautiful than the description of the New Jerusalem.[31] It will become the new Earth with a new heavenly atmosphere, now worthy of being a habitable place and home for Jesus and His Bride/Church.[32]

Theologians known as "**a-millennialists**" believe the end result will be the same. The difference between their belief and that of the pre-millennialists is that the a-millennial camp does not interpret Scripture to refer to two end-time comings of Christ with a thousand-year period in between. They see just one coming when all these end-time things happen. A third viewpoint on end-time events is the "**post-millennial**" theory. Those that hold to this position see the Scripture as indicating the return of Christ to set up His Kingdom on Earth will occur after the millennium. Post-millennialists believe that the Saints, empowered by the Holy Spirit, will bring in the great harvest and build the Kingdom, preparing the way for Jesus' glorious return.

Regardless of their different viewpoints, all these theological camps believe that God will establish a new Earth surrounded by Heaven where the Saints will work, rule, and live with Christ forever.[33]

Perspective of This Book: This book will not attempt to prove whether pre-, a-, or post-millennialism is the correct interpretation. Some truth can be found in each viewpoint. For instance, this book propagates the pre-mill view that Christ Jesus and His Church will reign for 1,000 years after the rapture of the Church. It presents a portion of the a-mill view that states, "Believers are already in heavenly places in Christ Jesus and reign in life by Him; Satan is a defeated foe and the Saints triumph over him in Christ."[34] It propagates the post-mill view that the Church will grow in power more and more until it demonstrates the fullness of Christ and His Kingdom. However, the "pan-mill" view is presented more than anything else: that is, everything is going to "pan out" according to God's pre-ordained eternal purpose, regardless of the different eschatological viewpoints that are being propagated by preachers and Christian authors.

Who Will We Be Throughout Eternity? The point I am trying to reveal is that we will always be God's real people made in His own image and likeness by our conformity to the image of the true God and Man, Jesus Christ.[35] Human beings will not become disembodied spirits floating around on clouds. Nor will we be reincarnated as someone or something else. We will have a human spirit, soul, and body forever. We will function in a kingdom that has structure, leadership, and principles for operating. Saints who learn to operate in their work and relationships according to godly principles will be the ones appointed to rulership in God's Kingdom.[36] Those who do not learn to "do business" like Jesus will go back to basic training in eternity until they are equipped.

So who is Jesus Christ, and who will He be throughout eternity? Most Christians know Jesus as the Son of God, God manifest in the flesh, and Savior of mankind.[37] Now let us look at Jesus in another area of His being.

Jesus—Saint in the Marketplace: Jesus was born with a body just as other members of the human race were. However, His blood type came from His Father, who was the Almighty God of Heaven and Earth. Jesus grew from babyhood to manhood in 15 years. Historians record that

Joseph, Mary's husband and the stepfather of Jesus, died when Jesus was 15 years old. Being the oldest child, He had to take on the full responsibilities as the male head of the household. His several brothers, His sisters, and His mother became His responsibility. As you know, that is a lot of responsibility upon the shoulders of a young man. Jesus had worked as an apprentice with His stepfather in his carpentry business. At 15 He now became the "CEO" of His own business. He no doubt employed the help of his younger brothers. He worked as a businessman in the business world for 15 years before He became a preacher and was manifested as the Son of God on the Earth.

God Was a Minister in the Marketplace: Since Jesus was God manifest in a human body, we could legitimately say that God was a Minister in the marketplace.[38] It is interesting to note that Jesus functioned as a natural human being for 30 years before He began to manifest His supernatural God-attributes to the world. He fulfilled His kingly ministry as a Saint in the marketplace before He entered His priestly ministry of preaching, teaching, healing the sick, and manifesting the power of the Kingdom of God. God did not give priority to Jesus' priestly ministry over His kingly ministry. In fact, Jesus spent 15 years in the kingly ministry and only three and one-half years in the priestly ministry. Ed Silvoso writes:

> Because of the roles He embodied—ruler, teacher and businessman—Jesus belongs in the marketplace rather than in a monastery. We easily see Jesus as a teacher by virtue of how well He taught and because in the gospels He is referred to as a Rabbi. We also recognize Him as the ultimate ruler

because He is the King of kings. However, picturing Him as a businessman is where we have the most difficulty today. Yet, in the gospels the opposite was true. At first Jesus was more easily recognized as a businessman than as a Rabbi or a ruler.[39]

God's thinking and purpose are different from man's. From our religious way of thinking, it is hard to imagine why God would seemingly waste 15 years of Jesus' adult life just having Him do secular work. I know several men who started ministry in their mid-teens. I was only 19 when I started full-time priestly ministry as a pastor. If God would have anointed Jesus to be His boy-wonder Evangelist with supernatural signs and wonders, just think how many He could have turned to God during those 15 years!

However, we must acknowledge that our way of thinking is not God's way of thinking. His ways are as high above ours as Heaven is above the Earth.[40] Yes, God knew that Jesus would spend only 34 years upon Earth from His conception to His crucifixion. Jesus spent 30 years becoming and being God's model Man and only three and one-half years being God's model Minister. That is a ratio of about ten-to-one in favor of being a true man of God over being a great minister of God. In God's divine order, He makes the person before He makes the minister. Father God is more interested in sonship of manhood than He is in sonship of ministry.

Manhood and Maturity: I have a teaching called the "Ten M's" which covers ten essential character attributes that every minister must possess to be godly and successful in ministry. They include manhood (or womanhood), maturity, ministry, message, marriage, methods, manners, money, morality, and motive.[41] The highest calling in God's Kingdom is that of being conformed to the image of His Son Jesus Christ, who is the perfect image and expression of Father God. Because this is so important, when I teach on the Ten M's, I spend almost half the teaching time on manhood and maturity. When these areas are in line, it is much more likely that the remaining eight will be as well.

God's Perfect Man—Man's Perfect God: Jesus Christ was and is God's perfect Man and man's perfect God. Becoming Father God's type of person is God's highest calling and purpose for any human being. God's predestinated purpose for all who are His is for us to be conformed to the image of His perfect Man, Jesus, **His only begotten Son**.[42] The Bible does not teach us to strive to be like God, who is a Spirit and consuming fire, but to be like God the man Christ Jesus.[43] Jesus will always be Son of Man-Son of God, eternal God-eternal man. The human body of Jesus was crucified on a cross and laid in a tomb, but after three days His Spirit re-entered that body, resurrecting and transforming it into an immortal human body.[44] He ascended to Heaven in that body and it is now sitting at the right hand of the Majesty on high.[45] There is now one Mediator between God and man and that is the *Man* Christ Jesus.[46]

God's Greatest Expression of Himself: At Creation, Adam became the highest expression of God in the universe. Man was the only creation that God made in His exact image and likeness.[47] Before man sinned he looked and functioned like God, and God looked and functioned like man. They were interrelated and compatible with one an-other. They related in the Garden as Father and created son. No doubt the angels were amazed at how much their God and man looked alike. Man walked like God walked and talked like God talked as they walked and talked in the Garden in the cool of the day.

All the other heavenly host watched as God created the body of man from the dust of the Earth and then breathed the breath of life into him. They were thrilled to see God's masterpiece creation immediately become a liv-ing, functioning God-like being. There are no biblical state-ments that the cherubim, seraphim, angels, or archangels were made in God's own image and likeness, only man. For that reason redeemed mankind is able to become the many-membered Body of the Bride of Christ. Redeemed Saints actually become co-equal heirs with Christ of all that He is destined to inherit from His heavenly Father. No other creation has such a calling and destiny.[48]

Saints—Mankind Beings Forever: When Christians die they are taken to Heaven, but not to become some other type of being. Mankind will never become angels, cheru-bim, or seraphim. When Jesus returns to resurrect and translate the bodies of the Saints, we will not be changed into any other form or likeness than how God made Adam as the first model man. Our eternal destiny as God's chil-dren and as Saints is to be redeemed spirit, soul, and body human beings, just as God originally created. There is no higher or greater being that God could make than man, since He had already made man in His own image and likeness, and there is no other being in eternal existence greater than Jehovah—the only Eternal Almighty God.[49]

God's Procreative Human Race: When God made man's body He made it to be exactly like the body that He wanted His only begotten Son to have as His own body forever. God established the human race through giving Adam and Eve the power to produce other human bodies which God would fill with the breath of life.[50] Man and woman could biologically conceive and birth a human body, but it could not become a living being able to function as a separate human being unless that body began breathing on its own. And so, through the procreative process, the whole human race was produced and populated the Earth.

The Eternal Body of God the Son: God planned to "**prepare a body for Jesus**" by the procreative process He had established. However, God Himself would be the Father by causing an **immaculate conception** in a young virgin woman.[51] Thereby, the body of Jesus became the only human body that was fathered by God Himself. For that reason Jesus became the only begotten Son of God.[52] Jesus was the only person that God ever begat.[53]

Adam was God's only created son; Jesus was God's only begotten Son. God Almighty, Jehovah, was not only the spiritual but also the natural Father of our Lord Jesus Christ.[54] This is the cornerstone of Christianity.[55] For if Jesus Christ is not the only begotten Son of God, then His blood is the same as other contaminated human blood and cannot cleanse us from all our sins. The life-blood of Jesus came from God. It was a sinless life and blood. We are cleansed from our sins by the blood of Jesus and saved by His life that was given for us on the cross of Calvary.[56]

How important is what happened to the body of Jesus? The human body of Jesus died on the cross and was placed in a grave. After three days God resurrected that body.[57] During those three days that Jesus was a disembodied spirit being, He proclaimed to the disembodied, human spirit beings what He had accomplished on Earth.[58] After three days Christ came back to His grave, reinhabited His body, changed it into an immortal body, and then ascended to Heaven in that body. This enabled Jesus to have His own human body throughout the endless ages of eternity. God did not leave Christ Jesus in His spirit-being body, nor create Him another natural body out of heavenly material. He resurrected that same earthly body that was conceived in the womb of Mary, walked the shores of Galilee, and died at Calvary. Jesus was not re-created but resurrected. Christians do not believe in re-creation but resurrection. The body of Jesus had to be made eternal not only for the redemption of man, but for God's eternal purpose for His Son and redeemed mankind. That resurrected earth body is the eternal body of God the Son.

The resurrection of the earth body of Jesus is the authenticity of Christianity. One has only to read First Corinthians chapter 15 to grasp the full importance of not only the resurrection of the body of Jesus but also of all human bodies who have ever lived on planet Earth.

> *Now if Christ is preached that He has been raised from the dead, how do some among you say that there is no resurrection of the dead? But if there is no resurrection of the dead, then Christ is not risen. And if Christ is*

not risen, then our preaching is empty and your faith is also empty [void, worthless, meaningless]. *Yes, and we are found false witnesses of God, because we have testified of God that He raised up Christ, whom He did not raise up—if in fact the dead do not rise. For if the dead do not rise, then Christ is not risen. And if Christ is not risen, your* [Christian] *faith is futile; you are still in your sins! Then also those who have fallen asleep in Christ have perished. If in this life only we have hope in Christ, we are of all men the most pitiable. But now Christ is risen from the dead, and has become the firstfruits of those who have fallen asleep* [bodies have died]. *For since by man* [Adam] *came death, by man also* [Christ Jesus] *came the resurrection of the dead* [human bodies]. *For as in Adam all* [mankind bodies] *die, even so in Christ shall all be made alive* [resurrected]....*But someone will say, "How are the dead raised up? And with what body do they come?" Foolish one, what you sow is not made alive unless it dies....The body is sown in corruption, it is raised in incorruption. It is sown in dishonor, it is raised in glory. It is sown in weakness, it is raised in power. It is sown a natural* [mortal] *body, it is raised a spiritual* [immortal] *body. There is a natural* [mortal] *body, and there is a spiritual* [resurrected, immortal] *body.*[59]

Immortal Bodies for Eternal Function: The apostle Paul explained in the remainder of the chapter that our mortal flesh and bone bodies, which are subject to death and corruption, cannot function in the eternal Kingdom of

235

God. They must be changed into immortal flesh and bone bodies. The bodies of the Saints who have already died will be restored for eternal functioning when Christ resurrects them at His second coming. Paul then reassures those who will still be alive when Christ returns that they will not be left with corruptible bodies but that they shall have their bodies immortalized:

> ...in a moment, in the twinkling of an eye, at the last trumpet. For the trumpet will sound, and the dead will be raised incorruptible, and we shall be changed. For this corruptible must put on incorruption, and this mortal must put on immortality. So when this corruptible has put on incorruption, and this mortal has put on immorality, then shall be brought to pass the saying that is written... "O Death, where is your sting? O Hades, where is your victory?"...But thanks be to God, who gives us the victory through our Lord Jesus Christ.[60]

The Day of the Saints will contribute much to hastening that glorious day of the ultimate triumph of Christ and His Church.

Natural Body-Spiritual Body: Time and space were given to this issue so that Christians can realize that man was created originally as spirit, soul, and body. He was created and called man. He was made like God, which was different from the way God had made any other creation. Man was given a flesh and bone body made from the dust of the Earth. This body was not intended to be a body man would use while on Earth and then be discarded forever when he died and went to Heaven. God knew that man would sin and cause his body to become mortal with the ability to die and go back to dust. But God already had a remedy to fix that problem—the resurrection. If Adam and Eve had not sinned they would have lived forever as spirit, soul, and body beings doing God's work on Earth. Redeemed mankind, the Church Saints, will need their earth bodies redeemed and immortalized to do the type of work God has planned for them to do with Him throughout eternity. Saints are called to rule and reign on new Earth forever. Yes, man is called to eternal work as well as to eternal worship and fellowship.

Both king and priest Saints need to realize that our natural bodies are not sinful throwaways. They are temples where God lives and are to be an extension and expression of the presence of God within.[61] Saints in the marketplace must be delivered from thinking, "My body is holy and spiritual when it is sitting in a church pew or standing singing and praising God, but it is worldly and natural when it is doing work in my profession." As a living mortal person who is a member of the eternal Body of Christ, each of us is the continuous dwelling place of God. Saints are those people who have been cleansed from all sin, sanctified and set apart for the Master's use. Whether day or night, at a church gathering or a workplace, we are to be one with Christ and doing His work continuously all the days of our life. Our life is His work and our work is to demonstrate His life in our worship, way of living, and the excellent manner in which we do our professional work. Work done in such a way that it glorifies God is just as spiritual to God as the things we do inside a local church. The criteria are whether it is biblically approved and whether it glorifies God and causes others to glorify God.

GLORIFYING GOD IN OUR WORK

What Does It Mean to Glorify God? The word *glorify* comes from the Greek word *doxazo*. It means "to extol, demonstrate and make known" the attributes of God. Words can explain and express, but actions can demonstrate. People are impressed more by what we do than by what we say. It is commonly said that what we do speaks so loud that people cannot hear what we say. Christians who do careless work, do not make it to work on time, or do not follow through on orders given will not be able to give a convincing testimony to their boss or fellow employees. They are not extolling the attributes of God's faithfulness, dependability, and trustworthiness.[62] They are not shedding Christ's life and light on people. They are glorifying not God's way of working but their own non-Christlike ways. When Christian employers and employees are committed to glorifying God in their work just as much as they do in a local church, then they will have faith for God to work with them in the supernatural gifts of the Holy Spirit right in their work.

Natural Work vs. Spiritual Work: There is no separation between spiritual work and natural work for a 24-hour-a-day member of the Body of Christ. For whatever we do in word and deed, we do it all in the name of the Lord Jesus.[63] In the Garden of Eden God did not command man to cut down the trees and build himself a tabernacle in which to stand worshiping God all day.[64] He told Adam to go to work by tending the garden, an action that would require physical labor.[65] God told him to name all the thousands of flying, swimming, and walking creatures.[66] That required creative mental work. He was to walk and talk with God in the cool of the day—relational work. God put high priority upon man's personal relationship with Himself and upon man doing the work that was assigned to him.

Worship and Work: Worship has a two-fold expression. One expression is what present-truth Saints are more familiar with—verbal expression through words and singing. There are numerous benefits and divine purposes for vocally expressing our praise and worship. Our worship leader, Dean Mitchum, has written a book on biblical purposes for worship.[67] Many Christians are familiar with some of these purposes, so we will not take time to cover them here.

Another expression of worship is just as meaningful to God as verbal expression. Philippians 1:11 says Saints are called to be a praise to God's glory. Jesus commanded us to let our light so shine that men may see our good works and glorify our Father who is in Heaven.[68] He said the way we let our light shine is by doing good work. Our good works glorify God. We are not saved by good works, but saved people will do good works.[69] This applies to doing good work on our job as well as doing righteous acts. For a Christian to work in a profession with faithfulness, integrity, skill, and a spirit of excellence is to let his light shine and be a praise to God. Remember that Jesus glorified God by doing good natural work for 15 years before He glorified His heavenly Father by doing spiritual work.

God Loves and Honors Work: God the Father puts a high priority on good workers, whether it is the work of the priest ministers in the local church or the work of the king ministers in the marketplace. Work in its different forms is mentioned more than 800 times in the Bible. This is as many as all the words used to express worship, music, praise, and singing. Work is one of the three most mentioned subjects in the Bible. It is not a bad word to God but a good word. Work was not a part of the curse to man, although after the Fall, it became a struggle to make work easy, enjoyable, and profitable. Man was commanded to work long before he sinned and was removed from the Garden of Eden.

Look at some Scripture phrases that quote Jesus:

*My food is to do the will of Him who sent Me, and to finish His **work**.*[70]

*My Father has been **working** until now, and I have been **working**.*[71]

*I must **work** the **works** of Him who sent Me.*[72]

*I have finished the **work** which You have given Me to do.*[73]

Notice a few other phrases about **work**:

*Abound(ing) in the **work** of the Lord.*[74]

*Let each one examine his own **work**.*[75]

*Be(ing) fruitful in every **good work**.*[76]

***Work** with your own hands.*[77]

*If anyone will not **work**, neither shall he eat.*[78]

*If a man desires the position of a bishop, he desires a good **work**.*[79]

*Do the **work** of an evangelist.*[80]

*For the **work** of ministry....*[81]

*God is not unjust to forget your **work** and labor of love.*[82]

Work is an eternal attribute of God. The Eternal Creator worked preparing all the resources man would need. God worked six days establishing Earth and all its inhabitants, including man.[83] God also set the Earth in rotation and in harmony with the universe. Jehovah rested on the seventh day, after He had completed all the things concerning Earth.[84] Then He went back to work on the eighth day continuing His eternal task of administering the affairs of Heaven and adding His new role of working with man.

Be Consistent and Established: The Saints who will participate in the next movement will be those who live and operate the same at work, at home, or in the local church. We should not talk or act in any way at home or work that we wouldn't behind the pulpit in church. Jesus is the same yesterday, today, and forever; we should be the same wherever we are.[85] Not only are we to live and function everywhere else as we would in church, but Jesus said for us to be as perfect as our Father in Heaven and to pray for His will to be done in our earthly bodies as it is in the heavenly bodies in heaven.[86]

Natural bodies and spiritual bodies, home, work, and play are all ordained of God. Being spiritual is not just a church activity but a way of life for the true Saints of God. Worship and work are both eternal attributes and activities of God. Saints are destined to work and worship forever.

"Let everything that has breath praise the Lord."[87] "And behold, I am coming quickly, and My reward is with Me, to give to every one according to his work."[88]

Be convinced of worship, work, and the importance of the resurrection. The Saints who participate in the coming Saints Movement must be thoroughly established in the faith that Jesus Christ is the Son of God. They must know and be able to proclaim the "gospel," which is the death, burial, and resurrection of Jesus Christ. They must know that their right to be a saintly child of God was authorized by the resurrection of the body of Jesus from the grave. Jesus Christ was declared to be the Son of God with power by the resurrection from the dead.[89] Apostle Peter declared that it was through the resurrection of Jesus Christ that God the Father has also begotten us to a lively hope and an inheritance incorruptible. We are kept by His resurrection life and power. He also declared that because of Christ's resurrection we are made ready to participate in God's great salvation that is going to be manifest in these last days when Christ Jesus comes to be glorified in His Saints.[90]

Let the Church Arise! In following chapters more details on specific ministries of the Saints are given. But here I want to establish the fact that fivefold ministers and Saints' membership ministries can function anywhere and anytime God so desires. If we are going to be co-laborers with Christ in bringing about the greatest harvest of souls ever recorded in Church history, and if we are going to make the paradigm shift to God's greater order for the twenty-first century Church, then we must let the Church arise and function wherever the Saints are positioned. Church is in session wherever kingly and priestly Saints are operating, not just weekly in a building. We must activate and empower all Saints to bring the Kingdom of God to their realms of influence, including the 98 percent who function primarily outside the local church.

ENDNOTES:

1. Revelation 1:6; 1 Peter 2:9.
2. Matthew 5:14.
3. Bill Hamon, *The Eternal Church* (Santa Rosa Beach, FL: Christian International Publishers, 1981), pp. 30-45.
4. 1 Corinthians 12:12-31.
5. Ephesians 4:7.
6. 1 Corinthians 12:7.
7. 3 John 2; Deuteronomy 8:18.
8. Ed Silvoso, *Anointed for Business* (Ventura, CA: Regal, 2001), Uncorrected proof, p. 18.
9. 1 Corinthians 12:12; John 3:5; 1 John 1:9.
10. Silvoso, *Anointed for Business*, pp. 6-7, 10.
11. For a more detailed explanation of God's Word, will, and way, please see *Prophets and Personal Prophecy* by Dr. Bill Hamon (Shippensburg, PA: Destiny Image, 1987), pp. 87-103.
12. Bill Hamon, "God's Earth Man," Bachelor of Theology Thesis, 1968, p. 13. Unpublished.
13. 1 Corinthians 9:27.
14. Hebrews 10:25.
15. John 14:12.
16. Acts 20:28.
17. Ephesians 4:11.
18. 1 Peter 2:5.
19. Ephesians 4:8b,11-16.
20. 1 Corinthians 3:16.
21. 1 Kings 5:17; 6:7.
22. 1 Peter 2:5.
23. Amos 3:7; Ephesians 3:5.

24. Exodus 25:8-27; Chronicles 22.

25. Ephesians 3:21.

26. John 1:29; Revelation 5:5.

27. Matthew 6:19-33.

28. 1 Thessalonians 4:15. Further explanation of these terms is given in the back of this book.

29. Revelation 20:6.

30. Revelation 20:7-15.

31. Isaiah 65:17; 2 Peter 3:13; Revelation 21:1-5.

32. Revelation 5:10; 11:15.

33. Isaiah 65:17-25.

34. Ernest Kavan, "Millennium," *Baker's Dictionary of Theology*, Everett F. Harrison, ed. (Grand Rapids, MI: Baker Book House, 1960), p. 354.

35. Romans 8:29.

36. Luke 19:17.

37. John 20:31; Acts 8:37; Galatians 2:20; 1 Timothy 3:16; John 4:14; Luke 3:6.

38. Colossians 2:9.

39. Silvoso, *Anointed for Business*, p. 21.

40. Isaiah 55:9.

41. Bill Hamon, *Prophets, Pitfalls, and Principles* (Shippensburg, PA: Destiny Image, 1991), pp. 66-101.

42. John 1:14.

43. Deuteronomy 4:24; 1 Timothy 2:5.

44. John 19:18; Matthew 27:60; Acts 10:40; John 11:25-26.

45. Mark 16:19; Hebrews 1:3b.

46. 1 Timothy 2:5; 3:16.

47. Genesis 1:26-27.

48. Romans 8:17.

49. Isaiah 45:22.

50. Genesis 1:26-27; 2:7.

51. Luke 1:35.

52. John 1:14.

53. John 3:16.

54. 1 Peter 1:3.

55. Ephesians 2:20.

56. 1 John 1:7.

57. Matthew 28:5-7.

58. 1 Peter 3:18-20.

59. 1 Corinthians 15:12-22,35-36,42b-44.

60. 1 Corinthians 15:52-57.

61. Colossians 1:27.

62. John 14:1.

63. Colossians 3:17,23.

64. Genesis 2:8.

65. Genesis 2:15.

66. Genesis 2:19.

67. Dean Mitchum, *Apostolic Kingdom Praise* (Santa Rosa Beach, FL: Christian International Publications, 2001).

68. Matthew 5:16.

69. Ephesians 2:8-10

70. John 4:34.

71. John 5:17.

72. John 9:4.

73. John 17:4.

74. 1 Corinthians 15:58.

75. Galatians 6:4.

76. Colossians 1:10.

77. 1 Thessalonians 4:11.

78. 2 Thessalonians 3:10.

79. 1 Timothy 3:1.

80. 2 Timothy 4:5.

81. Ephesians 4:12.

82. Hebrews 6:10.

83. Genesis 1.

84. Genesis 2:2.

85. Hebrews 13:8.

86. Matthew 5:44; 6:10.

87. Psalm 150:6a.

88. Revelation 22:12.

89. Romans 1:4.

90. 1 Peter 1:3-4; 2 Thessalonians 1:10.

CHAPTER 8

SAINTS IN THE MARKET-PLACE AND GOVERNMENT

One of the main contributions to the Saints Movement is the revelation of God's plan to use Christians in the marketplace (business and "secular" professions) and public square (government). During the decades of the 1970s and 1980s, I ministered personal prophecy to thousands of leaders around the world. I kept hearing the Lord prophetically expressing His desire to equip Christian businesspeople for ministry in the marketplace. The scriptural example for this is the prophets in the Old Testament who were ministers in the marketplace and public square. God wants to raise up a company of prophetic men and women who will function outside the church pulpit.

From a Prophetic Revelation to a Divine Commission: After I heard God speak His heart several times on this matter, a full picture of what He desired was formed in my spirit and mind. I began to preach about God's desire to raise up a company of Daniel- and Deborah-type prophetic Saints in the political and business arenas of the world. Scores of leaders received prophecies prompting them to fulfill the heart of God in teaching and activating Saints in this area. As far as I know, none of them responded. The Holy Spirit finally challenged me by declaring that He had planted the revelation of His heart and mind within my spirit and mind. He told me to take the leadership role, write the vision, and make clear His plans for Christian businesspeople in these last days. We called them the Joseph-Daniel and Deborah-Esther Company.

In 1984, the vision became a mandate from God for me to fulfill. It was born of God, which means it will require a commitment until it is fulfilled.[1] When something is born of God within a person, there is no option but to stick with it. The way of the Lord must be found and implemented for the vision to be fulfilled throughout Christendom.

The Essence of the Initial Vision: God plans to raise up a great company of committed Christians whose destiny is to fulfill their membership ministry in the Body of Christ not from behind a pulpit, but in the world outside the walls of the local church. This company will include all Christians who do not earn their income from church-related ministerial work. They will be the primary ones whom God will use mightily during the day of the manifestation of the Saints. Many Saints will become key political figures whom God will use to influence nations, as Daniel influenced the king of the Babylonian empire. Some Saints will serve as heads of great corporations and will cause the wealth of the world to come into the Church for reaping the great harvest and demonstrating the Kingdom of God. Others will equally demonstrate the Kingdom, but in a smaller circle of influence such as their classroom, shop, or local neighborhood.

As Christian International has been in the process of carrying out this vision, God has allowed us to meet others who are also committed to empowering God's people in the marketplace. One of these is Rich Marshall, author of the book *God@Work*. He writes:

> I am quite certain that the time has come to recognize not only that all of us are called of God, but that our calling is for ministry in all facets of society. I see that calling not only in what might normally be included in the business and professional arena, but also in government, sports, media, medicine, and in all areas of work life.[2]

APOSTLES AND PROPHETS IN THE MARKETPLACE

In the early 1980s, God began to bring revelation concerning prophets and apostles functioning in more places than inside the local church. He began to reveal that as the Church entered the twenty-first century, a great Apostolic Reformation would revolutionize the way the Church functioned and viewed itself.

Traditional theologians' teaching on local church structure and government have left the impression that ministers are called, ordained, and activated to function only in the religious/church portion of the Body of Christ. The concept of fivefold ministers fulfilling their anointed gift outside the walls of the local church and non-profit organizations is foreign to the average church leader today. To some it is almost sacrilegious to speak of apostles or prophets of God in government or business. They feel the same way Catholic priests felt about Martin Luther teaching that every Saint is a priest unto God. However, God is revealing this plan to those who will listen. Rich Marshall writes:

> Until recent years, the teaching from Ephesians chapter 4 regarding the fivefold ministry gifts of apostle, prophet, evangelist, pastor, and teacher were considered relevant by only a small minority of Christians. As the modern Pentecostal and Charismatic movements have enlarged and become such a powerful force in world missions and church growth, we are hearing more about the two forgotten gifts: apostle and prophet....
>
> C. Peter Wagner points out that there are "apostles of the city" as well as "apostles in the churches." The "apostle in the city" is a concept that we need to develop....We need to operate under the guidelines outlined in Ephesians chapter 4, not only in the Church, but also in the broader context of entire cities. It is important that we begin to see and identify the citywide leaders who can lead the entire Church within a city in strategic plans to reach that city....In the coming revival we need to identify the apostolic leaders in the marketplace arena. God is going to begin to reveal the fivefold ministry gifts to them as they operate in the marketplace.[3]

In his book, *Apostles & Prophets*, C. Peter Wagner devotes a section to marketplace apostles:

> God does not desire His kingdom to be limited to the existing Church....I believe that God wants to move His kingdom through the warp and woof of

society in general. Our prayer, "Your will be done on earth as it is in heaven" (Matt. 6:11), is proof enough of this assumption. The transformation of society for Christ, and nothing less, must be our goal.

...In many nations, the people of God are already scattered throughout most levels of society. We gather together with fellow Christians one, two or three times a week, but the rest of our time is spent out there in the marketplace. We realize that God has placed us out there in the world to be salt and light to those around us, but we live with a pervasive sense of frustration because we are not seeing the changes in the spiritual climate that we have desired....

Apostles and prophets are the foundation of the Church. The people of God are out there in force, but the critical mass for change has not been reached because the spiritual government is not yet in place. Individuals are doing what they can, but their best efforts are scattered in numerous directions, and therefore they do not make the desired impact on their surroundings.

It is more than likely that God has already placed true apostles throughout the marketplace. They have not been that effective in their ministries, however, because they have not been recognized for what they are. First, they have not recognized themselves as apostles....Second, marketplace apostles have not as yet been acknowledged and affirmed as apostles by the other believers already out there day after day....

I believe there are apostles of finance, technology, medicine, industry, education, the military, government, law, communications, business, transportation, nuclear science, agriculture and a hundred other segments of society. When these marketplace apostles begin to move into their rightful place under the powerful anointing of God—watch out! Revival will be right around the corner![4]

God's Apostles and Prophets Are Everywhere: I believe the Lord revealed to me that about 50 percent of the apostles and prophets who are being restored and brought forth will come from the business world. Some of them will eventually be called into pulpit ministry in order to equip the Saints. Some will become heads of nonprofit organizations. But the majority will fulfill their gifting in their own profession. There are God-ordained prophets and apostles in the world of business, finance, and government.

The Corporate Universal Church: Jesus did not say "I will build local churches" but "I will build My Church." Though local churches are to be miniature expressions of the worldwide corporate Church, yet they fall far short of expressing all the ministry of Christ's Church throughout the Earth, in every society and function of mankind. The Scripture does not say that Jesus gave fivefold ministers to serve the local church, but to equip the Saints. That commission includes ministering to Saints however and at whatever time and place is found for fivefold ministries to equip the Saints. Since the fivefold are to equip the Saints, and 98 percent of Saints are in the marketplace, it follows that a significant percentage of the fivefold should be operating there as well.

Buildings, places, and times do not make the Church. The Saints worshiping and ministering under the leadership of fivefold ministers is the Church functioning. We must make the quantum leap to God's way of thinking about "Church." The twenty-first century leaders must think of Church, whether corporate or local, as fivefold ministers and Saints functioning to fulfill God's purpose.

New Ways and Places for Local Churches: As we saw in Chapter 7, one of the greatest paradigm shifts evolving in the present Apostolic Reformation is concerning where and how we conduct local church ministry. The Church is wherever Saints are. The local church is wherever Saints and fivefold ministers meet. Let me emphasize again that this does not lessen the importance of the local church. However, it does bring adjustment to our way of thinking concerning who, where, and how local churches can be properly conducted.

Our apostle-prophet director of Christian International of Europe, Dr. Sharon Stone, established a local church in a business district in England for business owners and corporate leaders. She has also established local churches on university campuses for students. The "corporate church" meets in a technology center with the main church meeting and training sessions held on weekdays. Rather than trying to get the Saints to conform to traditional religious patterns, the goal is to provide equipping for Saints in ways that work for them and help them to reach the communities where they live and work.

Types of Old Testament Fivefold Ministers: We must remember that in the Old Testament all of God's ministers did not function inside the tabernacle, which is a type of the New Testament local church. The office of the **priest** in the tabernacle, which is typical of a New Testament

Church **pastor**, was fairly limited to work done in the tabernacle. The **Levites**, which are typical of **evangelists**, worked inside the tabernacle and also traveled throughout Israel ministering to God's people. The **scribes**, who are typical of the **teachers**, were students and teachers of the law of God. They mainly taught in the tabernacle but also traveled at times.

The Old Testament **prophets** are typical of Church **prophets** today. Very few of the prophets were of the Levitical priesthood. Therefore, the majority of them did not function in the tabernacle or operate out from it. Most of them earned their living from what we commonly call secular work. They were farmers, woodsmen, shepherds, government officials, and businesspeople who had the calling and gifting of prophet. The **patriarchs**, **judges**, and **kings** come closest to typifying the New Testament **apostles**. Abraham, Moses, and King David could exemplify the ministry of the apostle. Their primary callings were outside the tabernacle.

APOSTLES AND PROPHETS TO THE NATIONS

Two of the ten things that the Prophetic Movement restored to the Church were the ministry of the prophet and prophets to the nations. More heads of nations have been ministered to by Christian prophets and prophetic ministers during the last 20 years than has ever been recorded in the history of the Christian Church.

Numerous biblical examples show prophets prophesying to political leaders, both of their own governments and of foreign governments. **Prophet Samuel** prophesied to both Saul and David and anointed each of them to be king of Israel. He also had an ongoing relationship with them. **Huldah** is an example of a woman who had a godly reputation as an accurate prophetess. When King Josiah asked his assistants to inquire of the Lord for him, they went to Huldah, who delivered the word of the Lord for the king.[5] **Nathan, Elijah, Isaiah, Jeremiah, Ezekiel**, and **Daniel** are just a few more examples of prophets and apostles who prophesied to nations.

Prophesying to Foreign Government Leaders: We took a survey of our 600 Christian International Network ministers. The majority of our ministers have the calling of prophet or apostle. More than 400 of them are pastors of local churches. But many of these make several trips each year to different nations. One of the things the survey revealed was that our ministers had ministered in 150 nations. In 35 percent of those nations, the president and/or top government officials received prophetic ministry.

A Recent Example: Apostolic Prophetess Sharon Stone, who is Director of Christian International of Europe, has prophesied to 14 heads of nations. She received an invitation in the spring of 2001 to meet and prophesy to the president of Ghana. Before going, she contacted her Apostle-Bishop. She wanted me to seek the Lord for His word to Ghana. I did so and also requested the same of Prophetess Jane Hamon and Prophet Bill Lackie, who have previously given prophetic words to heads of nations. We are a company of prophets who work together in these matters.

The four of us sought the Lord separately, and together we received ten typewritten pages of prophecy.

Sharon arranged these in a professionally prepared folder to present to the president. The pages contained enlightenment, revelation, and direction concerning the government, economy, and resources of Ghana and its relationships with other nations. There were also words concerning God's will and destiny for the president personally. Sharon flew to Ghana and delivered the prepared prophecies, as well as prophetic words that came forth when she joined hands with the president and prophesied to him in person. The president then requested that she minister to most of his political cabinet.

One of the prophetic words to the nation was that a railroad should be built between the developed coast and the interior of the nation. After delivering the word of the Lord, Sharon sensed that God told her to help bring it to pass. This was a bit daunting to her, because she knows almost nothing in the natural about railways, but she recognized that the Church is no longer at a point where prophets just give the word of the Lord and leave. The apostolic helps to build and establish. So her assistant got on the phone and made a call to a businessman. God had properly positioned this Saint with access to the contacts and resources to get the railroad built.

We have been prophetically declaring for years that the time would come when heads of nations and great corporations would not consult the psychics, New Agers, witches, or occult practitioners, but would seek out those who represent the Most High God of Heaven. The prophets have the greatest calling and anointing from Christ to speak God's prophetic word to these leaders. I have reported on ministers from Christian International, but our network is not the only one ministering to government. I know of many other prophets in other camps who have also spoken to key leaders of different nations.

Prophesying to United States Leaders: One of the ministers who serves on my Board of Governors, Larry Bizette, has been privileged to prophesy to several U.S. government officials. He is a prophesying apostle who, along with his wife Brenda, pastors a church in Baton Rouge, Louisiana. Prior to becoming a pulpit minister, Larry served for many years as a bank vice president. He is helping to head up Christian International Business Network's School of Business and Government in Baton Rouge.

In 1997 we held a banquet for the launching of the School of Business and Government. We invited the mayors from the region and several state representatives. Following the meal and the program, Pastor Larry Bizette explained to the political officials that I was his Bishop and also a prophet of God who has prophesied to many government officials. Then he asked if they would like to receive personal prophecy. Although they admitted they did not know what that meant, they agreed. He offered for them to receive ministry either in private or in public, according to their choice. They felt comfortable receiving ministry before the 500 people present at the banquet. So we laid hands on, prayed, and prophesied to two mayors, four state representatives, and some other officials.

One of the state representatives present that night was Tony Perkins. He is a strong Christian and has the Daniel type of anointing to be a prophet of God in the political arena. Since that time, we have continued to develop a relationship with him. During February 2001, Representative Perkins took Larry Bizette with him to Washington, D.C. A special room was set aside near the Senate chamber at the Capitol for political officials to receive personal prophecy. They prophesied to several senators and congressional leaders, the attorney general, and other members of President Bush's cabinet. President Bush was not ministered to at that time, but we have reason to believe he will receive the prophets several times during his administration. He is a God-fearing man who loves God and respects His ministers.

The reason it is so important to have fivefold ministers in the arenas of government and business is the same reason we need fivefold ministers in local churches—to equip the Saints. As mentioned above, it is appropriate that many of the fivefold ministers live and work outside the local church, because that is where 98 percent of Saints are called to spend the majority of their time. As representatives of Jesus Christ and His Kingdom, it is vitally important that Saints in the marketplace be fully operational in hearing God's voice and doing His works. We need to change our thinking to realize that this is at least as important, if not more so, for kingly Saints than for the priests, because kings operate in realms that are largely still under the power of darkness.

HEARING GOD IN BUSINESS

It is essential that all Saints be able to hear the instructive voice of God for their business or field of employment. This is established by the fact that every successful endeavor in the Bible was based upon hearing God's voice and properly obeying that divine directive. **EVERY SUCCESSFUL BUSINESS ENTERPRISE IN THE BIBLE ACHIEVED ITS SUCCESS BASED UPON HEARING THE DIRECTIVE VOICE OF GOD AND PROPERLY FOLLOWING THOSE DIRECTIVES.**

Whether it was building a ship or the temple, leading in business, in government, or in ministry, God's people were successful in the projects they undertook if they heard and heeded the word of the Lord.

Noah was instructed by the Lord to go into a ship-building business. He built his ship (ark) according to revelation knowledge from God. He followed the prophetic directives and built a ship that stayed afloat during the greatest economic and natural disaster ever to hit planet Earth. While every business and living thing on Earth was "liquidated," his business survived and progressed to function in the new world.

Isaac had financial success while everyone around him was in economic recession. He received a prophetic word from God to stay in his geographic area, even though there was famine in that region. The Bible says he sowed at God's directive and timing and reaped a hundredfold in the same year. Then he became rich and kept increasing in wealth until he became exceedingly wealthy. He became so prosperous that all the surrounding businesses became envious of him.[6] There are many other examples of people prospering and gaining great positions of influence by following prophetic directives from the Lord, such as Abraham, Joseph, David, and Daniel.

People Can Still Hear from God Today: Regarding his experience in the business world, Ed Silvoso writes:

I thoroughly enjoyed dealing, buying, selling and hiring. The pressure was always on but every time it approached the boiling point I reached for "Jesus' chair." This was a chair I had deliberately placed in my office. Every time things became unmanageable I closed the door and I knelt by it to ask for divine guidance. Time and again He provided it. Sometimes He did it in a quiet way. Other times He gave me specific directions. More than once He performed business miracles in answer to those prayers. It was so reassuring to know that Jesus was there and that He had anointed me for the job I had.[7]

In the last chapter I mentioned Dr. Sanford Kulkin, one of Christian International's Board of Governors. He is a present-day example of a prophet in the marketplace. As a high-level business consultant, Sandy not only has God-given wisdom for consultation, but at times he also pulls upon his prophetic anointing to receive a word of knowledge and wisdom in giving wise recommendations. God has not only blessed him mightily, but has used him to help major corporations save millions of dollars and prosper abundantly. God is raising up prophets and apostles in the marketplace like Daniel and Joseph and Deborah and Esther. Christ's fivefold gifted anointings are given to Saints in every walk of life to build and establish His Church.

Hearing God to Be a Witness: Scripture makes it clear that God will speak to people to help them succeed in their enterprises. But He will also speak through them to be a witness to Himself to others. When those of us who function as priests encounter persons out in the marketplace and are asked what we do for a living, it is not too difficult to determine how they feel about spiritual matters based upon how they receive our response. Sometimes this leads to an opening to talk about the Lord. Many of our traveling ministers regularly have opportunities to lead people to the Lord or speak into their lives on airplanes. For example, when a young lady sitting next to my daughter-in-law, Jane Hamon, on an airplane found out that she was a pastor, she said, "Really? I've always wanted to become a Christian but never knew how."

Another time when Jane was traveling, she sensed the Spirit told her the man sitting next to her was a divine appointment. Although she really wanted to just keep to herself, she obeyed the Lord and struck up a conversation. When he asked what she did for a living and she replied that she and her husband pastor a church, he became angry and began speaking abusively about Christians. She silently prayed and the Holy Spirit showed her two specific areas where he had been deeply wounded in the past in regard to religion. She told him that she believes God loves people and speaks to them today and asked for permission to share with him what she felt He had to say. The man gave permission, and Jane shared what the Lord had showed her. He was in complete shock, admitted the truth of it, and nearly broke down and cried. She was then able to lead him to the Lord.

All Saints can be activated to hear the Lord this clearly. But Saints called as kings will need to trust the Holy Spirit not only for openings to speak to others, but also for the divine revelation to steer conversations toward spiritual matters.

Need to Recognize Divine Timing: Those called to "minister" in ungodly environments, especially those in environments that are openly hostile to the gospel, need to be able to hear the Holy Spirit at least as much as pulpit ministers do. If a pulpit minister fails to heed the leading of the Spirit, he or she may preach a message that lacks the anointing and power to impact the lives of those listening. If he is a traveling minister, he may not be invited back again. But public school teachers, university professors, police officers, or government employees could endanger their jobs as well as their influence if they speak out of turn. In some countries, Saints' lives are at stake every time they speak about Jesus. The Holy Spirit knows exactly when hearts are open and when the best impact can be made.

Miracles in the Marketplace: This is not to say that accurately hearing the Holy Spirit will keep Saints from persecution, because the Bible is clear that those who live godly in Christ Jesus will suffer persecution.[8] But if, like Paul and Silas, we are in the will of the Lord, carefully following the Holy Spirit, and we find ourselves in a "prison," we can rejoice, knowing that God will use it to bring a greater salvation.[9] Paul and Silas received a supernatural miracle (an earthquake) to release their chains and provide a witness to the jailer. We can expect to see this more often in the Day of the Saints. God can perform miracles just as easily in the marketplace as in the local church, at times even more so because there may be less unbelief.[10]

Today no believer who wants to be used mightily of God can expect to be able to without having the full arsenal of God at his disposal. In the Day of the Saints, average Saints will be like the prophet Elijah, who challenged the prophets of Baal and won, demonstrating the supremacy of God to all Israel.[11] But without the gifts of the Spirit in operation, Saints won't know when to speak up, when to stay quiet, when to move, or when to stay put. Nor will they have the power when they need to manifest it. Training in hearing the voice of God and ministering the gifts of the Spirit is urgently needed to prepare for the Saints Movement. It is no longer an option but vitally necessary for those who will be participants in the Day of the Saints.

There are more than 30 different Christian organizations dedicated to helping Christian businesspeople by producing magazines and having special conferences. But hardly any have special schools and colleges to educate and equip those who are called to be ministers in the marketplace. And only one of those organizations and networks, that I am aware of, is currently providing training in hearing the voice of God and in using one's gifts of the Spirit in the marketplace—Christian International Business Network.

The Christian International Business Network

We established the Christian International Business Network (CIBN) in the 1980s. The vision of the CIBN is to raise up a worldwide network of Christian businesspeople who practice biblical principles in their vocations and operate in the supernatural power of God. The network's mission is to teach, train, activate, and mentor Christian businesspeople and advance Kingdom businesses for the purpose of becoming an economic force, establishing the Kingdom of God, and fulfilling the Great Commission. We define Christian businesspeople as all those who conduct business in some way, not just those employed in business and commerce but all trades and professions, homemakers, retired persons, students, and any of the "kingly" Saints who primarily function outside the walls of the local church.

We sponsor several conferences each year for these ministers and Saints in the marketplace. We have also developed more than 40 teaching modules to teach, train, and activate those called to be ministers in the marketplace. These teachings and activations cover all the godly business principles for building a successful life and business. Most of this teaching and activation is done at the business chapters that we establish in local churches. Our special anointing is to teach and activate Saints to hear the voice of God, to know the proper guidelines for fulfilling prophetic revelation, and to draw upon and use the supernatural gifts of the Holy Spirit. This enables them to be more effective in fulfilling their membership ministry in their profession.[12]

Local Churches Provide for Ministers in the Marketplace: We believe pastors and the local church should provide the opportunity and training for the 98 percent of their congregation who are Saints in the marketplace. Christian International Business Network is not a substitution for, or competition with, the local church. It is designed to support pastors in ministering to their businesspeople. CIBN seeks to serve, support, and stimulate the unfolding of new and deep relationships between pastors and business professionals. These new relationships, built on love and understanding, will display how God is binding together His people as a team to go forth in accomplishing His will and His purpose in both the Church and marketplace today. We have spent $150,000 developing the modules and teaching manuals in order to have the resources for pastors to be able to establish a chapter in their local churches. We presently have established more than one hundred Business Network chapters in local churches. We expect to establish more than a thousand during the next few years.

We encourage pastors to appoint a man or woman of God who has prophetic and apostolic anointing in the business world to take leadership responsibility to establish a local church chapter for equipping their Saints who are called to minister in the marketplace. Local churches have a minister for the whole congregation, a youth minister for the young Saints, a music minister to teach and train the singing Saints, etc. Why not have a minister for the Saints in the marketplace?

Business Network Chapter Functions: The local chapter provides a place for Saints in the marketplace to network, fellowship, pray for one another, and have accountability with fellow Christians of like vision and purpose. Chapter members' callings, talents, and gifts in the workplace are identified, and prophetic and professional business counsel may be given. As mentioned, one of the key components is assisting the Saints to hear the voice of God for themselves so they can make the right decisions at the right time in the marketplace. Fortunes are made and lost based upon making the right decisions.[13] Education and mentoring are provided in applying biblical principles in what today is often a complex, stress-filled work arena.

A Testimony: Mel and Mona Ponder joined the CI Business Network chapter at CI Family Church in 2000. They had purchased three retail stores from relatives in 1999, but the market had begun drying up. To natural eyes, the only logical course was to liquidate as soon as possible. As they became involved in the CIBN, they sought the wisdom of the Business Input Committee. After considerable prayer and receiving detailed information about the business, the Business Input Committee felt the wisdom of the Lord was to open a new location. The Ponders agreed to move according to what they also felt was the word of the Lord. Despite the natural situation, they received favor to obtain a loan. The new location has provided an income for their family while the other stores are being phased out. It has also given them a new vision and opened other avenues, including a wholesale business.

The Ponders admit that, had they not gone through the Business Input Committee business review process, they probably would not be in business today. Relationships with businesspeople who have more background in finance, sales, and marketing gave them support in a challenging time and provided new insights in running a godly business. One idea they used was to have an intercessor pray on site once a week for the first several months. This gave them spiritual insight on how to keep past hindrances from affecting the new store. In addition to functioning for God in the marketplace, Mel has heeded the call to be a light in the public square. He was recently elected to his city council by a wide margin.

Business Saints Assisting Their Local Church: CI Business Network chapters also educate and encourage business Saints on understanding how they can financially help fulfill the vision of their local pastor and church. In the booklet *Kings & Priests*, David R. High agrees with the concept of educating business Saints so they can support their pastors' vision.

> If churches had an army of Word-trained, warring kings who were full of faith and the Holy Ghost, I don't know how a pastor could not want and appreciate them being on the team. When pastors hear from God and revival comes, one of the first problems to surface is a lack of space. The pastor says, 'Where do we put the people?' Wouldn't it be wonderful to have trained men who could hear from God and respond appropriately?

> A knowledgeable king might say, "Don't be concerned pastor. We have prepared with all our might for the house of God. We bought silver three years ago when it was down in price, and now it's up. We bought some real estate four years ago that has doubled in price. Our stocks are up. We have been listening to God for several years now and making preparation, and by listening to you, we knew that this day would come. We have mixed our faith with yours. It hasn't been easy, but we have resisted the devil. We haven't squandered our success on our own lusts. We have been waiting for God to tell us what to do with His wealth.

"Now don't concern yourself with all of the building details. We will build the buildings. We will deal with the contractors. And we have taken up some extra offerings to further invest in the kingdom we believe in. Don't worry about us. We are with you. As soon as this project is finished, we will prepare again for the next expansion of the kingdom."[14]

For some time, many have defined three major divisions in the army of the Lord: the preaching division, the praying division, and the paying division. In the Day of the Saints, all of these divisions will be active ministers. The pray-ers and pay-ers won't just pray and pay but will also operate like Christ Jesus in word and deed and in His heart of compassion. It is now time that we provide everything needed to help them with this mandate. However, many Saints in the marketplace are also especially gifted by God to procure the wealth of the world and to bring it into the Church to take the gospel of the Kingdom to the whole world.

The local church is the key place where these ministers for the marketplace should be trained to function. Those trained should then reproduce others to do the same thing. Several Christian business owners and employers are now having weekly training sessions for their employees. Biblical business principles and human relations are taught, including teaching and ministering the divine enablements of the Holy Spirit with wisdom and discretion. Testimonies have been received of greater harmony among workers and management and better work attitudes and practices. The results have been greater growth and prosperity for the business.

Thy Will Be Done in Earth as in Heaven: These Christians in business and government are seeking to fulfill the prayer Jesus gave us to pray and practice. Twenty-first century Christians must start living and doing business according to the prayer of Jesus for God's will to be done on Earth as it is in Heaven. In other words, let us live, do business, and conduct government like it is being done in Heaven. If you have no revelation of the business and government going on in Heaven, you need to search the Scriptures. Try to understand what it will be like when God creates a new Heaven and a new Earth and places His overcoming Saints to rule in His government, to make sure His work and righteousness is established and maintained throughout the new Earth.

In business language God is Chairman of the Board and Christ is the CEO (Chief Executive Officer) of Heaven. God made man the COO (Chief Operating Officer) of planet Earth. When Jesus Christ lived on Earth He spelled out the standards and principles of the Kingdom of Heaven. He personally demonstrated the revelation and power available to all officers of His Kingdom and then reproduced this power in His people through the gift of the Holy Spirit.

Fivefold Ministry Anointings in Business: Christ Jesus gave specific responsibilities to those He called to fivefold ministry. Apostles are like the founders or entrepreneurs who launch divisions of God's enterprise on planet Earth. Prophets are like strategists who plan and evaluate how to meet the Kingdom objectives. Evangelists are the sales managers who inspire their team to expand the business.

Teachers may be likened to trainers who ground the workers in the principles, products, and services of the organization. Pastors are similar to local business managers of units or branches who oversee the regular operations of their people, encourage them to meet their full potential, and help them work together as a team. The Saints, those who have answered the call to serve as officers of God's Kingdom, must now enforce Kingdom rule in the arenas in which they function. This often means overcoming the kingdom of darkness.

GOD'S KINGDOM IS INVADING THE DARKNESS

Isaiah 61:1-4 says:

"The Spirit of the Lord God is upon Me, because the Lord has anointed Me to preach good tidings to the poor; He has sent Me to heal the brokenhearted, to proclaim liberty to the captives, and the opening of the prison to those who are bound; to proclaim the acceptable year of the Lord, and the day of vengeance of our God; to comfort all who mourn, to console those who mourn in Zion, to give them beauty for ashes, the oil of joy for mourning, the garment of praise for the spirit of heaviness; that they may be called trees of righteousness, the planting of the Lord, that He may be glorified." And they shall rebuild the old ruins, they shall raise up the former desolations, and they shall repair the ruined cities, the desolations of many generations.

Isaiah 61:1-4 was Jesus' mandate and it is now the Saints' mandate. Just as Jesus came to destroy the works of the evil one, so His Saints must rise up and bring an overcoming power to challenge the powers of darkness and liberate those trapped in their grasp. As we saw earlier, we as Christians aren't just escaping this world. We are filling it with Christ's glory and eventually we're taking over. We are to enforce God's Kingdom throughout the Earth realm. Worldly, anti-Christ Jesus systems have brought desolation and ruin to cities and generations. If you are a Saint of God, get it clear in your head that you cannot just escape this world; get prepared to start taking over. The Holy Spirit and God's fivefold ministers have been commissioned to equip the Saints to bring Kingdom reform to every area of life.

The poor, the brokenhearted, the captives, the bound, those who mourn, and those in devastation are in all areas of society. Many of them are found in places where pulpit ministers do not have ready access. One billion Muslims are imprisoned in the darkness of Islam, including millions of Muslim women who live like near prisoners in their homes. Millions of Hindus, Buddhists, and followers of folk religions are bound by worship of demonic spirits. Others are controlled by Communism and atheistic governments, incarcerated in prison or bound by fear, depression, alcoholism, drug addiction, uncontrolled anger, bitterness, greed, or peer pressure. The poor include nearly one billion people in the world in extreme poverty, oppressed women and minorities, the illiterate who are unable to obtain gainful employment, those trapped in generational welfare, and even those in debt. The captives include the mentally ill—many of whom need deliverance more than they need medication—and those trapped by physical and emotional handicaps.

Spiritual Warfare in the Marketplace: As we saw in the last chapter, all Saints need to be equipped and activated in the weapons of their warfare, whether their ministry is within the local church or outside it. But some jobs are of such an intense nature that in order to succeed in them Saints really need to know how to operate in supernatural warfare. Ed Silvoso agrees:

> Jesus' promise that believers will be filled with the Holy Spirit, be able to cast out demons, expose lurking threats (serpents), survive evil schemes (surreptitious poisonous drinks) and make sick things well (see Mk. 16:17-18) has to do primarily with service in the marketplace. This is so for at least two reasons. First, the context for Jesus' words is definitely centrifugal and expansive. The entire world, the totality of creation, is the focus of our mission, not just a church building or a gathering of believers. Second, only demons with suicidal tendencies would dare hang around Spirit-filled church meetings. Most demons spend the bulk of their time in the pernicious command centers that control our cities— the still unredeemed business, educational and government circles. It is precisely in those places where God's power is desperately needed. And who is already strategically positioned to channel it? Those called to minister in the marketplace.[15]

Saints who function in roles where demonic activity is common especially need to be trained in the biblical principles of spiritual warfare, binding and loosing, recognizing the demonic, and having the revelation and faith to do deliverance. Correctional officers, prison guards, court workers, and police are among those who need to know how to take control of a situation in the spirit realm. They need wisdom on when to speak up or minister deliverance and help set captives free, and when to just bind evil spirits from operating and from harming them. In the recent past, the Church has taken a backseat to the world systems and allowed the devil to take over these realms. The world desperately needs Saints who will operate in a power greater than he who is in the world.[16] It is time to equip the Saints and send them back into the world to bring the life of Jesus.

Saints in Health Care Fields: Christian medical doctors, psychologists, counselors, nurses, and other health care specialists need to be able to operate in divine revelation to help their patients. They need to know how to bind spirits of infirmity, suicide, etc., in order to set their patients free. Some infirmities are caused by evil spirits, such as the deaf and mute spirit Jesus cast out.[17] Some ailments have natural causes, such as an immoral lifestyle of smoking and drug use. The life-giving power of Christ Jesus flowing through the believer will heal any problem, but understanding the cause helps ensure that the one who receives healing stays healed. If these Saints work in settings where they are not free to do in-depth ministry, they may refer patients to a present-truth church for further deliverance.

The Saints need to be taught and equipped in knowledge of the Bible to understand spiritual principles regarding health and healing. But they also need to be confident in their supernatural giftings. If Saints use their supernatural tools along with their natural training, they will be far more effective in treating illnesses and will find their "ministry" in high demand. The demonstration of Christ's love and power for physical healing will open patients' and their families' hearts to receiving emotional and spiritual healing.

Overcoming Sickness and Disease: God wants to give supernatural revelation and divine wisdom to His people to bring about advancements that will defeat the rule of satan in the natural realm. The devil comes to steal, kill, and destroy, and during his time as god of this world, he has extended his rule to bring destruction in all areas of life that he can.[18] He desires to bring premature death, affliction, and suffering to as many people as possible so they cannot fulfill their God-given destinies. As God's people invade the kingdom of darkness with the same power that raised Christ Jesus from the dead, we will see satan's hold weaken.[19] All Saints should be equipped to manifest supernatural miracles and healing in their ministry, just as Jesus did. But some Saints will be gifted by God to make scientific discoveries and advances that will help eradicate and cure diseases.

Levels of Faith: When it comes to finances, we know that one level of faith believes God to provide miraculous provision to meet one's immediate need. Another level of faith believes God to provide a steady income to supply needs on an ongoing basis without "crisis intervention." The third level of faith believes God for prosperity. Yet another level of faith believes God to abundantly spoil the wealth of the world and transfer it to God's Kingdom. The same principle is true in the physical realm. We can believe

God for healing after getting sick, or believe God for wisdom to be good stewards of our body/temple to keep us from ailing.[20] We can believe God for abundant energy and strength to work heartily for God.[21] But certain Saints are gifted to spoil the enemy's kingdom by defeating disease and suffering in a corporate way that brings freedom and life to many.[22]

Medical, Scientific, and Agricultural Reform: At our International Gathering of Apostles & Prophets conference in October 2000, Prophet Chuck Pierce gave a prophecy from the Lord which included the following:

> I'm going to send you to lands. And as I send you to these lands, you will **prophesy into the agricultural systems** all over this earth. Not only will you prophesy to agricultural states, but you will now **prophesy into medical reform**. For **the prophets will be consulted over how to bring about medical breakthrough**. I say to you, I am shifting you this day and reforming you. For lands will change, and the medical environment of this world will change. Also, I am beginning to create a synergistic wave that is about to hit you, knock you upward and lift you up, and bring you into new places, saith the Lord. Some of you even now I'm going to start putting nations within your heart. And those nations will begin to open up. The prophetic release is about to create a missionary sending force that will change nations.

When the prophets speak forth revelation from God, it has creative power. But prophetic words require the cooperation of God's people to bring them to pass. This word does not specifically state whether those prophesying into agricultural and medical systems will be prophets in those fields, or whether they will be "priest" prophets. Nevertheless, God's people in these fields must cooperate with the word of the Lord to bring it to pass. And intercession must take place to bring about the changes that the Lord desires.

In the Day of the Saints God will unleash new scientific and technological inventions to those who are positioned. Saints will come up with creative solutions to a wide variety of issues. Imagine Saints receiving revelation to cure Alzheimer's patients, solve the ozone depletion problem, or reconfigure highways to eliminate traffic congestion. Joseph was gifted by God to solve the problem of what could have been a devastating famine in Egypt and the surrounding nations. He came up with a 14-year plan for handling the agricultural production of a major world empire. Both Joseph's natural training in managing Potiphar's household and lands and his spiritual training in hearing God's voice were important to this achievement.[23] If all those called to be scientists, researchers, or other problem solvers thought the only way they could truly follow the Lord would be to give up their "secular" job and go into "ministry," some of the strongest Kingdom representatives would not be in place. This has happened in many industries as Christians have fled from so-called "worldly" occupations.

Saints in Broadcasting and Entertainment: One of the most notable examples of this is in the entertainment industry. As God's apostolic and prophetic government gets into place in various fields and regions, the potential for major changes is arising. Then the Saints of God will be able to be the "ground troops" carrying out the will of their Commander-in-Chief. At one of our major conferences, Cindy Jacobs prophesied that God was going to bring a turnaround in Hollywood and that we will see Christians owning major television and radio networks. In the Day of the Saints we may even see prophets telling the news. Who could better explain the significance of the day's events? And wouldn't it be helpful for people to hear what the prophets are sensing before it occurs? This is especially true if God's prophetic watchmen are sensing a warning about something that could occur that needs to be prayed against, or a different action taken, in order to avoid calamity. Holy Spirit anointing on the airwaves can reverse the deception and de-sensitizing to evil that have been taking place since Christians backed away from the forefront of the public forum some decades ago.

Psychic networks are making millions of dollars counterfeiting God's true prophets. God had Elijah face the false prophets on Mount Carmel in a power encounter between their god Baal and the one true God. Likewise, we will see prophets challenging the psychics and occultists on the airwaves. On more than one occasion the Lord has had me prophesy over individuals that God will use them to glorify His name in this manner. Moses outperformed the miracles of the magicians of Egypt; Joseph interpreted Pharaoh's dream better than the wise men of Egypt; and Daniel bested the wise men of Babylon.[24] Each of these encounters took place before the ruling authority of the most powerful nation in the world at that time.

So we should not be surprised if the Holy Spirit uses an "unknown" Saint, who has been well-prepared by God, to challenge prevailing wisdom by His power in a public forum.

Saints in the Arts: In the Saints Movement we will see new forms of expression of Kingdom principles and praise to God. New sounds will be brought forth in worship, praise, and warfare. New productions will bring the gospel to many in a new format. God will give some the anointing of Bezalel, who was filled with the Spirit of God and skill, ability, and knowledge in all kinds of crafts, to produce Holy Spirit-inspired works of art.[25] For example, at our annual Worship & Arts Conference held each June, we have held a class on prophetic painting. Esther Tubbs, the instructor, has helped the students to put visions they have received from the Lord onto paper. Then the revelation is able to impact all those who view the painting, not just the one who originally saw it.

Saints in Business and Finance: God will use His people to transfer the wealth of the wicked that has been stored up for the righteous into the Kingdom of God.[26] Saints who have been purified of God so that they are not given to the love of money will invade the financial realm and take it back from the devil.[27] God wants to empower His people to get wealth through Kingdom principles and supernatural insight.[28] Some Saints will be specifically used of God to help deliver others from bondage to poverty, debt, and financial lack.

In the parable of the ten minas in Luke 19, Jesus described the future king as distributing money to his servants and saying, "Occupy till I come" (verse 13b KJV). The New King James translates this phrase as, "Do business till I come," while the New International Version says, "Put this money to work...until I come back," and the Revised Standard Version says, "Trade with these till I come." The Living Bible says he "gave them each $2,000 to invest while he was gone." In other words, increase your money. The servant who turned his mina into ten was granted rule over ten cities; the one who multiplied his five times was given rule over five cities. Jesus used this parable to illustrate Kingdom business principles of servanthood, multiplication, and accountability. God cares about good business. He wants His people to prosper to bless them, so they can multiply His Kingdom.

Jesus said more about money than most other subjects. He also demonstrated success in business. He personally operated a traveling ministry with 12 full-time apostles and several other participants for three years. Jesus used supernatural wisdom from God to enable His disciples to catch more fish than their boat could hold, translating into great profit for them.[29] He also showed how God could supply the money for their taxes through Peter's livelihood of fishing.[30] All Saints can be trained to hear God for their business.

Saints in the School Systems: The public education system in the United States, and in many others countries, has come under the influence of an antichrist spirit that is hostile to Christian teachers and students. As we near the Day of the Saints, primary and secondary schools and colleges are becoming one of the more prominent forums where the confrontation between Christ's Kingdom and the kingdom of darkness will occur. Prophetic words have gone forth that God will start invading the school system of the United States. On school campuses power encounters will take place that will prove that Jesus Christ is more powerful than New Age, Wicca, the teachings of Harry Potter, secular humanism, and every other false religion that is trying to capture the hearts of young people. Christian students and teachers will be empowered by the Holy Spirit to speak truth and do miraculous exploits. Colleges such as Harvard that were founded on godly principles will experience revival. Adults who work in the field of education are among those who most need to be equipped in the supernatural weapons of their warfare. As those whom God has called to provide an apostolic and prophetic foundation in the schools stand strong in their workplace, they can expect to see anointed youth rise up to lead and equip the young generation.

YOUNG PEOPLE, HOMEMAKERS, AND MATURE SAINTS

God has always used young people in helping to bring forth restoration movements. The Day of the Saints will be no exception. Many prophecies have come forth that God is raising up a young "Joshua Generation" that will be radically on fire for Him. My grandchildren are among this group. The teen ministry at our headquarters church in Florida is called Rev-o-lu-tion. The youth pastors have raised up a dynamic group of young adults who are helping to empower the teenagers "to fight for justice and a national Holy Revolution." These young people are some of our most fervent prayer warriors and worshipers.

God is doing a similar work among youth at many churches. He is raising up an entire army of young people around the world who are crying out for spiritual revival.

Young Warriors for Revival: These youth are a preview of those God will use in the Day of the Saints. They are crying out for God to change them and bring revival, regardless of the cost. As mentioned earlier, the Saints Movement will not be about big-name ministers. God is going to use those who are sold out to Him and do not care who gets the credit. If those of us who have been in ministry for years cannot adjust to this change, God will pass over us and use the younger generation. I am committed to supporting the young generation as much as I can because I know they are destined of God to launch the Church into the future moves of God and bring back the return of the Lord.

No Junior Holy Spirit: There is not one Holy Spirit for children and another one for adults. The same Holy Spirit lives in all Saints. We regularly have youth and children give corporate prophecies in our church services. They know that they can hear from God just as well as the adults. Children can be just as anointed in healing the sick, raising the dead, and casting out devils. We need to teach them to be fearless young Davids able to defeat any mighty Goliath that would try to intimidate the army of God. In the Day of the Saints children will operate in the words and deeds of Jesus as easily as, or more so than, adults.

The Addulum Orphanage Revival: This is not fanciful, wild imagination, but reality. It has already been demonstrated during what was called the "Addulum Orphanage Revival" in China in 1952. Children in the orphanage got saved and filled with the Holy Spirit as a sovereign move of God swept into their midst. Those from six to nine years old were used the most. They had numerous angelic visitations, visions of Heaven and hell, and detailed dreams about people, places, and things happening. Their eyes were enabled to see into the spirit world of demons. It was so real that they chased the demons out of their midst and cast them out of people. The children would prophesy with great authority and vividly describe events from the Bible about which they had never been taught.[31] In the Day of the Saints we can expect greater things than in the past. Millions of radical, Jesus-loving, devil-hating young people will do exploits for their Lord and Master.

Homemakers and Workers From Home: If our children are going to be on fire for God, they need someone to impart a love for the Lord and lead them in salvation and baptism in the Holy Spirit. When we mention Saints in the marketplace, we are including all those who function primarily outside the local church, not just those employed full-time in corporations or businesses. Those who don't see themselves as holding a job, such as homemakers and full-time mothers, still participate in the marketplace on a regular basis. In addition, a growing number of people participate in the business world by working from their own homes.

One of our church members jokes that she has a "Wal-Mart ministry" because she has had several divine appointments at the local Super Wal-Mart. One day she was shopping and a man collapsed onto the floor nearby. She could tell he was close to death. She went over to him and rebuked the spirit of death, commanding it to let him go in the name of Jesus. A store employee witnessed this wide-eyed. One of the medics who arrived later told her he felt her actions had saved the man's life. This woman's husband travels with a miracle healing minister and sees amazing supernatural miracles on a regular basis. But the same divine principles of healing that work in a crusade will work at the local marketplace.

In New Testament times, evangelistic "crusades" were not planned events. As Ed Silvoso explains, they simply occurred whenever and wherever God's miraculous power caused people to take notice:

> Early Christians made the marketplace the focal point of their ministry. This was natural since they regularly went there to conduct business. It was also the place for them to witness to unbelievers. But they did more than witness, as we understand the word today. They performed signs and wonders in the marketplace. Being in the marketplace was so much a hand-in-glove part of their ministry that of the twenty-two power encounters recorded in the book of Acts, only one happened in a religious venue, the healing of the lame man seated at the Temple Gate called Beautiful (see Acts 3:1-11).[32]

The Older Generation: Young people are not the only ones the devil fears. In the United States, as in many other nations, the older generation is now greater in number than ever before. The devil wants to distract them through preoccupation with leisure and amusement, fear of the future, and health issues. But this generation of Saints is called to be an awesome workforce for God. In developed nations, people are living longer after retirement and have more free time to devote to working for God.

Don't Retire, Re-fire! Many years ago the Lord gave me a vision that we are still in the process of implementing—making land and housing available for Saints who have re-tired from their occupations. We know God is calling many older Saints to move to Florida, not to retire but to get "re-fired" and activated for the Kingdom. We are be-lieving God for mature believers, with pensions or some means of meeting their basic needs, who can function as dorm parents, counselors, prophetic team members, trav-eling ministers, prayer warriors, deliverance ministers, hospitality workers, office helpers, and many other things. Getting older is no reason to slow down.

As of this writing, I am 68 years old in the natural, but I have more energy than many 35-year-olds. It's not the age that matters but the attitude. If you allow the Lord to give you a vision, you will have the inspiration to get out of bed every morning. The only person I have met who told me that every prophecy they ever received had been fulfilled died within three weeks. If you have unfulfilled prophetic words, God isn't through with you yet! And if you haven't received prophetic words about your future, ask God to speak to you or seek out godly prophetic coun-sel and revelation.

Everyone, Find Your Place: The key to success as a child of God is to discover your membership ministry and faithful-ly fulfill it. It does not matter if another Saint's ministry is larger or more well-known. Just remain faithful to your calling, appropriating all the weapons of warfare and supernatural giftings that God has entrusted to His people. In his book *Turning Vision into Action*, George Barna discusses levels of vision. Regarding the first level, micro-vision, he states:

> Every Christian is called to be, at the very least, a micro-visionary. No believer can create a legitimate excuse for not having a sufficient measure of God's vision to leave some mark on the world he or she touches daily. The vision may be finite and restricted, but just as the Body of Christ needs people who have various gifts operating in cooperation and harmony to reach a global audience, the Church needs a broad-based foundation of micro-visionaries to influence their more limited but equally important worlds.
>
> You and I need to be supportive of micro-visionaries. Our churches are built on them. The reason churches don't make a dent in the postmodern culture is not that they have too many micro-visionaries. It is because they are weighed down with too many Christians—a majority—who have no vision whatsoever. Becoming a micro-visionary would be a major step up and a blessing to God, to their churches, to their families, to their friends and to themselves. Yes, "micro" means small; but it is better to have a person of small vision who faithfully and effectively executes that faith than to have a million people who attend church regularly, but never pursue God's vision. May God grant us more micro-visionaries in the days ahead.[33]

I sincerely hope that reading this book has given you a greater vision of God's overall purpose for His Church and planet Earth. But what Barna describes is what will happen in the Day of the Saints. Millions of God's people must get hold of God's vision for them to represent Jesus as Kingdom ambassadors and bring that Kingdom to their spheres of influence. In the next chapter, we will look at how Saints can be activated with the abilities to do just that.

ENDNOTES:

1. 1 John 5:4.
2. Rich Marshall, *God@Work* (Shippensburg, PA: Destiny Image, 2000), pp. 3-4.
3. Marshall, *God@Work*, p. 124.
4. C. Peter Wagner, *Apostles & Prophets* (Ventura, CA: Regal, 2000), pp. 54-55.
5. 2 Chronicles 34:21-28.
6. Genesis 26:1-22.
7. Ed Silvoso, *Anointed for Business* (Ventura, CA: Regal Books, 2002), Uncorrected proof, p. 15.
8. 2 Timothy 3:12.
9. Acts 16:19-34.
10. Matthew 13:58.
11. 1 Kings 18:1-40.
12. For information about Christian International Business Network chapters in your area or how to start a chapter in your local church, please call 1-800-388-5308 or e-mail cibn@cimn.net.
13. Genesis 30:25-43; 41:25-57; Luke 5:4-7.
14. David R. High, *Kings & Priests* (Oklahoma City, OK: Books for Children of the World, 1993), pp. 38-39.
15. Silvoso, *Anointed for Business*, p. 19.
16. 1 John 4:4.
17. Mark 9:25-26.
18. John 10:10.
19. Luke 10:17-18.
20. 1 Corinthians 6:19.
21. Luke 10:27.

22. Luke 9:1.

23. Genesis 39æ41.

24. Exodus 8:18-19; Genesis 41:15-27; Daniel 1:20; 2:27-28.

25. Exodus 35:30-33.

26. Proverbs 13:22.

27. Hebrews 13:5; 1 Timothy 6:9-10.

28. Deuteronomy 8:18; Proverbs 8:10-11,21.

29. John 21:6.

30. Matthew 17:27.

31. H.A. Baker, *Visions of Heaven* (New Kensington, PA: Whitaker House, 1996). See pages 37-39, 40-41, 46-48, 80-81, 121-123.

32. Silvoso, *Anointed for Business*, p. 6.

33. George Barna, *Turning Vision into Action* (Ventura, CA: Regal, 1996), p. 84.

CHAPTER 9

ACTIVATING THE SAINTS

As soon as a person is born again, he is entitled to every inheritance Christ Jesus has bought for a Saint of God. However, most people today do not automatically begin seeing the supernatural works of Jesus manifest through their lives the moment they pray the sinners' prayer. Jesus' 12 apostles spent three years with Him learning by example. When they experienced the supernatural visitation of the Holy Spirit, their faith had to arise and reawaken what they had heard from Jesus, the Word of God. Then they acted upon their faith by doing the works of Jesus.

We have been given the same spiritual resources as the early Church received, and now we have the words of Jesus written out for us in the New Testament. So how do we get Saints to move from hearing the Word to acting upon it? This chapter will explore some practical methods that we have found effective in getting people to personally experience God's power operating through them.

"**Activation**" is a word I chose in 1979 to explain what we do in getting Saints to minister their spiritual gifts. Since we first started, we have developed more than 50 different ways to discover what gifts a Saint has within them. We then teach them how to fulfill the scriptural command to "stir up the gift of God which is in you."[1] To describe this spiritual process of stirring up the gift which is within you, or making it become active, we gave it the one word name **activation**. This word also applies to the process used to appropriate all the gifts and graces of God.

Gifts God Offers to All: There are three major gifts individuals may receive from the Lord. The gift of eternal life, the gift of the Holy Spirit (often called the baptism of the Holy Spirit), and the gifts of the Holy Spirit. Revelation for how these gifts are received, activated, and manifested was restored during three different restoration movements: the **gift of eternal life** during the Protestant Movement in the 1500s; the **gift of the Holy Spirit** during the Pentecostal Movement around 1900; and the revelation and anointing for activating the Saints in the **gifts of the Holy Spirit** with the Prophetic Movement in the 1980s. The following chart reveals the time of restoration, the gift restored, and the movement that was used to restore it back into the Church.

TIME	GIFT	MOVEMENT
1500	Eternal Life	Protestant Movement
1900	Holy Spirit Baptism	Pentecostal Movement
1988	Gifts of the Holy Spirit	Prophetic Movement

Each of these movements brought the grace of God and faith to activate people into these different gifts. There was no scriptural understanding for receiving and manifesting these gifts within Christendom before a restoration movement came and brought enlightenment, application, and the experience of receiving and manifesting. This is what I call the restorational work of the Holy Spirit to bring "open revelation for faith appropriation and activation for manifestation."

FOUR BIBLICAL PRINCIPLES INVOLVED IN AN ACTIVATION

1. Hearing the Biblical Word of Truth on the Matter:

All divine gifts are given by God's grace but received by the faith of the individual. Faith comes by hearing God's Word of truth. You then know the truth and the truth makes you free to believe and receive.[2] So we first do biblical teaching to impart and build up faith. God-fearing, committed Christians cannot have faith to act upon something unless they can see that it is a scriptural truth. When they understand and believe the Word of truth on activating gifts, then their desire and faith arises to fulfill that ministry.[3]

2. Believing in the HEART:

Romans 10:10 declares that "with the **heart** one **believes**." When we believe in our heart, we come into right relationship with God, which the Bible calls righteousness. Faith does not operate out of the head but from the heart. The mind can feed to the heart (spirit) the biblical facts and other information that is needed to manufacture faith, but when faith is produced it will operate only from the heart. When the proper ingredients for faith to be formed are put in the heart, then faith is born and becomes alive and active. That is what the Word means when it says "faith comes." Faith comes into being when our spirit hears and believes the Word of God on the matter. Romans 10:8a says, "The word [of faith] is...in your heart." God has decreed that faith will function only from within the heart.

3. Confessing with the MOUTH:

Romans 10:10b further states that "with the **mouth** confession is made unto salvation." For faith to work from the heart, the mouth must cooperate by speaking, agreeing, and performing. James 2:26b says, "Faith without works is dead." This means it is inactive, not workable, non-productive, not useful, worthless. It would be the same to say, "Believing in the heart but not speaking it out with the mouth is non-productive." We can speak things with our mouth that are not motivated by faith, but living, biblical faith cannot fulfill its full function without the mouth speaking it. In other words, if we believe in our hearts the Scriptures that say, "Covet to prophesy" and "you can all prophesy one by one," then we will open our mouths and "prophesy according to the amount of faith in our heart."[4] When a Christian says, "I believe" a certain biblical truth yet does not practice that scriptural principle, it is not faith, but simply acknowledging that the truth is valid. King David said, "I believed, therefore have I spoken."[5]

4. Taking Corresponding Action:

If we really believe something in our hearts and are confessing it with our mouths, then we must take actions that are in alignment with what we are saying we believe. Faith without corresponding action is dead. Dead faith will not appropriate the promises of a living God nor produce the works of God. "Faith by itself, if it does not have works (corresponding action), is dead…Show me your faith without your works (if you can), and I will show you my faith by my works."[6]

Abraham took action in alignment with what he believed was the word of the Lord to him. He put Isaac on the altar and "by works faith was made perfect."[7] We must take corresponding action if we are going to activate and manifest the gifts of the Holy Spirit. You can determine how much faith you have by how much positive action you are taking in agreement with what you have been praying for and believing to receive.

ACTIVATION FOR THE GIFT OF ETERNAL LIFE

Before we can make the ministry of "**activation**" real, we must first cover the biblical principles for a person to receive the gift of eternal life. The Bible clearly teaches that eternal life is a gift from God.

*For the wages of sin is death, but the **gift** of God is eternal life….*[8]

By grace are we saved [receive eternal life] *through faith and that is not of ourselves, it is the **gift** of God.*[9]

*God so loved the world that He **gave*** [a gift] *His only begotten Son that…* [we might] *have eternal life.*[10]

The gift of eternal life is a sovereign gift of God for whosoever will receive it. Those who receive Christ as their personal Savior are cleansed from all sin by His blood.[11] Jesus takes all the sin away and comes and dwells within.[12]

He that has Christ within has eternal life, for Jesus is the resurrection and the life eternal.[13] Wages are earned, but a gift is given. If we have to become "good enough" to receive or do something to become worthy to receive a gift, then it is a reward for accomplishment, not a freely given gift. This is the belief of Protestant theologians concerning how one receives the gift of eternal life. Synonymous terms are *being born again, getting saved, repenting, accepting Christ,* and *receiving salvation.*

Why Do All Not Have the Free Gift? A true gift is given because the giver of the gift loves the receiver enough to purchase the gift and freely give it. Jesus purchased the gift of eternal life by His death, burial, and resurrection. The package is mailed to every person. But to get the gift in the package, each person has to personally sign for it and receive it. Sadly, millions have refused to receive the gift, and the package was marked "return to sender." In other words, eternal life was provided for every person on planet Earth, but that does not imply that every person automatically has the gift of eternal life.

Since it is God's will that none should perish but all have eternal life,[14] then why do all not have the gift? Because there is a requirement and a determining factor concerning who receives the gift of eternal life. That requirement is faith—believing and receiving! By grace are we saved through *faith.* Grace is God giving divine enablement from His loving favor. It is not based upon the merits or worthiness of the one receiving His grace. The Bible emphatically teaches that a person cannot receive Christ and His eternal life unless they believe. We must believe on the Lord Jesus Christ to be saved.

He who believes and is baptized will be saved; but he who does not believe will be condemned.[15]

Faith is the key that opens the door to Heaven's riches and procures them for the believer. Without faith it is impossible to please God or to receive divine things.[16] The gift is freely given, but only activated into the person by their faith. God's part was to procure the gift and make it available. Mankind's part is to believe God and receive the gift. Two areas are involved: God's sovereignty to give and man's free will to receive or reject.

Revelation for Activating Eternal Life: This was the main revelation and teaching that produced the Protestant Movement. Martin Luther started teaching that a person could be made right with God simply by believing on the Lord Jesus Christ. By the mysterious act of believing in the accomplished work of Christ on the cross, one could be cleansed from all sin and made righteous in God's sight. This could be accomplished without all the dead religious works that the Catholic church had established as requirements for meriting God's favor and escaping the fires of hell. If you are not familiar with all the religious works developed during the Dark Age of the Church, I urge you to become knowledgeable in order to fully appreciate the truths and spiritual experiences of the Protestant Movement. Volumes of books have been written on these things and we do not have space to cover them here.[17]

Radical, Foreign, and Revolutionary: Suffice to say, the concept that a person could be made right with God just by believing on the Lord Jesus Christ was completely foreign to the doctrine of the Dark Age Church. In fact, the Catholic church authorities excommunicated Martin Luther and declared his teachings to be heresy. To them his revelation was sacrilegious and contrary to their denominational doctrines. They declared it was absolutely preposterous and blasphemous for Protestant ministers to teach that a person could be made right with God without the pope's blessing, praying to Mary, doing penance, buying indulgences, and the numerous other religious works the church required. For more than 1,000 years, the church had been indoctrinated with the idea that salvation is obtained by good religious works, until it was incomprehensible for their leaders to accept the idea that a person could be saved simply by *believing*! But the truth of being saved by grace through faith without self-works became a living, consuming, burning revelation and life experience to the great reformer, Martin Luther.[18]

Revival vs. Revolutionary Reformation: The Protestant Movement was more than a revival. It was a revolution. The reformers revolted against the whole religious system. Martin Luther wrote 95 theses protesting the unscriptural practices of his Catholic church. Luther and like-minded believers were called "protesters" by their critics. Their cause was referred to as the movement of the protesters, which became better known as the Protestant Movement. A Protestant Christian is one who has rejected the old dead religious works for justification and has received justification by faith and faith alone. The great revelation and conviction of the reformers was that we are justified by faith and that the just shall live by faith.[19]

Freedom From Traditions Still Needed: Pentecostals and Charismatics need to receive this same revelation concerning the gifts of the Holy Spirit. Pentecostal tradition and various teachings have developed so many requirements, qualifications, and fears concerning ministering spiritual gifts that it has deadened faith and limited the Saints. Many of these groups need a liberation in the area of ministering the gifts, just as the Church of the Dark Ages needed to be liberated to be activated in the gift of eternal life, and the Evangelicals needed liberty to receive the gift of the Holy Spirit with speaking in unknown tongues. This is the day of liberation for all tongues-talking Saints to manifest their supernatural gifts.

FAITH—The Currency for Procuring Heavenly Things: It can rightly be said that **money** is the medium of exchange for **earthly things**, but **faith** is the medium of exchange for **heavenly things**. Money is the currency of Earth, and faith is the currency of Heaven. Heaven will not accept money, self-effort, good deeds, or religious works for the procurement of divine things. Living faith in a living Christ is the only thing that Heaven accepts. This is the reason the Bible exhorts mankind to have faith in God—simply believe and trust in the Lord.[20] God honors holy living, loving deeds, and righteous ways, but these attributes alone do not get answers to prayers. The five steps to answered prayer and receiving heavenly things are found in Mark 11:24 (KJV): (1) Desire, (2) Pray, (3) Believe, (4) Receive, and (5) Have. The key is the central word, *believe*. We must **believe** that we have **received** what we have been **desiring** and **praying** for before we can **have** it.

We have shared sufficient Scriptures and biblical principles to show how the gift of eternal life is received and activated into a person's life and being. Now let us look at the activation that the Protestant Evangelicals developed for helping people receive and enjoy this gift.

Activation for the Gift of Eternal Life: The activation that Protestant Evangelicals developed to lead people to salvation became known as the "sinner's prayer." The present-day minister who has demonstrated this the most is Billy Graham. He uses the four principles that are involved in an activation. **First**, the word of truth concerning eternal life is preached. **Second**, the listeners are encouraged to put faith in action by taking some steps: raise the hand indicating the desire to receive Christ, then walk down to the front. By these acts they are demonstrating that they believe in their heart. **Third**, they are asked to confess with their mouth by praying the sinner's prayer. The evangelist gives the words for the sinners to repeat after him as a prayer to God. After the prayer, the evangelist then tells the participants that they are now saved, born-again children of God. They now have the gift of eternal life, and their names have been written in the Lamb's book of life.[21]

 Fourth, they are asked to take corresponding action in agreement with what they have believed in the heart and confessed with the mouth. Those who have prayed the prayer to receive the gift of eternal life are taken to a side room and given instruction on how to maintain and appropriate the attributes of the gift they have received. The corresponding actions that help them maintain their Christian experience are attending church, reading the

Bible, praying, confessing their commitment to Christ to others, and living a holy life.

These are the four principles that are included in becoming a Christian. Through this process the gift of eternal life is activated into the life of an individual person. What the evangelist calls the "sinner's prayer," I would also call an activation. We have taken the time to review the activation of the gift of eternal life in detail because the same foundational principles and process activate any and all gifts of God.

Can One Person Help Another to Be Activated? To understand and accept spiritual activations, a few questions need to be addressed. Can one mortal person help another mortal person receive a divine gift? Our first response might be to say no, but the correct answer is yes. For if one person cannot help another person receive a divine gift, then why do we have evangelists? Why do Christians witness to sinners and pray for others to receive divine things? The Bible says Saints are the Body of Christ. Therefore, we have become Christ Jesus' mortal mouth, hands, eyes, etc. to carry out His will on Earth.[22]

So how does one mortal help another mortal receive a divine gift? By presenting the four biblical principles to the person and helping them follow through. If someone came to you asking for help to receive Christ, could you help? Would you say, "I can't help you. The gift of eternal life is a divine gift that only God can give"? Or would you lead in the sinner's prayer to activate the gift of eternal life within the person? Christians who believe that the sinner's prayer activation can activate the gift of eternal life should have no problem with activating Saints in the gifts of the Holy Spirit.

ACTIVATION FOR THE GIFT OF THE HOLY SPIRIT

With the Pentecostal Movement came the revelation for activating Saints in the gift of the Holy Spirit.[23] Prior to the twentieth century there was no open revelation for faith appropriation of the gift as it was received and manifest in the first-century Church. But the restoration of truth that came in 1901 brought the revelation that the gift of the Holy Spirit with speaking in other tongues was still for the Church. The students at Charles F. Parham's Bible College did an intensified study of Scripture to discover what was the most consistent sign or evidence that a person had received the baptism or gift of the Holy Spirit. They found that the only consistent manifestation was speaking in other tongues.[24] They saw that it was the word of truth and believed it in their heart. The college president laid hands on some of the students, and they began to speak in other tongues. A few years later it began to happen at the Azusa Street mission in Los Angeles, California. Then it spread all over the world. Now, 100 years later, hundreds of millions have received the gift of the Holy Spirit with speaking in other tongues.

Methods of Activating: The most common method of activating the gift of the Holy Spirit in Pentecostal churches was by gathering several people around the seekers to pray with them until they received the gift. We laid hands on them and encouraged them to believe, receive, and speak out. If they started speaking a little, then we encouraged them by saying, "That's it! Speak it out, speak it out." We used phrases such as: Send the rain, Lord, send the fire; press in; turn loose; and hang on. The early Pentecostals talked about "tarrying" for the Holy Spirit, which involved waiting and praying for hours until a manifestation was experienced. During my early Pentecostal days, I prayed with some people for up to three hours for them to receive the Holy Spirit and speak in tongues.

The Latter Rain Movement was used to restore the fourth doctrine of Christ, the laying on of hands.[25] The most common method of receiving the gift or baptism in the Holy Spirit in that movement was by laying on of hands with the expectation of the immediate impartation and activation of the gift.[26] This was carried over into the Charismatic Movement.

Principles and Attitudes in Activating: Regardless of the process, all Pentecostal/Charismatic churches believed and practiced activating Saints into the gift of the Holy Spirit. They all included someone's laying on of hands and praying for another person to receive. Their practices declared that they believed one mortal who has received the gift can help another mortal receive it.

This belief is demonstrated by the way Charismatic and Pentecostal ministers respond when someone makes a request for prayer to receive the gift of the Holy Spirit. The minister does not say, "Wait a minute. Let me see if it is the will of God for me to minister the Holy Spirit to you." Neither do they say, "I don't feel led to pray for that right now," or, "I don't sense the anointing is here for that gift to be ministered to you." They do not scrutinize the candidate to see whether there is sin in his life, neither do they ask if the person is in proper relationship with a pastor and local church. The minister does not ask if the person has the approval of his pastor to come to his/her church or conference and receive this gift. They will pray for anyone who wants to receive the gift, whether the person is a member of their church, another denomination, or no church at all.

Regardless of the persecution and rejection by the Evangelical/Holiness churches, the activation for receiving the gift of the Holy Spirit was restored. Millions are still being activated by the revelation for activating Saints into the gift of the Holy Spirit with other tongues.

Divine Consistencies: God is consistent and His Word works the same for all.[27] The same biblical principles work for the gift of eternal life, the gift of Holy Spirit, and the gifts of the Holy Spirit.[28] There is only one Holy Spirit, not one for the gift of eternal life and another for the gifts of the Holy Spirit. All divine gifts are received by grace and faith. There is not a Holy Spirit for the fruit of the Spirit and another Holy Spirit for the gifts of the Spirit. Both the gifts and the fruit come from the same Holy Spirit.[29] The fruit of the Spirit is just as divine and supernatural as the gifts of the Holy Spirit.

ACTIVATION FOR THE *GIFTS* OF THE HOLY SPIRIT

With the Prophetic Movement came the revelation that Saints could be activated in the spiritual gifts of the Holy Spirit by the same four biblical principles that activate the gift of eternal life and the gift of the Holy Spirit. Some of the old Pentecostal groups taught that one could not speak in tongues after their initial baptism unless they had a certain feeling, sensation, or unction. They had to be "moved by the Spirit" to exercise the gift of tongues. Some who came out of Pentecost into the Faith Movement and other independent churches kept these old Pentecostal ideas of having to be specially moved by the Spirit to speak in tongues or minister the gifts of the Holy Spirit.

However, most Charismatics taught that a Holy Spirit-baptized believer could speak in tongues anytime they so desired, whether or not they had a soulish emotion or physical sensation. In other words, one could speak in tongues whenever they willed to do so. This is based on the teaching of the specialist on speaking in tongues—apostle Paul. Here is an amplified version of what he said: "I will pray with my native tongue that I learned from childhood, and I will pray with tongues of the Holy Spirit wherever and whenever I will to do so."[30]

The Prophetic Movement taught that gifts are *given* (not loaned temporarily) to Saints by the sovereign choice and will of the Holy Spirit. But they are **activated** and **operated** by the **faith of the believer**. The main difference between the attitude of the Pentecostals and that of prophetic ministers concerning how the gifts of the Spirit are ministered is based on the interpretation of First Corinthians 12:11: "But one and the same Spirit works all these things, distributing to each one individually as He wills." The traditional Pentecostal view interprets this Scripture to say that gifts can only be manifested and ministered to others as the Spirit wills.

Charismatic and prophetic people interpret this Scripture as saying the **gifts are distributed to** (not operated by) each one at the choice and will of the Holy Spirit. It is up to the Holy Spirit to determine which supernatural ministry gifts He chooses to give to a particular Saint. But after the believer has received a gift, that Saint may minister the gift to others whenever and wherever he or she chooses to exercise faith to minister that divine gift. Membership ministry in the Body of Christ is by God's choice and placement, not the member's. "But now God has set the members, each one of them, in the body **just as He pleased**."[31] The same is true for the fivefold gift ministries that Jesus gives. "And [**Jesus Himself**] **gave** some to be apostles, some prophets..."; "**God hath set** some in the church, first apostles, secondarily prophets...."[32]

Sovereignly-Given but Faith-Activated: Membership ministries, gifts of the Holy Spirit, and fivefold ministries are all given at the choice and will of the Godhead. However, they are activated and operated by the faith of the believer. Gifts of the Holy Spirit can be stirred up and activated into ministry by the faith of the Saint.[33] Paul wrote to the Roman Christians and told them that each Christian has a measure of faith and special grace. "Having then gifts differing according to the grace that is given to us, let us use them: if prophecy, let us **prophesy in proportion to our faith**."[34] Notice he says we prophesy in proportion to our faith, not according to sensations or feelings. Everyone has received a measure or seed of faith.[35] That seed can be planted in the field of obedience. If watered, nurtured, and exercised, it can grow tremendously.

A key Scripture on activating and using spiritual gifts is Hebrews 5:14, which states that mature Saints are those who have their spiritual senses exercised to discern both good and evil. This includes discerning between our thoughts and the thoughts of Christ, between imagination and revelation, between prophetic revelations and personal convictions, and between sensing something from our soul versus receiving revelation from our redeemed spirit. Exercising our spiritual enablements is important because we learn and grow better by doing than just by hearing alone. It is the doers of the Word who are justified, not the hearers.[36]

Revelation for Activation Is Here: God has now given the open revelation for faith appropriation of the gifts of the Holy Spirit. With the grace, faith, and revelation that God has given, it is as easy for me to activate a Saint in gifts of the Holy Spirit as it is for Billy Graham to activate the gift of eternal life in a sinner. Remember that biblical faith and action are synonymous. We have developed numerous acts of faith that we use to activate Saints into prophetic ministry. Our broad terms "**the prophetic**" and "**prophetic ministry**" refer to all the supernatural manifestations of the Holy Spirit. This includes all the vocal, revelation, and power gifts of the Holy Spirit. With the restoration of apostles came the revelation for activating Saints in the power gifts of healing and miracles. We are now activating Saints in healing the sick and doing miracles, just as we activate them to prophesy and receive words of knowledge and wisdom.

Some Still Don't Know: There are multimillions of Catholics and members of Eastern Orthodox churches who do not know that God has brought revelation and restoration for receiving the gift of eternal life, even though this gift has been available for almost 500 years. Sadly, millions will die without ever being born again because they have never been taught the truth and biblical principles for receiving and activating the gift of eternal life. Many who do become exposed to the truth will not believe it because they reason that if it were true, their church would already be teaching it.

Multimillions of Evangelical Christians will never receive the gift of the Holy Spirit with speaking in other tongues, though it has been restored and re-activated in the Church for 100 years. Many who do hear of it refuse to believe and receive. Likewise, millions of Saints in Pentecostal, Charismatic, and Faith churches who are filled with the Holy Spirit and speak in tongues are not ministering the gifts of the Holy Spirit. They do not know that the Holy Spirit has brought open revelation for faith appropriation and activation. In other words, they do not have the revelation and faith that they can minister the gifts as easily as they speak in tongues. When they know the truth about activation of gifts, the truth will make them free to manifest spiritual gifts.[37] This truth is so essential for those who want to be properly prepared to be participants in the coming Saints Movement.

FROM OCCASIONAL PROPHECY TO CONTINUOUS PROPHETIC FLOW

To further clarify this concept, I will outline the process God took me through as I learned that personal prophecy can be ministered whenever and to whomever the one ministering chooses to release it.

Receiving Prophetic Presbytery: The ministry of laying on of hands and prophesying to people in personal prophecy was restored in the Latter Rain Movement during the late 1940s and early 1950s.[38] By the time I attended Bible College, the leaders of the movement had developed a pattern for "prophetic presbytery," which consisted of three or four ministers prophesying to one person or a married couple. The college had never had a prophetic presbytery ministry, but they were embracing the restoration movement truths and ministries, so they decided to have one in October 1953.

Protocol was established that those who wanted to be a candidate to receive prophetic presbytery had to fast from all foods and beverages, except water, for three days and nights. It so happened that I had started a water only fast six days before they made the announcement. I just continued and was on the ninth day of fasting when the special time arrived. All the candidates sat in one section of the church. After an hour of worship and praise, the presbytery team sought the Lord and decided whom they felt the Holy Spirit wanted to receive the prophetic ministry. The first man to be called had done some missionary work in Mexico. Those of us who were in our teens and early twenties wondered why they were calling up this old man in his mid-forties. *We* were the young Joshua generation that was going to take the world for Jesus. Nevertheless, he was invited to the platform and asked to kneel down in front of a chair. All the prophetic presbyters laid hands on him and prayed for a couple of minutes, then they began speaking personal prophecy. After the prophesying was finished, they all laid hands on him and prayed for the words to be sealed within him and for him to have faith and obedience to fulfill the prophetic words. He was sent back to his seat, and the ministers prayed together to determine who else God wanted to receive ministry.

After a few minutes one of the ministers pointed to me. They followed the same protocol in ministering to me. All of the prophecies over me were recorded on a seven-inch wire reel. This was long before the days of cassette tapes. It was later transferred to a seven-inch plastic tape reel and then typed on paper. The full prophecy was included in my first book on the prophetic, *Prophets and Personal Prophecy*. It was placed there to give an example of personal prophecies received in the early days of prophetic presbyteries.[39]

Prophetic Ministry Prophesied: After they prayed and four of the ministers prophesied, they had me stand and laid hands on me to be released in a greater prophetic flow because the prophecies spoke several times about my gifting and anointing being a strong prophetic ministry. I had been doing congregational prophesying before I left Texas and sometimes during the worship services at the Bible College. It was not difficult for me to release a flow of prophetic utterance, especially since there was such a strong anointing at the school. I shook like a leaf in the wind as I prophesied with great fervor. Because of my Pentecostal background, at that time I thought I had to feel a lot of emotional and physical sensation before I could believe I was anointed to prophesy.

Limited Ministry: After they had prophesied over me, they went back into their prayer huddle. The spokesman came back and said they believed that the missionary and I were the only ones whom the Holy Spirit wanted to receive prophetic presbytery. Eighty students had fasted three days to be candidates. You can imagine how discouraged and devastated the remaining 78 were! God used that experience not only to minister to me, but to teach me things which would bear fruit later in the future. The disappointment of the other students helped to plant in me seeds of revelation that not only do God's children want to hear from their heavenly Father, but that He wants to speak to all His beloved children.

A Sovereign Visitation of God: In 1954 I started traveling in ministry and ended up pastoring a church for the next six years. After that, I taught for five years in a Bible College. Then in 1968, I started building a distance-education ministry college which today is called Christian International School of Theology. We developed courses to help pastors establish an extension college in their local churches.

In the late '70s I started teaching, training, and challenging Saints to believe God for the gifts of the Holy Spirit to be manifested in their lives. I had been ministering in the prophetic since 1953, but 20 years later a divine visitation came to my life that activated me into a continuous flow of the prophetic. Prior to this time I prophesied to individuals here and there, usually no more than 15 to 20 people in one setting. I also ministered with other prophetic ministers in prophetic presbytery. The most I had ever seen receive prophetic ministry in one setting was five to ten couples.

Providential Preparation for Divine Visitation: In January 1973 on one of my traveling trips to establish CI extension colleges in several churches in the Northwest, my sovereign visitation from God took place. During the second week of traveling from our headquarters in San Antonio, Texas, I stopped at a church in Sacramento, California. After the preaching ministry they asked if I would minister to some of the congregation as the Lord directed. From about 9:00 p.m. to 10:00 p.m. I called out 15 Saints and ministered personal prophecy to them. I figured this was the maximum to whom the Holy Spirit would minister in one service, for that was the most I had ever seen receive personal prophecy in one setting.

When I finished calling people forth and prophesying to them, I had all the ministers come to the front and form a double line. We then asked the Saints to walk through the double line of ministers so we could lay hands on them and bless them. As I laid hands on the first person, a great prophetic anointing arose within me. Words of knowledge and wisdom and prophetic insight concerning the person's life and ministry filled my mind. I told myself that the quota had already been reached, so I restrained from prophesying and let the person go on by. With the second person the revelation increased. By the third person, it was like a volcano about to erupt in me. A tremendous amount of prophetic revelation concerning the person flooded my mind. I wasn't trying to make this happen; in fact, I was doing all I could to restrain it.

I asked the Lord if He was wanting me to prophesy over each one for whom He gave me the inspiration and words. He spoke back to me, "Yes, let it flow unrestrained."

To my amazement, every person who came before me received personal prophecy. There were 85 people in that line. I finished prophesying to the final person at 2:30 a.m.

Prophecy Fulfilled: When I arrived home, I read back over a prophecy I had received from a prophet in November of the previous year. Part of the prophecy said that within three months God was going to release an endless flow of prophecy through me to such an extent that it would go from one day into the next. The night of this divine visitation of an endless flow of prophecy, January 24, 1973, was within three months from the time of the prophecy. And the prophecy did flow through midnight from one day into the next.

Established as a Continuous Ministry: A few weeks later I was in Pennsylvania ministering to a congregation of 150 Saints. After preaching I started laying hands on the Saints. Again, with each one I laid hands on, a prophetic flow came forth. At 3:00 a.m. I finished prophesying to the 150th person. What I thought was a one-time sovereign work of the Holy Spirit was instead an abiding anointing that was received for continuous prophetic ministry. From that time on, every time I traveled in ministry I averaged prophesying to about 500 people per week. Once I had broken through my human mind-sets that were based on my experience and observation, rather than on God's will, my ministry was multiplied tremendously.

God Wants to Speak to Each Person: One of our ministers uses the example that he, as an earthly father, has something to say to each of his children every day. In the same manner, God always wants to speak to His children. It is not a matter of the Holy Spirit moving in some spooky experiential way on only a certain blessed few. God's blessings are for all His children. He even has something to say to all those who have not received Christ Jesus as their Savior. We have seen people brought to conviction and conversion to Christ through a prophetic word spoken to them. When God speaks about things in their lives that only they know, it convicts and convinces them that God is real and knows and cares about them.[40]

Prophecy Transforms Lives: I can personally testify that 85 percent of all my vision, knowledge of my personal gifting, and calling came from the voice of God through His prophets. No amount of soul-searching, research, or planning could have given me the same insight. Personal prophecy has enlightened and enabled me to fulfill 50 years of prophetic ministry. The personal words I have received are still giving me a hope and a future by enlightening me concerning God's purpose and destiny for my life. My first book on the prophetic, *Prophets and Personal Prophecy*, gives numerous testimonies of others who have likewise received vision, blessing, and transformation through God's personal prophetic words to them. Personal prophecy can bless people in every walk of life.

Ministers for Training Others in Prophetic Ministry: I continued to prophesy to hundreds each week that I traveled from 1973 till the mid-1980s. At that point I started staying home more to teach, activate, and mentor my staff and other ministers. We started Schools of the Holy Spirit and prophetic teaching/activating seminars to fulfill the commission I had received to raise up a company of prophets, prophetic ministers, and prophetic Saints. As we have seen, prophets are those sovereignly called to that fivefold office by God's choosing. Prophetic Saints are any and all believers who have been taught, activated, and trained to manifest the supernatural graces and gifts of the Holy Spirit.

We have developed a 300-page teaching manual called the *Manual for Ministering Spiritual Gifts.* After 13 years of training thousands, we have also developed a complete video set of the teachings and activations. It has 13 biblical teaching sessions which include several hands-on activations to go with each session. People learn best by participation. We teach the scriptural realities of supernatural manifestations. We then activate them into manifesting prophetic ministry. There is continual training in the areas of proper presentation, protocol, and timing. The participants learn not only how to receive a word of knowledge or prophecy, but how to deliver it with wisdom, grace, and maturity.[41]

We have an average of 15 ministers who travel to churches and take the Saints through the *Manual for Ministering Spiritual Gifts* in a seminar, which usually lasts two to four days. The manual is then left with the pastor to teach, activate, and mentor the Saints in properly ministering spiritual gifts over the next 13 weeks. We also hold intensified, week-long training seminars twice a year at our headquarters in Santa Rosa Beach, Florida, and once a year at our central U.S. location in Versailles, Indiana, and on the West Coast.

Our CI international headquarters (in Europe, India, eastern Asia, Australia, and Canada) and international representatives (in Latin America, Africa, the Caribbean, and elsewhere) are training thousands of Saints in their spiritual gifts and weapons of warfare. We also have a residential Ministry Training College in Santa Rosa Beach, Florida, for training in the Word and Spirit. We are very serious about obeying God's command to equip the Saints to participate in the coming Saints Movement so that Christ Jesus will have a prepared people He can use to fulfill His purpose.

A Sample Activation: I first started using activations in 1977. The Lord directed me to have the Saints pair up, join hands facing each other, and pray in the Spirit for a moment, asking the Lord to give them a sanctified thought, illustration, or something that would bless their fellow member. In places where this was the first time to participate, more than 90 percent of the participants would receive something to share with their fellow member. Since it was a faith exercise to receive and share a spiritual thought from the Holy Spirit, after they shared with each other I would instruct them not to make any major decisions on what they had received or to be too strongly affected. But what they received might be one of several confirmations they would need to receive before deciding something is the mind of Christ for them.

After conducting this activation thousands of times, we have discovered that about 60 percent of the thoughts shared are right on relevant things to the one for whom they were spoken. About 35 percent are what I call "wait and see" words, which means the person receiving the word will have to wait and see over a period of time to determine whether what was shared had any spiritual significance. About five percent would share strange non-relevant thoughts. The quality of thoughts shared is determined by whether the one sharing is more spiritually-minded, naturally-minded, or carnally-minded. Apostle Paul declared that we who are spiritually-minded have the very thoughts of Christ.[42] He also conveyed that those who are carnally-minded cannot perceive the thoughts of Christ.[43]

We have numerous testimonies of participatants in prophetic ministry activations who have experienced the joy of sharing a word with a fellow Saint and having it confirmed as a true prophetic word from the mind of Christ. A prophetic word is one which brings edification, exhortation, and comfort without any conflict with biblical principles.[44] It is a great encouragement to the one receiving the prophecy when it is an accurate prophetic word.

Hearing Spiritual Thoughts: Some beginners struggle to receive a prophetic thought to share with a fellow member. This restriction is caused by several things. Some Christians do not have a renewed mind. They need their thinking transformed by the renewing of their mind.[45] Some have thinking that is influenced by a carnal mind that cannot perceive divine thoughts.[46] Others are bound by negative religious teachings. These cause fears that block the thoughts of Christ from flowing into their conscious mind. Fear is the opposite of faith. Without faith a Christian cannot believe to receive an accurate word from the Lord. For Christians to properly minister in the prophetic they first have to be delivered from their fear. That is the reason we emphasize Second Timothy 1:6-7 to activate Saints in their gifts:

> *Therefore, I remind you to stir up the gift of God which is in you through the laying on of my hands. For God has not given us a spirit of fear, but of power and of love and of a **sound mind**.*

Those who participate in spiritual activations increase their spiritual sensitivity and ability to discern between their own natural thoughts and those that originate from the mind of Christ within them. Some have asked, "How does this work?" I usually answer by telling the person to explain to me how the red blood of Jesus washes away my blackened sins and makes me white as snow. Or, tell me how we speak in an unknown tongue which was never learned by natural knowledge. If you can tell me how these things work, then I can tell you how we prophesy and speak the mind of Christ to others.

To try to explain any of these three things mentioned, one would have to use biblical words such as: by grace, faith, anointing, gifting, divine enablement, etc. I can't explain how the blood of Jesus can cleanse me from all sin and make me a new creation in Christ Jesus. All I know is that God said it would, ordained it to do so, and established it as a workable reality. When I believe and receive it according to how God has established it, then it works in my life. People who insist on being able to understand and describe a spiritual work with the natural mind are destined to frustration and unbelief. The natural mind cannot perceive the spiritual things of God because they cannot be perceived and received by the natural mind. They can only be understood and explained by the spiritual mind.

But the natural man does not receive the things of the Spirit of God, for they are foolishness to him; nor can he know them, because they are spiritually discerned.[47]

Thousands of people have testified to the value of activations in helping them grow in their ability to discern the thoughts of Christ and to minister the mind of Christ to others one-to-one. Sharing activations has resulted in people getting saved, filled with the Spirit, healed physically, and receiving edification, exhortation, and comfort. Our training sessions begin with simple, short activations and progress to longer and more challenging ones. But the principles for hearing God remain the same.

QUALIFICATIONS FOR MANIFESTING THE SUPERNATURAL

It is simple and easy to activate Saints in the gifts of the Holy Spirit. The same principle applies as for activating people in the gift of eternal life or the Holy Spirit. The real challenge is to train and mature the Saints in the proper use of gifts. It is easy to get a person to receive Christ as their Savior, but it is more difficult and challenging to get them to live the life of Christ. The main reason is that God gives gifts to Saints without any qualifications on their part except to receive and manifest. Gifts are received and operated by grace and faith alone. Gifts are manifested by those who receive, believe, and demonstrate regardless of their personal imperfections, failures, and immaturity. In my 50 years of involvement in supernatural ministry, I have seen ministers with moral problems, bad character, very little integrity or honesty, and even with erroneous doctrine who still manifested prophecy, healing, and miracles.

How Can That Happen? Saints ask, how can this be? It should not be! But the fact is that gifts are not received or ministered by good works. They are grace gifts, meaning they are given at the choice of the Giver and not based on the worthiness of the receiver. The ideal is gifts operating from the fruit of the Spirit and godly character. The reality is, God uses what He has. For better or for worse, you and I are the best God has. Space does not permit an in-depth discussion of all these issues here. Our teaching manual and other books go into greater detail of the Scriptures and principles to bring revelation, clarity, and wisdom in these areas.[48] However, the good news is that if even unscrupulous persons can operate in the gifts of the Spirit, then Saints whose hearts' desire is to honor God certainly can, even if they do not feel perfectly worthy in their own efforts.

Four Hindrances to Manifesting the Supernatural: In the Day of the Saints average Saints will powerfully manifest the supernatural. But you don't have to wait until then! Following are the four greatest hindrances to Saints who want to move in this area:

    1. Lack of knowledge of the gifts and your rights and privileges as a Saint to minister in the supernatural. The gifts of the Holy Spirit are listed later under "The Saints' Arsenal" (see page 322). If you are not very familiar with the various gifts and their workings, I particularly encourage you to attend one of our "Ministering Spiritual Gifts" training seminars. If that is not feasible, the recommended resources listed in the back of this book will give you more information. Also, Christian International School of Theology has a self-study course on the gifts of the Holy Spirit which may be taken for either personal enrichment or college credit.[49]

2. Fear of making mistakes, being embarrassed, offending people, or bringing reproach by failing to do everything right. Our training programs that we have developed over the years, "Schools of the Holy Spirit," and gift activation seminars are designed to give Saints a safe place to exercise their faith in manifesting their spiritual gifts. It is like a military training exercise where soldiers learn to use their weapons of war. The spiritual manifestation in which Saints need the most teaching, training, and maturing is properly ministering prophetic words. This is because prophecy, especially words spoken with a "thus saith the Lord," can drastically affect a person's life. Saints not ministering a perfect word are not called false Saints or false prophets in these training sessions. We follow the same process and principles used in teaching a child to walk and talk. Walking and talking are children's God-given abilities, but they have to be trained to do so properly. Much greater detail and scriptural support for these principles can be found in my books *Prophets and Personal Prophecy* and *Prophets, Pitfalls, and Principles*.

3. A sense of unworthiness. I find that the biggest hindrance to sincere Christians manifesting their spiritual gifts is a sense of unworthiness. Most Christians are still trying to merit being worthy enough to being used of God. Many are waiting on something to qualify them, yet nothing ever will except divine gifting and faith. Ask yourself, "As a born-again, Spirit-filled Saint, what am I waiting on to manifest the supernatural?"

4. Lack of desire and willingness to be instrumental in blessing others. Because of their lack of desire or willingness to bless others, apostle Paul commanded the Saints to "earnestly desire spiritual gifts" and "covet to prophesy." The Holy Spirit gift of one's spiritual prayer language is for "self-edification," but the gifts of the Spirit are for blessing others. "He who speaks in a tongue edifies himself, but he who prophesies edifies the church."[50] Selfishness and the lack of Christian passion to bless others and glorify Christ are major hindrances to manifesting spiritual gifts.

The Compassion of Jesus: One of the ways we become more like Jesus is to develop a compassionate desire to minister to others. Apostle John declared that Jesus came not to be ministered unto but to minister and to give His life for others. Jesus declared that He was commissioning His disciples just as His Father had commissioned Him.[51] We can stay in our comfort zone, or we can overcome our fears and become more like Jesus Christ.

There are those who do have a desire to be a blessing to others by their supernatural enablements. However, their church does not promote Saints manifesting the supernatural or make opportunity for Saints to minister. As those who are determined to fulfill their full calling as Saints cry out to God to make a place for them, God will help them find the people and places where they can be trained and allowed to minister the supernatural. The Holy Spirit is searching for some to be like the household of Stephanas, who had "addicted themselves to the ministry of the saints."[52] God hates bad habits and addictions, such as drug addiction, but He loves godly addictions. The household of Stephanas had become not just sniffers and pill poppers; they had become main-liners in their ministry to the Saints. They even became peddlers—getting others addicted to the same ministry of the supernatural.

Some Limitations Are in Order: Some churches will not allow place for Saints to learn to develop their giftings because of their fear of potential problems.[53] In their efforts to heed First Corinthians 14:40, some have emphasized "decently and in order" to the point where they no longer "let all things be done." We believe that for churches to obey Christ, they must allow opportunity for the equipping of the Saints. However, church leadership must learn how to effectively handle any issues that may arise, and they must establish godly protocol for the use of the gifts.

While Christian International provides ample opportunity for Saints to have a safe place to learn and grow in their spiritual giftings, we also have protocol that we expect people to follow. Conferences and Sunday morning services are not proper times for those who are being trained in the gifts to minister. We do not support Saints ministering to one another without proper covering. All mature prophetic ministers and churches have proper protocol concerning when, where, and how prophecies are ministered and the supernatural manifested. As Saints seek to grow in their giftings, part of the maturing process is learning to submit to proper protocol and stay within godly boundaries.

We have taught and activated hundreds of thousands of Saints and ministers into manifesting the gifts that have been given to them. We have had opportunity not only to teach and activate, but also to mentor, train, and mature hundreds in proper ways to minister spiritual gifts. We are using the revelation, scriptural teaching, activations, and experience that God has given us to equip the Saints. Then the Saints can fulfill the scriptural command for them to desire and minister the supernatural manifestations of Christ that we call the gifts of the Holy Spirit.

THE SAINT'S ARSENAL

Three different places in Scripture list the gifts that Christ Jesus has given to His Saints.

GIFTS OF CHRIST Ephesians 4:11	MINISTRIES Romans 12:4-8	GIFTS OF THE HOLY SPIRIT 1 Corinthians 12:7-11
Apostle	Prophecy	Revelation Gifts: Word of Wisdom
Prophet	Administration	Word of Knowledge
Evangelist	Teaching	Discerning of Spirits
Pastor	Exhortation	Power Gifts: Gift of Faith
Teacher	Giving	Gifts of Healing
	Leadership	Working of Miracles
	Mercy	Verbal Gifts: Prophecy
		Tongues
		Interpretation of Tongues

No Longer an Option but Essential: Activating Christians in the gifts of the Spirit is absolutely essential at this time, for several reasons. Gifts are some of the main tools the Holy Spirit uses to build up the Church. Jesus said, "I will build My Church." Prophetic ministry is a major tool in building the Church members.[54] The gift of healing delivers the Saints from satan's sicknesses and afflictions.[55] Word of knowledge reveals hidden things and enables Saints to supernaturally know certain things.[56] The word of wisdom gives supernatural strategy for accomplishing the work of the Lord. The gift of discerning of spirits reveals what spirit is motivating the attitude and actions of individuals.[57] If discernment reveals that a demonic spirit is present, the Saints have the ability to bind it or cast it out, and the Saints also have divine protection from harm.[58]

The working of miracles brings miraculous provisions and supersedes nature to preserve the Saints.[59] The gift of faith supernaturally appropriates resources and enables things to happen that would be impossible in the natural.[60] The gift of prophecy brings edification (building up), exhortation (stirring up), and comfort (cheering up) to the Saints.[61] Prophesying also brings enlightenment, education, and revelation concerning God's heart and mind on specific matters.[62]

Space does not permit in-depth coverage of each of the gifts here. For those who are interested in a detailed, scriptural study of these various gifts, including examples of their use in the Bible and in recent life experiences, we have produced a self-study course on the Gifts of the Spirit.[63]

Training for Reigning: As mentioned earlier, Christian International has trained hundreds of thousands of Saints in hearing from God and ministering a word to others. We have four different modules in our Apostolic Prophetic Training seminars geared to help activate the revelation gifts. We are working on modules to activate Saints in the power gifts of healing, faith, and miracles. We also have raised up a deliverance team whose members specialize in getting Saints set free from demonic oppression and generational curses. Hundreds of our church members and visitors have been set free in individual sessions or corporate meetings. The team leaders travel nationally and internationally raising up deliverance teams in other churches so they can get their people set free.

As history progresses to the end of the age, a greater dichotomy is forming between those who are in Christ and those who are in the world. The world is getting more and more demon-possessed and oppressed, while the Church is becoming more and more glorious in Jesus. Those who want to maintain peace with both sides will not be able to for long. "Fence-walking" Christians are going to have to make a choice. We are either going to be aggressively advancing the Kingdom of God using all the divine enablements Christ has provided, or we will find ourselves actively opposing the move of God in His Church.

Supernatural Fruit: We have been discussing activation of the gifts of the Spirit, but the "fruit" of the Spirit are just as divine and supernatural as the gifts.[64] They are not natural attributes but supernatural Spirit attributes. I am believing God to give us more revelation to help Christians know how to activate the fruit of the Spirit, similarly to how we activate the gifts of the Holy Spirit. Most Christians do not know how to draw upon and activate supernatural love, joy, peace, patience, etc., any more than they know how to draw upon and activate the gift of prophecy, word of knowledge, gifts of healing, etc. The same principles work for divine fruit as for divine gifts. Both are attributes of the same Holy Spirit.

Weapons for Warriors: Saints must be given opportunities to become familiar with their weapons of warfare—the gifts of the Spirit. A soldier can be taught all the parts and workings of a rifle, but until it is put in his hands and he is given opportunity to shoot at a target, he will never become a skilled rifleman. It is time for the fivefold ministers to develop spiritual military training camps for the Saints to be trained in their gifts of the Holy Spirit. The Holy Spirit has already distributed the weapons of the Spirit to the Saints. "The manifestation [gifts] of the Spirit is given to each one for the profit of all."[65] Apostle Peter gave the Christians this charge, "As each one has received a gift, minister it to one another, as good stewards of the manifold grace of God."[66]

Manifesting Gifts—Choice or Command? Paul didn't make a suggestion. He commanded the Corinthian Christians to earnestly desire spiritual gifts, especially that of prophesying. He didn't say, "If you feel inclined or led to do so," or, "If God will lead me to, I will." God's will concerning the gifts of the Spirit in relation to the Saints has been made known and written down in First Corinthians 12:7-11. We don't need to pray about His will regarding spiritual gifts. We need to read His will, receive our inheritance, and begin manifesting the gifts. Paul commanded the Saints to develop a driving passionate desire for the gifts of the Spirit to be active in their lives by telling them to "**covet to prophesy**." Those who speak in tongues bless themselves, but those who prophesy bless others. Paul encouraged zeal for spiritual gifts, as long as the motive is to edify the Church.[67] These gifts are to be active in the Spirit whether in our local church, home, or professional life.

The gifts of the Spirit are the weapons of warfare for God's army of Saints. They are the powerful tools that will be used to manifest the gospel of the Kingdom of God. The gifts of the Spirit will be used to convince sinners that Jesus Christ is the only true Savior of mankind and to demonstrate His lordship. In the Day of the Saints, the Church will demonstrate that Jesus is the only true God who created Heaven and Earth. He is Owner of the Earth and everything in it. Jesus will be glorified in His Saints until all the so-called deities of other religions will be exposed as powerless and meaningless. The full demonstration of God's power and wisdom will cause the greatest harvest of souls ever recorded in Church history. More souls will be saved during the last century of the mortal Church than have been saved during all the former centuries of the Church combined. It is time for the Saints to be equipped in their powerful weapons!

ENDNOTES:

1. 2 Timothy 1:6.
2. John 8:32.
3. Romans 10:17.
4. See 1 Corinthians 14:1,31,39 (v. 39 KJV); Romans 12:6; Matthew 12:34-37.
5. Psalm 116:10a KJV; see 2 Corinthians 4:13.

6. James 2:17,19b AMP.

7. James 2:22.

8. Romans 6:23.

9. See Ephesians 2:8.

10. John 3:16.

11. 1 John 1:9.

12. 1 John 5:11-12.

13. John 11:25.

14. 2 Peter 3:9.

15. Mark 16:16.

16. Hebrews 11:6.

17. Bill Hamon, *The Eternal Church* (Santa Rosa Beach, FL: Christian International Publishers, 1981), pp. 169-186.

18. Ephesians 2:8-9; Hamon, *The Eternal Church*, p. 151.

19. Romans 1:17; Hamon, *The Eternal Church*, pp. 174-176.

20. Mark 11:22.

21. Revelation 20:15.

22. 1 Corinthians 12:12-27; Ephesians 5:30; John 17:18.

23. Acts 2:38.

24. Hamon, *The Eternal Church*, p. 215.

25. Ibid, pp. 242-268.

26. Ibid, p. 244.

27. Hebrews 13:8.

28. Ephesians 4:4.

29. 1 Corinthians 12:7-11; Galatians 5:22-23.

30. 1 Corinthians 14:15.

31. 1 Corinthians 12:18.

32. Ephesians 4:11; 1 Corinthians 12:28 KJV.

33. 2 Timothy 1:6.

34. Romans 12:6.

35. Romans 12:3.

36. James 1:22.

37. John 8:32.

38. Hamon, *The Eternal Church*, pp. 249-268.

39. Bill Hamon, *Prophets and Personal Prophecy* (Shippensburg, PA: Destiny Image, 1987), pp. 61-69.

40. 1 Corinthians 14:24-25.

41. The *Manual for Ministering Spiritual Gifts* is taught several times each year at Christian International and various

local churches. For more information, please contact Christian International at 1-800-388-5308.

42. 1 Corinthians 2:16.

43. Romans 8:7; 1 Corinthians 2:9-16.

44. 1 Corinthians 14:3.

45. Romans 12:2.

46. 1 John 2:16; Romans 8:6-7.

47. 1 Corinthians 2:14.

48. See the books and accompanying study manuals to *Prophets and Personal Prophecy*; *Prophets, Pitfalls, and Principles*; and the *Manual for Ministering Spiritual Gifts*. See the back of the book for ordering information.

49. Christian International School of Theology may be reached at 1-800-388-5308 or www.cimn.net.

50. 1 Corinthians 14:4.

51. John 17:18; 14:12.

52. 1 Corinthians 16:15b KJV.

53. Proverbs 14:4.

54. 1 Corinthians 14:3-5; 1 Timothy 4:14.

55. Matthew 10:1; 1 Corinthians 12:28,30.

56. 1 Corinthians 14:6; Hebrews 4:12-13.

57. Mark 9:25; Acts 16:16-18.

58. Psalm 91; Matthew 16:19.

59. 1 Kings 17:4,6; Luke 9:13-17; Acts 8:13; 28:3-6; Galatians 3:5.

60. Mark 5:34; 10:52; 11:22-23; Acts 6:8; Hebrews 11:5, 11,29,32-35.

61. 1 Corinthians 14:3-5.

62. 1 Samuel 3:1; Proverbs 29:18; Acts 21:11; Galatians 2:2; Ephesians 3:3; Revelation 1:1.

63. Available through Christian International School of Theology. Please call 1-800-388-5308 or visit our website at www.cimn.net.

64. Galatians 5:22-23.

65. 1 Corinthians 12:7.

66. 1 Peter 4:10.

67. 1 Corinthians 12:7,31; 14:1,3-4,12,31,39.

CHAPTER 10

THE CALLING AND MINISTRY OF THE SAINTS

THE LAST WILL AND TESTAMENT OF JESUS CHRIST

Tremendous insight and expanded understanding will come to each of us as we go to the Scriptures and find out all that is included in our inheritance in Christ Jesus. The New Testament contains the details of the last will and testament of Jesus Christ. A will does not go into effect until the person making the will dies. Jesus wrote His will by His life and words while He was here on Earth. He then died, arose from the dead, and ascended to Heaven. The apostles and a few other Saints were the attorneys who put all the details of the will together, totaling 27 documents. These became the 27 books of the New Testament of the Bible. All that is in these books are the things that are willed to God's children, the Saints, His corporate Church.

Everything in "the will" is given to the corporate Church. However, the Holy Spirit reveals what each member receives as his or her portion of the inheritance. Each member has access to all the inheritance but is given grace to receive and manifest certain portions of the full inheritance of the Church. "But to each one of us grace was given according to the measure of Christ's gift."[1] Each one was given gifts according to his abilities. Jesus gifted some to be prophets, some apostles, and everyone to be something. He gives to each according to his/her own ability.[2] Divine ability to manifest one or more of the gifts of the Holy Spirit is given to every Saint.[3] The Holy Spirit distributes to each one individually as He wills.[4] There is one Body of Christ but many members; each has a different gifting and ministry to manifest, as different as members of the human body.[5]

The Good News and the Bad News: Each Saint has received a divine inheritance from Christ which becomes his or her commission and responsibility to fulfill as a particular member of the Body of Christ.[6] The inheritance is the good news. The bad news is that each Saint will be held responsible and will have to give an account of how he handled the inheritance. In Jesus' parable of the talents, the two faithful servants who used and multiplied their talents were rewarded greatly. The Saint who had received only one talent did not use or multiply his talent. He was declared an unprofitable servant and was cast into outer darkness where "there will be weeping and gnashing of teeth."[7]

From all these scriptural statements we can see that we have received an inheritance in Christ and He has an inheritance in us. There is a day of reckoning for the

Saints when Christ Jesus comes to claim His inheritance. He expects us to be as faithful with His inheritance in us as He is with our inheritance in Him. "In [Christ Jesus] also **we have...an inheritance**," "the riches of the glory of [**Christ's**] **inheritance in the saints**."[8]

Make Your Bible Reading More Purposeful and Enlightening: To make the Scriptures more meaningful concerning being a Saint, do the following: Whenever you see the words *we, us,* and *you,* substitute the word *Saint.* Whenever the words *He, His,* or *Him* are used in reference to God or Christ Jesus, use their proper names. As an example, let us read a few verses from Ephesians chapters 1 and 2:

> *Blessed be the God and Father of the Lord Jesus Christ, who has blessed the Saints with every spiritual blessing in the heavenly places in Christ, just as God chose the Saints in Christ before the foundation of the world, that the Saints should be holy and without blame before Christ in love, having predestined the Saints to the adoption as sons by Jesus Christ to Himself, according to the good pleasure of God's will, to the praise of the glory of Christ's grace, by which God made the Saints accepted in [Jesus] the Beloved. In Jesus the Saints have redemption through Jesus' blood, the forgiveness of sins, according to the riches of Christ's grace which Jesus made to abound toward the Saints in all wisdom and prudence, having made known to the Saints the mystery of God's will, according to Jesus' good pleasure which Christ purposed in Himself....[All of this is] because of God's great love with which Jesus loved the Saints, even when the Saints were dead in trespasses,*

made the Saints alive together with Christ (by grace the Saints have been saved), and raised the Saints up together, and made the Saints sit together in the heavenly places in Christ Jesus, that in the ages to come God might show the exceeding riches of His grace in the Father's kindness toward the Saints in Christ Jesus.[9]

Inserting the word *Saints* for the personal pronouns that mean the same in these verses magnifies our understanding of the calling, ministry, and destiny of the Saints. I encourage every Christian to do this often in Bible reading. To make the scriptural truths even more personal, put your own name where you were putting *Saints*. To gain a greater understanding of Christ's will and purpose for the Church, place *Church* in each place referring to Saints.

Many different terms are used to describe the calling, ministry, and destiny of the Saints. We will now look at **THE CALLING AND MINISTRY OF THE SAINTS REVEALED BY THEIR VARIOUS NAMES.**

Saints As Children of God

Saints are the children of God through faith in Christ Jesus.[10] "The Spirit Himself bears witness with our spirit that we are children of God, and if children, then heirs—heirs of God and joint heirs with Christ."[11] Saints are those who have been born again by the Spirit of God, making the Almighty, Eternal God their Father.[12] Jesus was a physical, human child of God by being the only begotten Son of God, with Mary as His natural mother and God as His Father.[13] Jesus became an eternal body, soul, and spirit Son at His resurrection, where God said, "You are My Son, today I have begotten You."[14] Christ was "declared to be the Son of God with power...by the resurrection from the dead."[15] Jesus was the "firstborn from the dead" and thereby became the "firstborn among many brethren," enabling all Saints to become members of "the church of the firstborn who are registered in heaven"[16] This makes Jesus the elder Brother and Head over the whole family of the children of God, the Church.[17] The Bible never calls us the children or sons of Jesus Christ; nevertheless, Jesus and His Father are one. The prophet Isaiah prophesied that one of the names given to the Christ child who was to be born and the Son who was to be given would be "Everlasting Father."[18] Jesus Christ is our everything. In Him we live and move and have our being. He is the Life and being of the Saints.[19]

When Saints can grasp the reality that their Heavenly Father is the One who created the heavens and the Earth, who owns everything and who has all power in Heaven and Earth, then their faith will be unlimited and their accomplishments will be world shaking.[20] The ones who participate in the Saints Movement will come to that revelation and do great exploits for God.[21] Since most children of God would verbally acknowledge these things, then why are they not able to manifest their inheritance as heirs of God and joint-heirs with Christ Jesus? Galatians chapter 4 reveals the main problem. "Now I say that the heir, as long as he is a child, does not differ at all from a slave, though he is master of all."[22] Children cannot receive their full inheritance until they become of age. Parents do not give great wealth or weapons of war to children. Children must grow to maturity and become adult men and women of God. The Bible exhorts the

Saints not to be immature children who can be tossed to and fro by every wind of doctrine, but to grow up in all things in Christ, the head of the Church.[23]

Saints Who Are Immature and Dull of Hearing: Why don't all Saints understand and grasp present truth? Many Saints do not grow beyond the elementary teachings of being born again and going to Heaven. Some become dull of hearing, while others refuse to eat the solid food of mature teaching. Others will not allow themselves to be challenged to exercise their spiritual senses so they can discern between good and evil, or will not exercise their spiritual gifts and ministries until they are effective demonstrators of the life and ministry of Christ.

Paul expressed his frustration about this in his letter to the Hebrew Saints abroad. He was seeking to educate, activate, and motivate them to maturity and powerful ministry.

> *...we have much to say, and hard to explain, since you have become **dull of hearing**. For though by this time you ought to be teachers, you need someone to teach you again the first principles of the oracles of God; and you have come to need milk and not solid food. For everyone who partakes only of milk is unskilled in the word of righteousness, for he is a **babe**. But solid food belongs to **those who are of full age**, that is, those who by reason of use have their senses exercised to discern both good and evil. Therefore, leaving the discussion of the elementary principles of Christ, let us go on to perfection.*[24]

A Foundation or Whole-Building Saint: Every Saint needs to be firmly established on the fundamentals of the Christian faith, but that is just the foundation of the life as a Saint. Some people have been Christians for decades but have remained baby Christians and have never advanced beyond the basics. In the Saints Movement, God will not be able to use those who have been His children for some time, but who are still immature and childish. As the Commander of His army of Saints, Jesus cannot put these believers in the front line of battle or give them a heavy load of responsibility and ministry. That is one reason I am writing this book and trying to make the vision plain. I hope all who read it may be inspired to run their race to the finish, go on to perfection, and be established in all present truth. As you can tell, my passion is to help everyone know and fulfill their calling, membership ministry, and destiny.[25]

Two Things That Hinder Maturity and Mighty Ministry: Two more things that will keep children of God from receiving their inheritance and advancing beyond babyhood Christianity are *carnality* and *materialism*.

> *And I, brethren, could not speak to you as to spiritual people but as to carnal, as to babes in Christ. I fed you with milk and not with solid food; for until now you were not able to receive it, and even now you are still not able; for you are still carnal. For where there are envy, strife, and divisions among you, are you not carnal and behaving like* [unregenerate] *men?*[26]

The phrase *not able to receive "it"* represents one's maturity, ministry, and full destiny. Adjust the "it" in your life and become a mature, victorious, overcoming Saint ready to be a joint-heir and co-laborer with Christ Jesus in His next move to accomplish His purpose in and through His Church.[27] Jesus also made it clear that to truly inherit the things of the Kingdom, one must not be given to the love of money. The deceitfulness of natural riches is one of the traps that hinders some from progressing on to their full spiritual inheritance as children of God.[28] These issues of maturity and money are two of the "Ten M's" that must be in order for a minister, or any Saint, to be successful.

SAINTS AS THE LIGHT OF THE WORLD

"You [the Saints] are the light of the world."[29] Jesus said that He came as the Light of the World and told His followers to believe in the Light while they had the Light that they might be the children of the Light.[30] He declared, "As long as I am in the world, I am the light of the world."[31] After Jesus returned to Heaven, His Church Saints became the light of the world. There is meaning in these words that escapes the average Christian. One major truth we want to reveal here is that when the Church is walking in the light as God intended, it has a definite effect upon the world.[32]

The Church—The Light of the World: For instance, when the light of the Church was reduced from a thousand-watt bulb during the first century to a mere candle light during the Dark Ages, nearly the whole world lived in ignorance, superstition, and wickedness. There was very little progress in the world for the 1,000 years when the light of the Church was not shining brightly. While there were some major developments and inventions, world population in general did not increase much, and the average person remained in a state of poverty and ignorance. This began changing when the Church began increasing its light at the time of the restoration of the Church.

The preparation for the restoration began with John Huss 100 years before Martin Luther nailed his 95 theses to his church door in 1517, which was the year Church historians have set for the beginning of the restoration of the Church.[33] After 25 years of studying Church history and the correlating events that were happening in the world, the following truth was made real to me: Every time the Church received more light of restoration truth from the Word of God, a corresponding increase in technology, inventions, and culture took place in civilization.

Church Fulfilling Proverbs 4:18: Proverbs 4:18 says that the path of the just is a light that shines brighter and brighter until the perfect day. World historians call the early 1500s the great Renaissance or "rebirth" and the time of the Enlightenment. With each restoration movement that has taken place through the centuries, the world has also increased in "enlightenment." Many discoveries and inventions came through Saints of God, but others came through non-Christians. The offer of increased revelation was given to the whole world, whether they were personally appropriating the restored spiritual truths or not.

For example, in the arena of weaponry, explosive power was discovered in the natural—from gun powder to dynamite, to TNT, to atomic bombs. In travel, technology has advanced from horse-drawn stagecoaches to trains, automobiles, planes, jets, and spacecraft; from boats powered by oars and sails to gigantic engine-powered ships and atomic submarines. Written communication has gone from handwriting, to the printing press, to typewriters, and now to computers. Wire and air communication has changed from smoke signals to the telegraph, telephone, radio, television, fiber optics, satellites, computer chips, and the Internet. Knowledge has increased in medical science from the times of blood-letting and sawing off legs and arms without anaesthetics, to operations with anaesthetics, penicillin, x-rays, transplanting human organs, and the understanding of DNA. Modern technologies, such as cloning of animals and possibly humans, have become so advanced that the possibilities and resulting implications are mind-boggling.[34]

During this same period of time, there have been advances in ethical and moral areas in many parts of the world. These include recognition of the individual rights of people; outlawing of slavery and child labor; improved status of women; democracy and the rights of average people to participate in government; universal education and widely increased literacy rates; fair trials for the accused and outlawing inhumane methods of torture; Social Security and charities to feed the poor. Over the centuries the emphasis has shifted from the rich and powerful, such as those born into royalty, to the ability of average citizens to achieve something worthwhile in their own lives. In the same way, the Holy Spirit is showing the supernatural ability of Christ to flow through any "average" Saint.

In the last 50 years, as the Church has experienced a movement taking place every ten years, inventions have also soared at a tremendous rate. The world has advanced more in technology and inventions since the Holy Spirit baptism was restored to the Church in 1901 than it has in all the history of mankind. Spaceships have now taken man beyond the limitations of Earth. Through restoration, the Holy Spirit is taking the Church beyond all religious -isms, traditions, and limitations. We cannot yet imagine what kind of advancements will be made when the Saints Movement and subsequent movements take place. The Church will advance further and accomplish more in its last 100 years than in all the previous centuries combined.

When does the light of revelation cease? According to Proverbs 4:18, restorations will continue illuminating the Church with Christ-light. As this light of revelation becomes more and more complete and perfected it will take over and drive out all the darkness of this world. "The lawless one will be revealed, whom the Lord will consume with the breath of His mouth and destroy with the brightness of His coming."[35] Jesus will truly be the Light of the World, and the kingdoms of this world will become the kingdoms of our Lord Jesus and His anointed Church.[36]

SAINTS AS BELIEVERS AND REPRODUCERS

> ... *"Go into all the world and preach the gospel to every creature. He who believes and is baptized will be saved; but he who does not believe will be condemned. And these signs will follow those who believe: In My name they* [believers] *will cast out demons; they will speak with new tongues; they will take up serpents; and if they drink anything deadly, it will by no means hurt them; they will lay hands on the sick, and they will recover."*

*So then, after the Lord had spoken to them, He was re-
ceived up into heaven, and sat down at the right hand
of God. And they* [believers] *went out and preached
everywhere, the Lord working with them and confirming
the word through the accompanying signs. Amen.*[37]

According to the Gospel of Mark, these were the last
words of Jesus before He ascended back to the Father. He
gave the signs of the true believer. Believers first accept
Christ as their personal Savior and identify with His death
by being baptized in water.[38] They become empowered by
receiving the gift of the Holy Spirit and speaking with
other tongues.[39] They have confidence that God's protect-
ing and preserving power will keep them from harm, such
as anyone trying to poison them or a snake biting them.
This can mean natural protection, such as from a real
snake bite, or protection from the venom of the devil and
his demons. Thus empowered, they proclaim the gospel of
the death, burial, and resurrection of Jesus Christ.[40] Their
witnessing and preaching is not with just words, but with
the accompanying signs of casting out demons and healing the sick.

Saints with the characteristics of a true believer are
Saints who will be used mightily during the Saints Movement. Many prophetic and apostolic leaders are training
the Saints to heal the sick and deliver people from demonic influence. We have been teaching and activating
Saints in the verbal and revelation gifts of the Holy Spirit
for 20 years, during the Prophetic Movement. Now the
Apostolic Movement has brought revelation and anointing for activating Saints in the power gifts. Along with this

we are activating the believers into their ministry of casting out of demons.

Demonstrators vs. Reproducers: Some who are knowledgeable of the great Deliverance Evangelism Movement of the 1940s and 1950s and the ministry of casting out demons that came during the Charismatic Movement might ask, "What is different and new concerning healing the sick, prophesying, and casting out demons today?" The difference is this: In those meetings, great ministers such as Oral Roberts, T.L. Osborne, and Derek Prince ministered these things to the people, but they did not reproduce these ministries within the Saints so that they could do the same. A similar scenario was present during the Latter Rain Movement. At that time, many were doing some of the work of apostles and prophets. They taught that apostles and prophets were being restored back into the Church, but they did not call themselves by those names, nor were they reproducing like kind.

Forty years later, in 1988, the Prophetic Movement came, and men and women were willing to be called by their fivefold ministry of prophet or apostle. A new anointing that was restored in the Prophetic Movement was the anointing for spiritual "reproducing." That was my God-given portion to pioneer and demonstrate within the Church. In March 1984, during a prophetic conference where I was a speaker, an older prophet prophesied to me that within five years God was going to give me a special divine endowment which would be a "reproducing anointing." The following is an excerpt from that prophecy:

*...There is going to be a whole new wave of God's glory that is going to be ignited through your ministry...and it's going to be the multiplying of yourself, for you are to have a ministry of **producing reproducers who will reproduce reproducers who also will reproduce re-producers**...*[41]

Double Portion for Reproducing: I had been teaching and training others in the prophetic ministry for several years. But when the Prophetic Movement was birthed in 1988, the double portion anointing for reproducing was given by the Holy Spirit. It came within the five-year period that the prophet had prophesied. God birthed in my life and ministry the reproducing anointing that has enabled me to teach and activate others into being prophets, prophetic ministers, and prophetic people. All of the more than 600 ministers under my apostolic oversight in the Christian International Network of Churches are prophetic ministers. They are not all prophets, but as five-fold ministers they can each manifest prophetic ministry. We have trained and activated more than 200,000 Saints into prophetic ministry.

The "Genesis Principle" of every seed reproducing after its kind is alive and productive in our midst.[42] Most of the pastors that we have birthed into ministry are also re-producing reproducers who are reproducing others. From those I have ministered to prophetically, to all the ones they have personally prophesied to, to the ones to whom they have in turn ministered, a chain-reaction has occurred. The result is that over one million people have been ministered to prophetically. The company of prophets, prophetic ministers, and prophetic people now totals in the millions around the world.

Reproducing Generations: My wife and I became great-grandparents on January 22, 2001. This came by the re-producing principle. Tim, the son we had birthed and raised, had a daughter (Ruth) whom he and Karen raised. Then Ruth married Yancey and birthed a son whom they are now raising. My mother came from Oklahoma to our home in Santa Rosa Beach, Florida, so that we could take a photograph of five generations of our family.

In the natural I am a great-grandparent, but in fathering prophetic people, we could take a picture of six or seven generations of prophetic Saints that have been reproduced. This reproducing anointing is not just for the ministry of Christian International. It has been restored into the Church at large. Every fivefold minister needs to receive it and start reproducing the anointing that God has given them in the Saints, so that each Saint can be activated and enabled to fulfill their membership ministry.

SAINTS AS LOVERS AND WORSHIPERS OF GOD

Praise and Worship: Saints must have a revelation of the power and purpose of praise and worship. There is so much important revelation in this truth, it would require another book to cover it all.[43] A couple of major reasons will be sufficient here. Praise prepares a habitation for God to come, bless us, and minister through us.[44] Saints desperately need the manifest presence of God that praise and worship to God produces. And praise is one of the greatest weapons of warfare found in the Bible.[45] The Saints in the coming move of God will be fanatical worshipers of the Lord. They will worship and praise with the revelation of what they are doing and faith in its value and purpose.

In order to be worshipers of Jesus Christ, the Saints who participate in the next move of God must be filled with the love of God. Apostle John was the Apostle of Love. He talked more about God's love in his Gospel and three small Epistles than did any other writer of Scripture. I believe every Christian is convinced that we need the love of God, so let us go beyond the basics and cover some specifics. It is understood that the first and greatest commandment is to love God and the second is to love one's neighbor as oneself.[46] We can define love in two categories: how much love we have toward God and how much of God's love we have within us.

Our love to God can be demonstrated by our verbal worship to God and by keeping His commandments. Jesus said those who love Him will keep His words.[47] Therefore, we show our love to Jesus Christ by reading His love letters to us, the Bible. We only love God to the degree we love His Word. We also show our love to God by spending fellowship time with Him in prayer and worship. We demonstrate our love to God when we trust Him, lean upon Him, and don't murmur and complain when things do not go our way, but continually acknowledge Jesus as a faithful and true Savior who works all things together for our good.[48] We also show the greatest love to God when we willingly submit to His transforming process to conform us to His image.[49] This gives Jesus great joy, for it makes it possible for Him to fulfill His purpose of bringing many sons unto His full glory.[50]

Measuring God's Love Within: Let us now see what reveals how much of God's love is in us. During 52 years of being a Christian, I have seen a few Saints and ministers who could express their love to God through worship and reading their Bible, but they had very little of God's love incorporated into their life, being, character, and personality. The second of the two greatest commandments is to love our neighbor as we love ourselves. In other words, how we treat others and handle life's situations reveals how much of God's love has become a living part of our lives. God's love is more than an emotion; it is actually the very characteristic of God Himself.[51] Demonstrating love is portraying the nature and character of Christ Jesus.

When First Corinthians 14:1 says to "pursue [and make your aim] love, and desire spiritual gifts, but especially that you may prophesy," it is not contrasting love against the gifts of the Spirit. It is telling Saints: Make your greatest goal and ambition to be conformed to the image of Jesus Christ.[52] But while you are pressing toward that goal, keep blessing others by ministering the gifts of the Spirit, especially the gift of prophesying. There is no competition between gifts of the Holy Spirit and the love of God. They are both attributes of the one true God and His Holy Spirit.

WHAT IS GOD'S LOVE?

This love of which I speak is slow to lose patience—it looks for a way of being constructive. It is not possessive: it is neither anxious to impress nor does it cherish inflated ideas of its own importance. Love has good manners and does not pursue selfish advantage. It is not touchy. It does not keep account of evil or gloat over the wickedness of other people. On the contrary, it shares the joy of those who live by the truth. Love knows no limit to its endurance, no end to its trust, no fading of its hope; it can outlast anything. Love never fails.[53]

So what is love? Scripture does not say it is an emotional fervor or sweet sentimental talk. It is patience, kindness, goodness, right attitude, and righteous ways of handling life.

How important is it to have this love character of Christ? If we phrased this Scripture in present-day terms, it would describe Christians as follows:

Though we are Charismatics who speak with the tongues of men and angels; or prophetic people who prophesy and understand all mysteries; or faith people who have faith to move mountains; or religious humanitarians who sacrifice all we have to feed the poor, but we have not LOVE, it profits us nothing![54]

That should motivate everyone to make sure we have and live the character of Christ's agape-love.

We have spent a lot of time discussing the equipping of the Saints in the supernatural works of Jesus. The outward manifestations of miracles, signs, and wonders will compel nonbelievers to come hear the gospel. But Scripture tells us that Saints are recognized as disciples of Christ by their love.[55] Jane Hansen, President of Aglow International, writes:

When our relationships are right, when we are walking in true intimacy with God and others, we will have a testimony before the world that those who are truly seeking the meaning of life will be unable to resist. It is this, our genuine love for one another, that Jesus said would testify of His life in us (see John 13:34-35). His disciples would not be recognized by physical healings, nor by miracles, signs or wonders, as wonderful and exciting as these are, but by love. In the atmosphere of such love, God's anointing for the miraculous and the power that "breaks the yoke" of our enemies is poured out.[56]

The Saints who will be used of God will need to be "filled with all the fullness of God." They must be "rooted and grounded in love," knowing the love of Christ in its full width, length, depth, and height. This enables the Saints to comprehend and exercise their faith to believe that God can do exceedingly, abundantly above all that they can ask or think.[57]

SAINTS AS WARRIORS AND OVERCOMERS

The victorious Saints in the Saints Movement will definitely be warriors and overcomers. Seven times the Book of Revelation says that the overcomers are the only ones who will get the rewards it describes and who are privileged to rule and reign with Jesus Christ.[58] The three major things that Saints must overcome are the world, the flesh, and the devil. Those who participate in the Saints Movement will have been delivered from all worldliness, having crucified the flesh, and will be living a sanctified holy life.[59] This puts them in position to have power to fight the good fight of faith and overcome the devil.[60]

Too many present-day Christians are so bound up in worldliness, materialism, and fleshly activities that they

347

are unable to be free and to cast out demons and destroy the works of the devil. "For this purpose the Son of God was manifested, that He might destroy the works of the devil."[61] Jesus said, "As the Father has sent me, I also send you."[62] We have the DNA of the "Mighty Man of War" within us.[63] Mature sons of God are devil destroyers. For Saints to be prepared, they must get off of their leisure cruise boat and get on God's destroyer battleship, learn how to man their guns, and blow the devil out of the water! They must exchange their "Santa Claus" Jesus for Jesus the Mighty Warrior. Too many Christians see Jesus as just a big jolly fellow with gifts to give and joy to bring, who thinks everybody is great and would not destroy anything.

Why God Anointed Jesus Above All Others: The Scriptures declare that God anointed Jesus above all others because He loved righteousness, but equally hated iniquity and all evil.[64] The Bible talks almost as much about what God hates as it does about what He loves. God hated wickedness so much that He destroyed an estimated 20 million wicked people with a flood to cleanse the Earth of evil.[65] He found only one righteous family. He loved righteous Noah and his family and saved them from destruction. God's compassion and mercy caused Him to save eight people, but His righteousness caused Him to destroy 20 million.

Not an Old God and a New One: Some will say, "But that was the God of the Old Testament." There is not one God of the Old Testament and another God of the New; there is only one God. There is an Old Testament and a New Testament, but one God of both. The God who killed millions in the Flood, sentenced a million Israelites to death in the wilderness, served as Commander-in-Chief of Joshua's army and fought along with them to destroy the people who were in Israel's promised land, is the same God who so loved the world that He gave His only begotten Son to provide salvation for mankind.[66] Those who say there is no judgment for Christians in the New Testament need to tell Ananias and Sapphira that and see what answer they get![67]

The Saints will be warriors with great compassion for mankind, but no mercy for the devil or the works of darkness.[68] They will be overcoming warriors who love righteousness but hate all kinds of evil. They will be soul savers and devil destroyers. Those who lack either of these aspects of Christ are unbalanced. Saints, it is time to put on the whole armor of God and pull your sword of the Spirit out of its scabbard! Raise your shield of faith and be ready to march forward as an overcoming warrior when the trumpet sounds for the launching of the Saints Movement.[69]

SAINTS AS MARTYRS

For the Saints to be fully ready to be used of God for unlimited service, they must come to phase number three of overcoming grace: "And they overcame [satan] by the blood of the Lamb and the word of their testimony, **and they did not love their lives to the death**."[70] In this great battle over the souls of mankind, there may be some Saints who will face martyrdom. This third phase has two applications. First, some Saints may be killed for the cause of Christ. Millions of Christians already have been put to death for their faith, especially in the first three centuries of the Church. Even today some reports estimate that hundreds of thousands are being martyred each year because they are Christians. In places such as India, Indonesia, China, and the Sudan, Saints are being tortured and killed for their faith. The Saints will come to the place where they do not hold back because of suffering and death, for they will love not their lives unto death.

Second, Saints must daily live a martyr's life. We are dead and our life is hid with Christ in God.[71] Like Paul, we are to be:

> ...always carrying about in the body the dying of the Lord Jesus, that the life of Jesus also may be manifested in our body. For we who live are always delivered to death for Jesus' sake, that the life of Jesus also may be manifested in our mortal flesh.[72]

Jesus said that if we are willing to lose our lives, then we will save them. But if we try to save ourselves, then we will lose our lives.[73] The Saints will learn to live the crucified life daily, and, if God so allows, give up their lives as martyrs for the gospel of Jesus Christ. They will have the spirit and attitude of Paul who said, "For to me, to live is Christ, and to die is gain."[74] In the Day of the Saints, Saints will come to the experiential reality of Galatians 2:20.

SAINTS HELP DETERMINE SHEEP AND GOAT NATIONS

Sheep Nations vs. Goat Nations: Jesus said that when He returns the second time, one of the first things He will do is separate the sheep nations from the goat nations. All citizens of every nation should definitely pray and work toward making their nation a sheep nation.

> When the Son of Man comes in His glory, and all the holy angels with Him, then He will sit on the throne of

*His glory. All the **nations** will be gathered before Him, and He will separate them one from another, as a shepherd divides his sheep from the goats. And He will set the sheep [nations] on His right hand, but the goats [nations] on the left. Then the King will say to those on His right hand, "Come, you blessed of My Father, inherit the kingdom prepared for you from the foundation of the world"....Then He will also say to those on the left hand, "Depart from Me, you cursed, into the everlasting fire prepared for the devil and his angels."*[75]

New Earth and New Jerusalem: The Book of Revelation declares that when God establishes the new heavens and new Earth, then the foursquare city of New Jerusalem will descend to new Earth. It does not reveal whether it will sit upon the Earth or orbit around new Earth. Apostle John wrote what he saw:

*I saw no temple in it, for the Lord God Almighty and the Lamb are its temple. The city had no need of the sun or of the moon to shine in it, for the glory of God illuminated it. The Lamb is its light. And the **nations** of those who are saved shall walk in its light, and the **kings of the earth** bring their glory and honor into it. Its gates shall not be shut at all by day (there shall be no night there). And they shall bring the glory and the honor of the **nations** into it. But there shall by no means enter into it anything that defiles, or causes an abomination or a lie, but only those who are written in the Lamb's Book of Life.*[76]

There will be sheep and goat nations when Jesus returns. What are we doing to help our nation obtain a sheep nation status? One way is to have kingly apostolic and prophetic ministers in key government positions to influence and direct our nation to righteousness. God is desirous to raise up ministers in the marketplace and public square who can bring forth sheep nations to go into God's eternal Kingdom on Earth.[77] Those who will be used in these areas will need God's supernatural revelation knowledge and divine wisdom.

Paul prayed for the Ephesian Christians to fully understand and appropriate all that God provided for His Saints when He raised up Christ from the dead.

> [I] *do not cease to give thanks for you, making mention of you in my prayers: that the God of our Lord Jesus Christ, the Father of glory, may give to you the **spirit of wisdom and revelation** in the knowledge of Him, the **eyes of your understanding being enlightened**; that **you may <u>know</u>** what is the hope of His calling, what are the riches of the glory of His inheritance in the saints, and what is the exceeding greatness of His power toward us who believe, according to the working of His mighty power which He worked in Christ when He raised Him from the dead and seated Him at His right hand in the heavenly places, far above all principality and power and might and dominion, and every name that is named, not only in this age but also in that which is to come. And He put all things under His feet, and gave Him to be head over all things to the church, which is His body, the fullness of Him who fills all in all.*[78]

The Saints in the Saints Movement will have a workable revelation of this prayer. When he wrote Ephesians

3:21, Paul was revealing that the Church will forever be manifesting God's glory as the Saints co-labor as joint heirs with Christ Jesus throughout the endless ages of eternity: "To [God] be glory **in the church** by Christ Jesus to all generations, forever and ever. Amen."

Overcomer Saints Will Rule the Nations:

> [The Saint] *who overcomes, and keeps My works until the end, to him I will give power over the nations—* "He shall rule them with a rod of iron."[79]
>
> *To him who overcomes I will grant to sit with Me on My throne, as I also overcame and sat down with My Father on His throne.*[80]
>
> *...we are children of God, and if children, then heirs—heirs of God and joint heirs with Christ, if indeed we suffer with Him, that we may also be glorified together.*[81]
>
> *Then the kingdom and dominion, and the greatness of the kingdoms under the whole heaven, shall be given to the people, the Saints of the Most High. His kingdom is an everlasting kingdom, and all dominions shall serve and obey Him.*[82]
>
> *The kingdoms of this world have become the kingdoms of our Lord* [Jesus] *and of His Christ* [anointed one—the Church], *and He shall reign forever and ever!*[83]

Jesus has redeemed us by His blood out of every tribe, tongue, people, and nation. Jesus has made us kings and priests to our God, and we shall reign on the Earth.[84] We have the joyful privilege of participating with Christ Jesus in helping the nations of the Earth turn to righteousness now and throughout the Day of the Saints, before the appointed time of judgment. We have recently seen God move in the United States in response to the prayers and efforts of the Saints of God.

A Prophetic Word and Intercessory Prayer: In 1996 there was a great Christian gathering in Washington, D.C., called "Washington for Jesus." Approximately one-half million Christians attended. One morning several recognized prophets gave prophecy concerning the United States of America. A portion of the prophecy I gave stated that if the leadership of the Church and the U.S. government did not turn the nation back toward righteousness by the end of 2002, then God would lift His hand of blessing and protection from the nation.

On September 11, 2001, the Church in America had a "wake-up" call. I believe that God took His hand of protection away from this nation for one hour that morning to show us a small glimpse of the types of situations we could face if He removes it entirely. How the Church responds in intercessory prayer, repentance, and spiritual warfare will make a tremendous difference. One can also see now why the recent presidential election was so crucial. This president and his cabinet have the greatest potential of cooperating with God to turn the nation back to its Christian heritage and God's righteousness.

Not Political or Personal, but God's Purpose: The unusual events and outcome of the election of 2000 were not a matter of the desires of Republicans or Democrats, nor of citizens who are Anglo, African, Asian, Hispanic, or Jewish, nor of the young or senior citizens. It was a matter of the intercessory prayer of the Saints for our nation. During that time, the Holy Spirit was pressing Saints to intercede in prayer not for their choice, but for the man who could be most instrumental in turning our nation back to God. The future of our nation was being weighed in the balance. The next few years would determine its future. Modern technology enabled the mobilization of more intense prayer for this election than for any other election of a president of the United States. Even Christians in other nations were interceding for America. The Holy Spirit was pressing God's Saints to pray that the right man would win the election.[85] We must conclude that God answered our prayers and the right man won.

Holy Angels and Saints Working Together: It was not just a battle between two political parties, nor the state of Florida trying to get all the ballots properly counted. It was a battle being fought in the heavenlies for the destiny of a nation. It was a war being fought by the holy angels of God against the wicked angels of the devil. The authority of the angels not only comes from God but also is dependent upon the prayers of the Saints. The praying of the Saints and the prophesying of the prophets authorize and empower the angels. Who wins is determined by the intensity and perseverance of the Saints in intercessory prayer. The battle was heavy and the final outcome was not determined immediately. Like some football games, it extended into several overtimes before the winner was declared.

Potential to Be a Reformer: Now President Bush not only has the awesome responsibility of presiding over the nation, but also the responsibility to be instrumental in fulfilling the prayers of the Saints and the purpose of God for the nation. I believe President Bush has the calling to do for America what Josiah did for Israel when he became king. He brought restoration of righteousness and sought to turn the nation back to God and His ways. For President Bush to be instrumental in bringing this about, it will require even more intense prayer by the Saints than what was done before the election. He does not need our criticism, but rather our prayers. For one thing, he does not have the freedom to function that the kings of Israel had, for they had sovereign headship in making decisions. Our president has to deal with the Congress, Supreme Court, and many other factors in bringing change. The Bible does not make a request for us to pray for our governmental leaders; it makes a command.[86] I believe God wants America to be a "sheep nation" and we, the Church, can help bring this to pass. God is giving every natural, political nation the opportunity to align with Him and His purposes.

Overcome the World, the Flesh, and the Devil: One of the reasons for writing this book is to let the Saints know that they have a destiny of ruling and reigning with Christ. This is not automatic for everyone who has been cleansed from their sins by the blood of Jesus. Each Saint must overcome the world, the flesh and the devil. We must learn God's ways of doing business according to His biblical Kingdom principles. Those who overcome all things and become conformed to the image of Jesus Christ will inherit all things that God has destined for Jesus Christ. When we realize our potential power and full inheritance in Christ, we will willingly do all that is necessary to reach our full potential and fulfill our ultimate destiny.

SAINTS AS MEMBERS OF THE BODY OF CHRIST, THE CHURCH

Throughout this book, references are made to the Saints being members of the Body of Christ. First Corinthians 12 and Romans 12 explain how the Body of Christ is one Body but has many members. "Now you are the body of Christ, and members individually."[87] Paul uses the analogy of the human body and its members to portray how every Saint is a particular member with a different function. Although science may not have the complete understanding yet, there is no such thing as a member of the human body that does not have a function. The same is true for all members of the Body of Christ. **The Saints are members of the Body of Christ 24 hours a day, not just when they enter the doors of the local church.** When this truth becomes a reality, it will bring a revolutionary transformation and activation of the Saints into the next move of God. The local church and fivefold ministers will go through an apostolic reformation that will change their vision of God's purpose for the Saints and the way local churches are to function.

Every member is important, valuable, and necessary for Jesus Christ to have a perfected Body of Christ. Ephesians 4:13 says that fivefold ministers must function until they bring the corporate Body of Christ to a "perfect man"/ Church. What is a perfect human body? It is one with all of its members in place and every member functioning as it was created to function. A "perfect Church" simply means one in which every member is present and is performing his or her ministry as was predestined. The member is alive, active, and healthy; has the right attitude; is living righteously and manifesting mature character. Clearly, there is much work yet to be done to have sufficient Saints ready as perfected members to be used in the Saints Movement.

Transformation Must Take Place: The Saints must be **changed** from an **audience** to an **army**, from **spectators** to **participators**, from just **church pew sitters** to **preachers in their profession.** Time and place must be given for teaching, training, activating, mentoring, and maturing the Saints in their membership ministries in the Body of Christ. This can never be accomplished with just regular Sunday morning and Wednesday night services. Fivefold ministers must provide the Saints "schooling for ruling," "training for reigning," and maturing for ministry.

This is no longer an option for ministers. The timing has become imperative, now more than ever before in the history of the Church, that the Saints be trained. The Holy Spirit has been commissioned by Christ to make sure this happens. Jesus Christ is not making it a suggestion or something to pray about; it is a commandment He has already given. Jesus said, "I will build My Church!" He ascended to Heaven and commissioned the fivefold ministers of apostles, prophets, evangelists, pastors, and teachers to be the building contractors. The Saints are their building material. Until recently, all fivefold ministers were not actively functioning in the Church. But now this present-day portion of the building of the Church can be fully implemented.

Saints Will Make Judgments and Reign with Christ: There are some other ministries and titles that could be used to describe the various ministries of the Saints, but the ones already given cover the major areas. The Saints are also those who are to judge the world, judge angels, and execute the judgments written.[88] This will take place in two moves of God which will come sometime after the Saints Movement.[89] The Saints will also be eternal joint-heirs of Christ in their ministry and reign with Him in the ages to come.[90] That, too, is beyond the Day of the Saints. Here we will concentrate on what we must prepare for now.

Telescopic Prophets and Apostles: Some prophets and apostles are like gigantic telescopes that can see far into the future, much as astronomers look into space at the distant stars and galaxies. They do not always know what they are seeing, but they know it is there. The Old Testament prophets saw things that would happen hundreds and sometimes even thousands of years in the future. They were looking through a darkened glass and could not make out the exact details, but they knew something of a certain nature was going to happen.[91] Apostle Paul revealed that we prophesy in part and we know in part, but when the prophecy is perfectly fulfilled, then everyone can understand what the prophecy was all about.[92] When the Saints Movement starts being revealed and fulfilled, then we will understand more fully what we have been seeing and saying prophetically. But at this time we do see something coming that is for real and will be fulfilled.

Throughout this book we have described what I see as different aspects of the Saints Movement. Each restorational move of God had been prophesied by prophets and apostles before it actually came. John Huss prophesied 100 years before the Protestant Movement happened that such a thing would come to pass.[93] Holiness ministers preached about a great Pentecostal outpouring coming to the Church. Pentecostal preachers proclaimed a coming great outpouring of the Latter Rain.

Nevertheless, many who declared these restorations and outpourings were coming rejected them when they did not come through their denomination. The Pharisees also rejected their anticipated Messiah because He did not come in the location and manner that they wanted. We all must stay open to wherever God activates the Saints Movement, whether it starts with our group or with someone else's. If we don't, we risk "going around the mountain again" or missing out altogether. The Day of the Saints has been prophetically seen and declared, and some Saints will fulfill it. I am determined to help prepare these Saints and be one of the participants.

Saints Who Will Not Participate Are a Contradiction of Terms: The full meaning of *Saint* is one who is 100 percent sold out to God, on fire for Christ, holy and set apart for the Master's use. Even the term *lukewarm Saint* is a contradiction of terms. A true Saint is not lukewarm. Even saying that there will be "Christians" who will not participate is a contradiction, for the word *Christ* in Greek means "the anointed one." So a Christ-ian is an anointed one who is a faithful and ardent follower of Jesus Christ. Jesus addressed the church of the Laodiceans, describing the condition of some of the members:

> *I know your works, that you are neither cold nor hot. I could wish your were cold or hot. So then, because you*

are lukewarm, and neither cold nor hot, I will vomit you out of My mouth. Because you say, "I am rich, have become wealthy, and have need of nothing"— and do not know that you are wretched, miserable, poor, blind, and naked—[94]

Jesus went on to say that if they would overcome all of these things by responding to His rebuke with repentance, by letting Him purify them like gold and clothe them with white garments of His righteousness, and by becoming zealously on fire for Him, then He would not remove them from being members of Christ's Body, the Church.[95]

Above All, Be an Overcomer: Jesus declared that He would grant to all those who overcame to sit with Him on His throne, just as He also overcame and sat down with His Father on His throne. Jesus then gave the same challenge in all of His letters to the seven churches in Asia. "He who has an ear, let him hear what the Spirit says to the churches."[96] Let us all have hearing ears to hear what Christ Jesus is saying (through His prophets, by His Holy Spirit, and by the Word of God) to each of us as members of His Body who are called to be Saints.

ENDNOTES:

1. Ephesians 4:7.
2. Matthew 25:15.
3. Ephesians 4:11; 1 Corinthians 12:7,28.
4. 1 Corinthians 12:11.
5. 1 Corinthians 12:12-27; Romans 12:4.
6. Ephesians 1:18.
7. Matthew 25:30b.
8. Ephesians 1:11,18; see also Ephesians 3:7,11; Matthew 25:14-30; 1 Corinthians 12:7-11.

9. Ephesians 1:3-9; 2:4-7.

10. Galatians 3:26.

11. Romans 8:16-17a.

12. John 3:7-8.

13. John 3:16,18.

14. Acts 13:33; Hebrews 1:1-5; 5:5.

15. Romans 1:4.

16. Revelation 1:5; Colossians 1:18; Romans 8:29; Hebrews 12:23.

17. Ephesians 1:22-23.

18. John 10:30; Isaiah 9:6.

19. Colossians 3:3-4; Galatians 2:20; Acts 17:28.

20. 1 Chronicles 29:11-12; Isaiah 40:26,28; Revelation 4:11.

21. Daniel 11:32b.

22. Galatians 4:1.

23. Ephesians 4:14-15.

24. Hebrews 5:11–6:1a.

25. 2 Peter 1:12; Hebrews 6:1-2; Philippians 3:14.

26. 1 Corinthians 3:1-3.

27. Galatians 4:7; Romans 8:17; 1 Corinthians 6:3.

28. Matthew 6:24; 13:22; 1 Timothy 6:6-11.

29. Matthew 5:14a.

30. John 12:36,46.

31. John 9:5.

32. John 4:9.

33. Bill Hamon, *The Eternal Church* (Santa Rosa Beach, FL: Christian International Publishers, 1981), p. 170. For more information on "The Restoration of the Church," see pp. 115-305.

34. Special Report on Human Cloning, *Time* (Sunday, Feb. 11, 2001).

35. 2 Thessalonians 2:8.

36. Revelation 11:15.

37. Mark 16:15-20.

38. Romans 6:1-5.

39. Acts 2:3-4.

40. 1 Corinthians 15:1-10.

41. Bill Hamon, *Prophets and the Prophetic Movement* (Shippensburg, PA: Destiny Image, 1990), p. 105.

42. Genesis 1:11-12.

43. For more information on this subject, see *Silencing the Enemy* by Robert Gay (Orlando, FL: Creation House, 1993). Available from Christian International.

44. Psalm 22:3; Colossians 3:16; 2 Kings 3:15.

45. 2 Chronicles 20:22; Psalm 149:6-9.

46. Mark 12:30-31.

47. John 14:15,23.

48. Romans 8:28.

49. Romans 8:29.

50. Hebrews 2:10.

51. 1 John 4:8.

52. Romans 8:29.

53. 1 Corinthians 13:4-8a (Phillips).

54. 1 Corinthians 13:1-3.

55. John 13:35.

56. Jane Hansen, *Fashioned for Intimacy* (Ventura, CA: Regal Books, 1997), p. 188.

57. Ephesians 3:14-21.

58. Revelation 2:7,11,17,26; 3:5,12,21. Also Revelation 5:10; 21:7; 22:5; 2 Timothy 2:11-12.

59. 1 John 5:4; Galatians 2:20; 5:24.

60. Revelation 12:11.

61. 1 John 3:8b.

62. John 20:21b.

63. Exodus 15:3-4; Isaiah 42:13; Revelation 19:11.

64. Hebrews 1:8-9.

65. From the footnote to Genesis 6 in the Amplified Bible.

66. Genesis 7:4; Numbers 14:29; Deuteronomy 7:1; Joshua 6:2; 8:1; 9:24; 10:7-10,19,36,40; 11:6,20; John 3:16.

67. Acts 5:5-10.

68. Deuteronomy 7:2.

69. Romans 6:10; Ephesians 6:10.

70. Revelation 12:11.

71. Colossians 3:3.

72. 2 Corinthians 4:10-11.

73. Mark 8:35.

74. Philippians 1:21.

75. Matthew 25:31-34,41.

76. Revelation 21:22-27.

77. Revelation 11:15

78. Ephesians 1:16-23.

79. Revelation 2:26-27a.

80. Revelation 3:21.

81. Romans 8:16b-17.

82. Daniel 7:27.

83. Revelation 11:15b.

84. Revelation 5:10.

85. C. Peter Wagner, ed., *Destiny of a Nation* (Colorado Springs, CO: Wagner Publications, 2001), pp. 16-17,21-23,44-45, 74-77,79-80.

86. 1 Timothy 2:1-2.

87. 1 Corinthians 12:27.

88. 1 Corinthians 6:2-3; Psalm 149:9.

89. These moves are mentioned in my books *The Eternal Church* and *Apostles, Prophets and the Coming Moves of God.* They will also be covered in more detail in a future book.

90. Romans 8:17; Ephesians 3:10,21.

91. 1 Corinthians 13:12.

92. 1 Corinthians 13:9.

93. David Huebert, "Outlined Study on Church Restoration" (Chilliwack, BC). For more information see Hamon, *The Eternal Church*, p. 126.

94. Revelation 3:15-17.

95. Revelation 3:18-19.

96. Revelation 3:22.

CHAPTER 11

THE OMEGA-
TRANSITION GENERATION

A Beginning and an End: In all things concerning mankind, there is a beginning and an end—a first and last. In the English alphabet the first letter is "A" and the last is "Z." In the Greek alphabet the first letter is "Alpha" and the last letter is "Omega." Jesus said of Himself, "I am the Alpha and the Omega, the Beginning and the End..., the First and the Last..., and who is and who was and who is to come, the Almighty."[1]

Jesus as God is the Eternal without beginning of days or end of life. However, Jesus as a mortal man had a beginning at conception and birth. He continued on Earth for 33 and one-half years and then His mortal body was crucified on a cross. Jesus' time living in a mortal body came to an end as that body died and was placed in a grave. But three days later God's resurrection power caused His body to make the transition from a mortal body to an immortal body.

The human race had a beginning when God created Adam and Eve and placed them in the Garden of Eden. Their time in the Garden and their access to the tree of life ended when they sinned. That event began mankind's time of mortality. Ever since that time, every individual on planet Earth has had a time to be born and a time to die. Solomon wrote, "To everything there is a season, a time for every purpose under heaven: a time to be born, and a time to die..."[2]

Everything progresses toward its final state. Every living thing on Earth has a beginning, progresses in growth to maturity, then finishes its purpose and dies. Most plant life produces seeds that reproduce like kind and continue its existence on Earth. The Bible declares that every human being who has ever lived in a human body and has died will be resurrected into immortality. Those who lived for God during their mortality will be resurrected with immortal bodies that cannot ever feel pain again or die. Persons who lived unrighteous lives will be resurrected with indestructible bodies and cast into the lake of fire to suffer eternal torment for endless eternity.[3] The Church Saints have a special designated time for their dead bodies to be resurrected—1,000 years before the rest of humanity.[4] At the same moment, the Saints who are still alive will have their mortal bodies changed into immortal bodies.[5]

In God's divine plan for man and planet Earth, everything is moving toward an ultimate fulfillment and final eternal state. At this time we want to discuss how we will progress from our present state to that eternal state. We will discover that the Saints Movement is designed to progress the Church, mankind, and planet Earth one step closer to that final eternal state. We have shown that the Church had a glorious beginning for several centuries, then began to fall away from its original truth and life experiences. It went into a thousand-year Dark Age. In approximately A.D. 1500 the Church was launched into its great period of restoration. The times of restoration have continued up to the present. We are currently in the Holy Spirit's commissioned time to restore the ministry of prophets and apostles to their God-ordained position and ministry within Christ's Church. The Holy Spirit is now in the process of completing God's full purpose for the Prophetic-Apostolic Movement. Part of that purpose is to fully equip the Saints for their predestined Day to manifest God's power mightily throughout the Earth.

The Saints Movement will activate a chain reaction of divine events which will escalate the final events and will bring about the consummation of the ages, resulting in the fulfillment of all things. The coming Day of the Saints is definitely on the Holy Spirit's schedule as one of the times of restoration needed to bring about the complete restoration of all things which are necessary for the return of Christ to take place. Let us now look at all the Scriptures concerning the final status of all things relating to mankind. We will discover what has not yet been fulfilled, accomplished, and established as God has predestined for all things to be in their final state. If we want Christ Jesus to return soon, we can hasten His return by working with the Holy Spirit to bring about the restoration of all things.

For, as we have seen, Christ Jesus is being held in the heavens until the restoration of all things which have been spoken by the prophets since the world began.[6]

THE FINAL OUTCOME

The Bible gives a clear picture of the final outcome and status of all things in Heaven and Earth. It gives a complete revelation of the future eternal state of Earth and all the inhabitants who have ever lived on planet Earth. The Word of God also reveals God's purpose and final destination for His Church. It speaks of the Church's progressive restoration until it reaches full maturity and destiny in Christ. We can also see in Scripture the final state and destiny of planet Earth, the nations of the Earth, and especially the nation of Israel. The final place and state of all the ungodly who have ever lived on Earth is vividly described. That part is clear. But the all important question is, how do we get **from here to there**? What are the progressive steps the Church and the nations must take before we arrive at our eternal state? What part do the Saints play in "hastening the coming of the Day of God"?[7]

HOW DO WE GET FROM...

Here	to	There?
Temporal	to	Eternal?
Progressive	to	Permanent?
Mortal Church	to	Immortal Church?
Prophecy-Future	to	History-Prophecy Fulfilled?

Three major groups must come to prophetic fulfillment for the day of God to arrive. (1) The Church must come to the fullness of Christ. (2) The world's cup of iniquity must become full. And, (3) Israel must come to full restoration. The Church is the key to the others reaching their fulfillment. The Church must first reach its fullness before Israel is restored. When the Church and Israel are both in proper alignment with God, He will then proceed with executing His judgments upon the ungodly.

Different Theories, but Agreement on the Final Outcome: Most of Christendom would agree on what the final status of all these things will be. The different opinions come from the various theological concepts concerning how we progress from here to there. What are the progressive steps that God has planned to reach that ultimate, eternal state? The biggest difference in the beliefs of Evangelical, Pentecostal, Charismatic, and Prophetic-Apostolic Christians relates to how much involvement the Church of Jesus Christ has in the progressive process to arrive at the final stage. Some preachers see the Church removed from the Earth for seven years, and others for three and one-half years, before the Saints return to co-labor and reign with Christ on Earth for a thousand years (the "millennium").[8] Others see the Church co-laboring with Christ through the entire process until they are changed to immortal Church members at the last trumpet, in a moment, in the twinkling of an eye.[9] However, other than that seven-year period at the end of the age of the mortal Church, these believers are in general agreement concerning the final outcome of all things.

Some have asked me what I believe concerning the "rapture" (the resurrection and translation of the Saints). First of all, let me say that I believe the Bible emphatically states that it will take place. Second, I have my own ideas and convictions concerning when and by what means it will take place. The Scriptures give some indications as to what will activate the rapture. Evangelicals and Pentecostals are especially interested in what a minister or Christian author believes concerning the timing of the rapture. Theologians have given names to different beliefs concerning how the end of this age will be consummated.

The three major theological concepts concerning the end times are: pre-millennialism, post-millennialism, and a-millennialism. Most Evangelicals and Pentecostals are pre-millennial. The pre-millennial preachers all propagate the rapture of the Church but present four different views as to when the rapture will take place. The different thoughts are all based on interpretations of a seven-year period and a three and one-half year period mentioned in the Books of Daniel and Revelation.[10] These seven years are generally called the seven years of the great tribulation. The four views of a pre-mill rapture in relation to those seven years are: a pre-tribulation rapture with seven years in Heaven before returning; mid-tribulation rapture with three and one-half years in Heaven before returning with Christ to establish His Kingdom; a post-tribulation rapture with just a few minutes with the Lord in the air before beginning the 1,000-year millennial reign with Christ over the Earth. The fourth view is that the Saints will be changed immediately here on Earth and never take the trip to Heaven before beginning to rule and reign with Christ for 1,000 years. These periods of time are more commonly referred to by preachers in abbreviated terms as the pre-trib, mid-trib, post-trib, and "no-trip" views.

What Does the Author Believe? Technically, what I believe is not relevant, for what anyone believes and propagates will not change the way God is going to fulfill all things. The only way an author's viewpoint would be relevant to the reader is if that author has an accurate revelation of God's plans for His Church. Each year during the five years I taught in a Bible College I had the third- and fourth-year classes spend three weeks debating these four rapture views. I could take any one of the four views and, just by using certain Scriptures, convince a new Christian that the view presented was the right one. I have a personal opinion of which view I feel is more apt to be the way it happens, but when and how long are not the most important issues. What part we are to play and what preparation is needed for us to do our part are the keys.

Here is my attitude: If God gave me a vote and it counted for anything, then I would vote for a seven-year sabbatical in Heaven before starting to rule and reign with Christ here on Earth. If God would not give me seven years, then I would take three and one-half years. And if not that, I would take five minutes. If none of these were my options, then I would just be changed from my mortal body into an immortal body along with the rest of the Saints and begin immediately ruling and reigning with Christ.

The seven years are not as important as what we are going to do when they are completed. At this present time, the most important thing is the preparation needed to enter into our eternal co-laboring ministry with Christ in fulfilling His eternal purpose, both now and throughout the ages to come. Present-day Saints in the Church need to relate to what part we are to play personally and corporately in progressing things until the temporary becomes the permanent and all prophecies are fulfilled, thereby becoming established facts of history. Now let us look at what the Bible says about the destiny of Earth and all its inhabitants.

THE CHURCH—THE ONE, UNIVERSAL, MANY-MEMBERED, CORPORATE BODY OF CHRIST

The revelation that God wanted a Church came when Jesus declared, **"I will build My Church."** Jesus purchased His Church with His own blood, authorized it by His resurrection, and brought it forth and empowered it by His Holy Spirit. As we have seen, Jesus built it on the foundation of His apostles and prophets with Himself being the Chief Cornerstone. The building material of the Church is redeemed mankind. They are being built together as a many-membered corporate Body of Christ. This corporate Body of Christ is the body where Christ dwells and does His work on Earth, just as the personal body of Jesus was God's human body to dwell in and to do His work on Earth for 34 years. The New Testament first-century Church manifested God's power, wisdom, and grace as revealed in the Book of Acts.

The Epistles of the New Testament reveal the destiny and ministry of the mortal Church in this age and that of the immortal Church in the ages to come. They reveal various stages the Church would go through after the first-century apostles passed from the scene. The Scriptures declared that men would begin to teach and practice things that would cause the Church to fall away from its original glory.[11] That great falling away came to pass within a few centuries after the Church was established. Church historians call it the "Dark Age" of the Church. It lasted for 1,000 years until A.D. 1500. Then apostle Peter's prophecy about the "period of restoration" for the Church began in A.D. 1517.

Beginning, Progressive Growth, and Ultimate Fulfillment: Most of the prophecies concerning Church restoration have become history. Five major restoration movements have restored the Church back to its present status. Only two or three more major movements are yet to take place to bring the Church to full restoration. Expectations are that they will be fulfilled within the first 30 years of this third millennium.

Everything alive in God's natural creation has a beginning, progressive growth unto maturity, and then ultimate fulfillment of God's purpose for it. The Church has already had its beginning and most of its progressive growth, with only a few more restoration steps to reach its full stage in Christ's ministry and maturity. The Church will then be ready to fulfill the ultimate destiny for which God brought it forth.

The present-day apostles and prophets must discover and reveal by the spirit of revelation the times and seasons of God and the prophetic Scriptures the Church has yet to fulfill. Some prophetic Scriptures are in God's destiny and will happen simply because God has ordained it. However, there are some things relating to the Church that require the involvement of the Saints to be fulfilled.

In order for us to know where we are and how much farther we have to go to reach our destination, we must know our beginning and ending point. If we left one location at six in the morning and were supposed to arrive at another location at midnight, we could look at our watch and determine distance covered and time left to reach our destination. If a person was making a trip from New York to Los Angeles and knew the route he was taking, then by looking at the map and seeing what state and city he was passing through, he could determine how much farther he had to journey to reach the destination. But if the driver did not know the ultimate destination, he could not determine how many more cities and states he would have to go through to reach his predestined place of arrival.

God has put in His holy, written Word a description of the final destiny and state of planet Earth and everything on it. Let us see what the Bible says is the ultimate destination, state, and place for each one of the following: the Church; planet Earth; the nations; the ungodly; the devil; and all natural creation.

THE DESTINY OF THE CHURCH

- The Church is destined to come to the unity of faith and knowledge of the Son of God unto a perfect man, unto the measure of the stature of the fullness of Christ.[12]

- The Church will be glorious and holy without spot, wrinkle, or blemish.[13]

- The Church will be victorious and overcoming, subduing all Christ's enemies under His feet.[14]
- We will grow up in all things in Christ, the head of His Body, with every member functioning properly.[15]
- We will be conformed to Christ's image, that Jesus might be the firstborn of many sons of God.[16]
- As overcomers we will sit with Jesus on His throne, ruling powerfully over all nations.[17]
- The Saints are destined to judge the world and even the fallen angels.[18]
- The Saints have the honor of executing all the judgments written.[19]
- The Saints will receive the Kingdom, and possess the Kingdom forever and ever.[20]
- The Saints will be vindicated by the Ancient of Days and given worldwide powers of government.[21]
- The Saints will be given power to rule over every nation under Heaven, and all shall obey them.[22]
- Jesus and His Saints will execute judgment on all the ungodly for all their ungodly deeds.[23]
- The Saints will become heirs of God and joint-heirs with Christ in all He shall ever be and do.[24]
- The Church will make known the manifold wisdom of God to all in the natural and spiritual world.[25]
- The Church will fulfill the eternal purpose which God accomplished in Christ Jesus our Lord.[26]

- The Church will manifest the glory of God throughout all ages, world without end.[27]

- The Church will become the Bride of King Jesus, thereby making them King and Queen of eternity.[28]

- The Church will fulfill God's original mandate for mankind to rule and subdue all things on Earth.[29]

- The Saints will inherit and rule on new Earth where righteousness will dwell forevermore.[30]

- The righteous Saints shall shine forth as the sun in the Kingdom of their Father God.[31]

THE DESTINY OF PLANET EARTH

- The Earth will be filled with the glory of the Lord as the waters cover the sea.[32]

- The Earth will be purified by fire from the fall of lucifer and the sin of man.[33]

- All things on Earth will be made new, pure, and beautiful for the habitation of the Saints.[34]

- All kingdoms on Earth will become the kingdoms of Jesus Christ and His Church.[35]

- Earth will become the center of Heaven with the New Jerusalem orbiting around it.[36]

- New Earth and the new heavens will be the home and headquarters of Christ Jesus and His Church.[37]

- The Earth will be redeemed from decay and death when the Saints are fully manifested.[38]

THE DESTINY OF THE NATIONS OF THE EARTH

- All nations of the Earth shall have the gospel of the Kingdom preached to them for a witness.[39]
- God will gather all nations to the Jehoshaphat Valley to enter into judgment with them there.[40]
- All nations will have become goat or sheep nations by the time Christ returns.[41]
- Jesus will separate nations when He returns: sheep nations on His right; goat nations on His left.[42]
- Sheep nations will be allowed to remain and function on new Earth during the millennial reign of Christ.[43]
- Goat nations will be cast into everlasting fire with the devil and his angels.[44]
- All wicked nations who forget God will be turned into hell.[45]
- Sheep nations shall walk in the light of the New Jerusalem and kings will bring in their glory.[46]
- The leaves of the Tree of Life on each side of the River of Life will bring healing of the nations.[47]
- The nations are destined to be ruled with a rod of iron by Jesus and His Church.[48]
- All nations and kingdoms shall be consumed or brought under the rule of the Kingdom of God.[49]
- The nations and kingdoms of this world will become the kingdoms of our Lord Jesus Christ.[50]
- All nations shall come to the Desire of All Nations (Jesus) and be filled with God's glory.[51]

- The nation of Israel shall be redeemed and restored, becoming the center of activity of new Earth.[52]

- God shall inherit all nations and they shall serve Him.[53]

- All nations shall flow into the house of the Lord—the Church of Jesus Christ.[54]

THE DESTINY OF THE WICKED, UNGODLY, NON-CHRISTIANS, ALL ANTI-CHRIST RELIGIONS

- The wicked will be separated from the just and cast into the furnace of fire where there is wailing and gnashing of teeth.[55]

- The eternal place of the fearful, unbelieving, abominable, sexually immoral, occult practitioners, idolaters, and all liars is in the burning lake of fire and brimstone, which will be their final state of eternal death.[56]

- All whose names are not found in the Lamb's Book of Life will be cast into the lake of fire.[57]

- The ungodly will be judged, convicted, and then sentenced by Jesus and His holy Saints.[58]

- The proud and wicked will be burned up and righteous Saints shall trample them under their feet.[59]

- Those who do not obey the gospel of Jesus shall be punished with everlasting destruction.[60]

- Wicked, lazy servants who are unprofitable will be cast into outer darkness where there is gnashing of teeth.[61]

- The unjust, presumptuous, and self-willed are reserved unto the day of judgment to be punished forever.[62]

- The armies of wicked kings will be conquered and cast alive into the lake of fire by Jesus and His army of Saints.[63]

- Saints living on new Earth will be able to view the wicked burning in the lake of fire.[64]

- The world's cup of iniquity will become full, as happened with the Amorites, Sodomites, and the pre-Flood race.[65]

THE DESTINY OF THE DEVIL, EVIL ANGELS, AND DEMONIC SPIRITS

- Everlasting fire has been prepared for the devil, his angels, and all evil spirits.[66]

- Satan, the devil, will be bound in the bottomless pit for 1,000 years so he cannot deceive nations.[67]

- The destiny of the devil is to be cast into the lake of fire and tormented day and night forever and ever.[68]

- Death and hell will be cast into the lake of fire with the devil and demons bound there forever.[69]

THE DESTINY OF ALL NATURAL CREATION

- All creation earnestly expects and eagerly awaits the revealing of the sons/Saints of God.[70]

- Natural creation will be delivered from the bondage of corruption into the liberty of God's children.[71]

- All creation will be delivered from the dross, dullness, and decay caused by the fall of lucifer and the sin of man.[72]

- Planet Earth will be cleansed by fire, causing rocks and plants to be as brilliantly beautiful as the New Jerusalem.[73]

- The curse of hurting and destroying each other will be removed from both man and animals. Former enemies such as the wolf and lamb will "not hurt nor destroy" any longer.[74]

- Redeemed natural men will receive the redemption of their mortal bodies into immortal bodies.[75]

The revelation from all these Scriptures is that all people who have ever lived on Earth will either spend their eternity with Jesus in Heaven's new Earth or with the devil in the hellish lake of fire. All those who do not know the true God and obey the gospel of His Son Jesus Christ will be removed from the Earth at the end of this age. As the old saying goes, we read the last chapter and found that we won. We will inherit all things that are life-giving and good. All non-Christians will lose and be cast into the lake of fire with their master, the devil, and all his evil spirits. The Earth will be cleansed from the dross and death caused by the fall of lucifer and the sin of man. When this takes place, everything on Earth will radiate with the brilliance of the gemstones described in the New Jerusalem. All the evil and darkness will be removed from the Earth and all its atmosphere will be purified as Heaven's atmosphere engulfs Earth. The new Earth will then become the center of Heaven and all universal activities. Jesus and His

Church Bride, under the authority of God the Father, will rule and reign over all things together.

Future Glory: No wonder Paul declared that the sufferings of this present time are not worthy to be compared with the glory which shall be revealed in us.[76] Our eyes have not seen nor have our ears heard all that God has prepared for them that love Him.[77] What our eyes have seen and our ears have heard of His plans for us makes us willing to sell out to God 100 percent. Some of us will be allowed to live and overcome all things with Christ. Some will be Christian martyrs. And some will die of natural causes and remain with Christ in Heaven until the resurrection-translation of the Saints. Then seven years later, or three and one-half years, or five minutes, or immediately, Jesus will come to Earth with tens of thousands of His Saints to execute judgment upon the ungodly for all their ungodly deeds and for all harsh things which they have spoken against Him.[78]

Regardless of how all end-time things come to pass, if you are a member of Christ's Body and a Saint of the Most High God, you are a joint-heir with Christ. You will be with Him in all He shall ever be or do, both now and throughout eternity. Let us all follow the admonition of apostle Paul to press toward the goal for the prize of the high calling of God in Christ Jesus.[79] Whether we live or die, we are continuously with the Lord and co-laborers with Christ whether here on Earth, in Heaven, or throughout eternity.

The final state of the Saints is all glorious, especially after we reach our resurrected, immortal, eternal state. Nevertheless, we must live, function, and fulfill many things before all the Saints of all ages can move into that position. Many purposes of God must be brought forth and fulfilled. Every purpose of God to be accomplished on Earth has to be birthed by a mortal person. Numerous fivefold ministers and Saints are "pregnant" with divine purposes that God wants birthed in His divine timing. Many Saints will yet be born, live, and die before all things are fulfilled.

The Omega Generation: However, God has predestined a generation that will live and never die. They will be changed in a moment, in the twinkling of an eye. They will be the "Transition Generation" that will make the transition from mortal Saints to immortal Saints. They will be the last generation of the mortal Church—"The Omega Generation." They will transition from mortal life to immortal life without going by way of the grave. They will make the transition from the Church Age to the Kingdom of God Age. I believe many are alive now and more are being born daily who will become that generation.

Let us now look at what purposes of God may yet need to be fulfilled and what we can do to help birth and fulfill God's final purposes for planet Earth and all its inhabitants.

Birthing God's Purpose

As we have seen, the Day of the Saints is about believers entering into partnership with Jesus Christ in such a way that they manifest His works on Earth on a daily basis. The Saints will be executing the will of Christ Jesus upon the Earth. In order to execute God's will, or purpose, we must have it birthed as a living reality within us.

In the book *Birthing God's Purpose,* I brought forth some vital biblical truths concerning how Saints can co-labor with God in birthing something He wants brought forth in His Church and manifested on the Earth.[80] I then shared a revelation God gave me in 1992. It was a divine vision/revelation revealing how God's end-time purpose for the Omega-Transition Generation was going to be fulfilled. The Holy Spirit revealed steps that I would need to take to fulfill my part in the Omega Generation. The six major steps that a Christian man and woman take in order to properly birth a child were used to reveal how we can birth a divine purpose of God.

STEPS TO BIRTH GOD'S PURPOSE:

1. **You need to get a revelation and conviction concerning whether you and the present truth are meant for each other.** Are you compatible? Do your desires, vision, and theology line up with what God is doing today? If not, are you willing to seek God for new vision? You must get a clear revelation of your membership ministry and destiny in Christ.

2. **Make a covenant like a marriage vow to God that you will stay with His purpose and ministry regardless of the ways it may affect your life.** In other words, you become bound to the purpose of God. Remember, God will not let you conceive a revelation that is destined to bless His Church unless

you are committed to bringing it forth and working with it until it reaches maturity.

3. **Maintain a close relationship with Jesus Christ until you get pregnant with present truth and the future purposes of God for yourself and His corporate Church.** Revelation is birthed from intimate relationship with God and His Word, prayer, and walking in His ways. When you are close enough to God to know His heart, the desires of your heart become aligned with His purposes.

4. **Maintain the pregnancy, by keeping faith and confidence in what you are pregnant with, until it progresses to God's time for its birth.** Do not abort the vision regardless of the persecution, rejection, difficulties, and inconveniences it may bring to your life. Keep interceding and standing in faith for the vision to become reality. Being pregnant with a spiritual restoration truth, a vision, a personal membership ministry, or a divine purpose of God may continue for many years before God's time for birthing. Keep in mind that while a woman is pregnant others cannot see the baby inside, nor can she show it to anyone so that they can see what it looks like, but when it is born all can see the results of the waiting time. God will not leave us eternally pregnant. He will bring us to the time of birth.[81]

5. **Allow God to bring you into labor and birthing at His *kairos* time.** Be sensitive to

His timing. Don't become impatient and try to force premature labor. Don't be discouraged if you have some false labor pains that don't produce. But press on until the Holy Spirit induces the true labor pains that produce the birth of the baby. Stay strong and courageous during the struggle of travail and birthing, knowing that the momentary affliction will produce a great result. Trust God to give you strength for fully birthing a healthy revelation or ministry that is destined to bless many.

6. **Grow the baby to maturity.** Make room in your life for a long-term commitment to the purpose of God. Be prepared to be a parent in the coming Saints Movement. Become equipped to teach, train, activate, mentor, and mature others in their ministry and in God's present truth and corporate purpose for His Church. Make sure you are fully established in every restoration truth that has been restored to the Church over the last 500 years.

As each of us follow these divine principles, we will be able to fulfill God's original command for us to be fruitful by birthing and then multiplying and bringing to maturity that which He enabled us to produce.

God has purposes for individual Saints and He also has purposes to be fulfilled for each generation. The Bible declared that David fulfilled God's will and purpose for his generation.[82] God showed me some of His purpose for three generations—not a generation of 100 years, but three generations of certain age groups. As you read and find yourself in one of these age groups, remember that we are using natural age, but that spiritual age has more application than the natural.

CHALLENGE TO THREE PROPHETIC AGE GROUPS IN THE OMEGA GENERATION

I want to enlighten and challenge you with some things that the Lord shared with me in 1992. As I was talking to the Lord about some particular things I said, "Lord, ever since my early twenties I have preached about the Joshua generation. Expectations were that I would be part of that generation and cross over Jordan before I was 30 years old. Now I am more that twice that age." Jesus began to share some encouraging and enlightening things with me. He reassured me that I would be a part of the Joshua generation, but that I was not of the new generation group but of the older Joshua group.

To convey the reality of what God was seeking to reveal, He used the three generations of my wife and me, our children, and our grandchildren. In 1992 our three children were in their thirties and our grandchildren were 13 and under. He said, "Those 40 and older will be the generation that will cross over Jordan. Those your children's ages, 39 down to 14, will be the generation that will begin to dispossess the '-ites' of Canaan. And those 13 and under, including a generation yet to be born, will be the ones who will see the consummation of the ages, bring back the King, overcome all things, and see My Kingdom established on planet Earth."

In the year 2002, these age groups are ten years older. The first group would be those Saints 50 and above, the second group those 24 to 49, and the last group those ages 23 and younger, including those yet to be born. The older group will be the generals, lieutenants, and mature leaders who have been established in present truth. They will lead the Church into its end-time promised Canaan land. The participating Saints ages 24 to 49 will be the ones who drive out the "-ites"—and possess Canaan by making sure the Apostolic and Prophetic Movements fulfill their destiny and purpose. They will become the prophetic-apostolic intercessors who will function like midwives, nurses, and doctors to help birth the Saints Movement. They will be the main propagators of the present restoration movements and the major leaders. Those ages 23 and under will be the group that fulfills all things, overcomes the last enemy in Canaan, completes the way, and makes ready a people for the coming of the Lord. They are going to be the most God-fearing, Jesus-loving, radical, fanatical, unstoppable, unquenchable, dead-to-self, alive-to-God, possessing, overcoming, fearless, devil-hating, bold generation of God's people ever!

Take Action—Respond—Make a Prayer Commitment: It is no accident that you are reading these things now. You have a destiny to be part of one of these groups. Every Saint has a strategic place and destiny in God's army. Fulfillment of that destiny will be based on the spiritual receptivity and maturity of each Saint.

Spiritual Age More Applicable than Natural Age: Where you fit is not so much according to natural age as to the spiritual maturity that these age groups represent in the natural. In other words, a 60-year-old who has just been born again and has become turned on to God's purposes would not necessarily be part of the older group. However, for the sake of simplicity, I will use the natural ages now to make the challenge to each group. These ages are as of the year 2002.

To Saints Ages 50 and Older: I challenge those 50 and older to have the Caleb spirit and attitude. Caleb requested the right to lead his tribe to take the land that he had claimed for himself when he originally spied out Canaan. Then he declared to Joshua:

> *Here I am this day, eighty-five years old. As yet I am as strong this day as on the day that Moses sent me; just as my strength was then, so now is my strength for war, both for going out and for coming in. Now therefore, give me this mountain* [to go and take for my inheritance].[83]

I have been claiming this promise for years, that I will be as strong for warfare ministry at 85 as I was at 42. I have been, and will continue to be, a major leader in the apostolic and prophetic. However, I am not going to stop there. I am "pregnant" with the Saints Movement, and I am moving the pregnancy along by preaching and writing on the revelation and scriptural reality of the coming Day of the Saints.

Let us declare that we are not stuck with the status quo! We are not the over-the-hill gang. We are still warriors. We have the Caleb spirit and attitude! Let us make the declaration, "Although I am this age in the natural, yet my strength and vision are vibrant and alive. I can swing my sword and fight with the warriors. I will use my years of wisdom and maturity to help bring to maturity the 14-year-old Prophetic Movement and the 4-year-old Apostolic Movement, and to carry and nurture the Saints Movement until it is birthed in the midst of the Church." If you are in this group and are ready to make a commitment to God, then pray this:

> I make a legal commitment in the spirit realm, like a legal marriage vow, to stay with God's purpose for me and the Saints Movement until birthed, then help bring it to maturity and fulfillment. I dedicate myself now to raise this child, to give all my resources to it, and to bring it forth to fulfill destiny. It is being recorded in Heaven right now that I am making this covenant with God. I will be completely and continually sold out for God's purposes. I will not abort. I will not stop. I will press on and possess my promised land. Amen.

To the Age Group 24 through 49: You are the group that must fully demonstrate the Apostolic-Prophetic Movement and bring forth the Saints Movement. You may not be the main demonstrators, but you will be the teachers, trainers, activators, and the ones who will go before and prepare the way. You have received a revelation that has caused a conception within the womb of your spirit. Something has been activated in your spirit that will make you want to see God's last-day apostles and prophets do the work of preparing the way and making ready a people for the coming Day of the Saints. Are you willing to stay in the womb of preparation until you are ready to be birthed?

Now God is preparing you to be leaders, sergeants, lieutenants, and generals to help lead this great army, and to be demonstrators of His great power. Right now you are going to be the older brothers and sisters of the Saints Movement.

The next generation—the group of 23 and younger—will work with all the babies that are going to be born into God's family. They are the main ones who are going to be the harvest reapers. But the 24 to 49 group are the major demonstrators and standard bearers, the ones who have to go out to prepare the way, demonstrate it, take the Apostolic and Prophetic Movements on to fulfillment, and lay the foundation for the Saints Movement. In some places people don't even know there has been a Prophetic Movement. There are places that don't even know there are still apostles and prophets in the Church today. Numerous Saints and pastors do not know the history, restoration, and destiny of the Church. Many do not know that the Church is being prepared to fulfill a great end-time purpose with Christ Jesus. We have the divine commission to make this truth known throughout the Body of Christ around the world!

If you are sincerely ready to commit to help make this happen, pray this prayer of commitment:

> Father God, I am Your child. You have given me a calling and destiny to birth something. There has been a conception within the womb of my spirit. I have a vision to see the Saints come forth. I have a desire to be, to do, and to demonstrate the truth. Here I am, Lord. I am committed. I make a vow, a marriage relationship with

You, that I will stay close to You until this is accomplished. Now let the Saints Movement that I am pregnant with begin to grow within me until miracles, signs, wonders, and the supernatural are demonstrated through my life. I will be an older brother/sister to the arising Saints. I will be whatever You want me to be, and I will fulfill whatever part You assign to me. You are writing my name in Your book of remembrance.[84] You wrote my name down today afresh and anew. God, I want You to be able to say, "Child, I can depend on you." Here am I, Lord. Use me for Your own purpose. Amen.

To the Saints Ages 23 and Under: I believe the college-age group, teenagers, children, and babies being born are the ones who are going to bring back the King. They must become the most fanatical, radical, devil-hating, Jesus-loving, fearless, bold, and courageous generation that has ever lived on planet Earth! This is the generation that really excites my spirit, for I know their destiny. I am believing God to keep me alive and active another 20 to 30 years so that I can be with this group in all that they are going to be and do.

If you are in this age group, you must come to the place where your life is the standard for showing those around you the way to live. You must come to the place where nobody can intimidate you about your Christianity or about your God. You must be convinced that Jesus Christ is the one and only true God. Jesus is the only Way, the only Truth, and the only Life. The world and old-order Christians will call you fanatics, but you will not be a lukewarm generation, for you are going to get too fiery for the devil to handle! Become bold now! You do not have to wait until you are a certain age. Your generation is going to experience and demonstrate the supernatural Kingdom of God until it is established and covers the Earth as the waters cover the sea.

There is coming not just a youth revival, but a youth revolution! You are going to the public schools, private schools, church schools, and colleges. A revolutionary revival is coming to schools from kindergarten through college. You will invade all areas of the world with the supernatural Kingdom of God. Many will get activated by becoming involved in intercessory prayer walks, Bible studies, and spiritual renewal meetings. You are the "Transition Generation." Your group will be the generation that will fully manifest the Day of the Saints, become the army of the Lord, and bring forth the "Kingdom Establishing Movement" which will finalize the restoration of all things, releasing Jesus to come from Heaven and take dominion over all the Earth.[85]

Jesus is still saying today that we should allow the children to come unto Him, for He is going to use them mightily.[86] Jesus is excited about this age group, for they will be the ones to bring Him back as King. Even now God is going to sovereignly visit the teenage and junior-age Saints, moving them into the Holy Spirit realm of visions and supernatural visitations. They will prophesy very specific things and heal the sick. They will receive such a revelation of Jesus that they will lose all fear of the devil and evil spirits. They will know that the smallest child of God, cleansed by the blood and clothed with the robe of righteousness and the garment of praise, can whip the biggest demon hell has to offer. They will be little Davids, boldly going against and defeating great Goliaths.

I challenge youth pastors to begin preaching and imparting this vision and faith to the youth. This is not fanciful, wild imagination but reality. As we saw in Chapter 8, it has already been demonstrated during the "Addulum Orphanage Revival" in China in 1952. Believe for God's visitation and be prepared to allow it to happen when it starts.

Young people, get pregnant with this visitation. Get such a hunger and thirst until you are filled with God's righteousness, revolutionary revival, and another restorational move of God! Start preparing now so that you will be prepared to participate in all God is about to do. Your generation is going to experience all that the prophets have seen and longed to participate in.[87] Do not miss your day of visitation, for you are a predestined and privileged generation.[88]

The first step to take is to let the Lord Jesus know that you are willing to fulfill His purpose for your age group. If this is your strong desire, pray this prayer of commitment:

> Father God, in Jesus' name, I present myself to You for Your purpose. I surrender my whole life—spirit, soul, and body—to You for Your use. I want to be one of the Saints who are destined to be part of Your young Joshua group that will become the Kingdom of God Demonstration and Transition Generation. I do not understand in my head all that this will entail, but my heart

says I receive and believe to become all that You want me to be. You are writing my name in Your record book now.[89] I submit to Your process. Amen.

An Apostolic Charge: When I first preached this message and the groups finished praying these prayers, I made some apostolic decrees and prophetically prayed for each generation. By the power of the Holy Spirit, God can apply the same decrees and prophetic prayers to you who have prayed just now.

> Father God, in the name of Your Son, Jesus Christ, I ask You to release upon all the Saints who have committed to You the eight major anointings You have given to me and the ministry of Christian International. May all who receive this message also receive the impartation of the:
> - Prophetic anointing
> - Apostolic anointing
> - Family and team anointing
> - Activation of spiritual gifts
> - Reproducing and restoration anointing
> - Warfare praise/intercessory warfare prayer
> - Prophetic-apostolic evangelism
> - Anointing to minister as Saints in the marketplace
>
> Lord, let them conceive a revelation and become pregnant with Your purpose for them, as individual Saints and as Your corporate Church.

Give each one the ability to conceive and bring forth Your destiny within the Church. If they are not already pregnant with the Day of the Saints, then we decree that the seed of the Saints Movement, and future movements such as the "Army of the Lord" and the "Kingdom Establishing Movement," will be in all three of these age groups. May each fivefold minister fulfill his calling. Make them into apostolic and prophetic leaders in the local churches and in the marketplaces. Activate within them such revelation that they will become Your visionaries, miracle workers, and believers who cast out devils and heal the sick, demonstrating signs and wonders for Your glory. May they please You in all they do, hastening the Day of the return of Your dear Son, Christ Jesus.[90] Amen.

I apostolically decree and prophetically charge you to know and fulfill your prophetic destiny! We also agree and decree for you to come forth into God's destiny for His Church and planet Earth, in Jesus' name.

COME FORTH, OMEGA GENERATION!

Lord, we call forth those ages 23 down to those yet to be born, for they are the Transition Generation to become the greatest ever Demonstration Generation. Lord, make them fanatics for You. They are destined to be the third and final group of the Joshua Generation, the Omega Generation of the mortal Church. Jesus, birth Your end-time purpose and zeal within them so that the zeal of the Lord of Hosts may perform this.[91] Lord, may all of us in the older generations help this last generation birth every revelation they need to accomplish Your final work. We decree your prophetic purpose and make intercession on behalf of this generation.

It is the appointed time for you to come forth, "Generation to Come." This is the generation that prophet David, the king, prophesied about in Psalm 102:12-22. These prophetic Scriptures reveal who they are and what they shall accomplish. As verse 18 declares, "This will be written for the generation to come." You are the Esther Generation that has come to the kingdom for such a time as this.[92] The great cloud of witnesses in Heaven are waiting for you to fulfill your ministry, for without you, they cannot be perfected.[93] Not only are the heroes of the faith witnessing and waiting, but the whole creation is groaning in travail with laboring birth pangs and with earnest expectation for the Day of the full manifestation of the Saints so that it can be "delivered from the bondage of corruption into the glorious liberty of the children of God."[94]

I implore all the age groups to do their part to bring the divine purpose to full term so that the Day of the Saints may be birthed. Older ones, you are the spiritual midwives to help bring forth the Omega Generation. God has solemnly promised that He will deliver what has been shut up in the womb and definitely cause delivery to take place at the time of birth.[95] The woman clothed with the sun is in labor pains to bring forth the man-child (the matured

Church-Saints). He shall not be devoured by the dragon but shall take his throne rights alongside King Jesus and rule the nations with a rod of iron.[96]

> Lord Jesus, we do not know all that will transpire as we make our journey from "here to there," from progressive restoration to full restoration of the Church, and until the mortal Church becomes the immortal Church. We do not see all the things that will happen along the way, but Your Word has revealed the end result of our journey. We know the Day of the Saints is drawing near.

> We will do all in the power and wisdom You give us to make ready a people and prepare the way for the full manifestation of the Saints. The manifestation of the Saints will cause the gospel of the Kingdom of God to be demonstrated in all nations for a witness to all nations. Then the end can come, causing the restoration and fulfillment of all things. We will co-labor with You, Christ Jesus, until the glory of the Lord fills the Earth as the waters cover the sea and all the kingdoms of this world become the kingdoms of our God. We will continue in faith until the Ancient of Days makes the divine decree in favor of the Saints. Then the Saints will be given the right and authority to make all Christ's enemies His footstool. Jesus, by Your grace we will overcome all things so that we may sit with You in Your Father's throne, establishing Your righteousness

and reign throughout Your new Earth. We will not stop until all that God has prophetically declared has become historical fact and a living reality. So be it.

Omega Generation of Saints, the Spirit and the Bride say, "Come!" The witnesses say, "Come!" The whole creation says, "Come!" It is the appointed time to birth and to come forth! It is all in, by, and through You, Lord Jesus. We pray for Your Kingdom to come, Your will to be done on Earth as it is in Heaven. Even more so, may **You** come, Lord Jesus![97] Amen.

ENDNOTES:

1. See Revelation 1:8,11.
2. Ecclesiastes 3:1-2.
3. Revelation 20:14-15.
4. Revelation 20:4-6.
5. 1 Corinthians 15:52-53.
6. Acts 3:21.
7. 2 Peter 3:12.
8. Revelation 5:10; 20:4-6.
9. 1 Corinthians 15:51-52.
10. Daniel 7:25; 8:14; 12:7; Revelation 11:14.
11. 2 Peter 2:1-3; 1 Timothy 4:1-2; 2 Timothy 4:3-4.
12. Ephesians 4:13.
13. Ephesians 5:27.
14. Hebrews 1:13; 10:13; Psalm 110:1.
15. Ephesians 4:15.
16. Romans 8:29; Hebrews 2:10.
17. Revelation 2:26-27; 5:10.
18. 1 Corinthians 6:2-3; Revelation 19:11-15.
19. Psalm 149:5-9; Revelation 19:11-15.
20. Daniel 7:18.
21. Daniel 7:22.

22. Daniel 7:25-27.
23. Jude 11.
24. Romans 8:17.
25. Ephesians 3:10.
26. Ephesians 3:11.
27. Ephesians 3:21.
28. Revelation 19:7-8.
29. Genesis 1:26-27.
30. 2 Peter 3:13.
31. Matthew 13:43.
32. Numbers 14:21; Isaiah 40:5; Habakkuk 2:14.
33. 2 Peter 3:10-13.
34. Revelation 21:5.
35. Revelation 11:15.
36. Revelation 21:2.
37. Revelation 1:6; 5:10; 21:1; 2 Peter 3:13.
38. Romans 8:19-22.
39. Matthew 24:14.
40. Joel 3:2.
41. Matthew 25:31-46.
42. Matthew 25:33.
43. Matthew 25:34.
44. Matthew 25:41.
45. Psalm 9:17.
46. Revelation 21:24-27.
47. Revelation 22:2.
48. Revelation 19:15.
49. Daniel 2:34-35,44-45.
50. Revelation 11:15.
51. Haggai 2:7.
52. Romans 11:25-26; Isaiah 1:26.
53. Psalm 82:8; 72:11.
54. Isaiah 2:2.
55. Matthew 13:49-50.
56. Revelation 21:8.
57. Revelation 20:15.
58. Jude 15.
59. Malachi 4:1-3.
60. 2 Thessalonians 1:7-10.

61. Matthew 25:26-30.
62. 2 Peter 2:9,17.
63. Revelation 19:11-21.
64. Isaiah 66:24.
65. Genesis 15:16; 18:20; 19:24; 6:13.
66. Matthew 25:41.
67. Revelation 20:1-3.
68. Revelation 20:9-10.
69. Revelation 20:14.
70. Romans 8:19.
71. Romans 8:21.
72. 2 Peter 3:10-13.
73. Revelation 21:9-21.
74. Isaiah 65:25.
75. Romans 8:23; 1 Corinthians 15:51-55; 2 Corinthians 5:1-8; 1 Thessalonians 4:14-17.
76. Romans 8:18.
77. 1 Corinthians 2:9.
78. Jude 14-15.
79. Philippians 3:14.
80. Bill Hamon, *Birthing God's Purpose* (Santa Rosa Beach, FL: Christian International Publications, 2001).
81. Isaiah 66:9.
82. Acts 13:36.
83. Joshua 14:10c-12c.
84. Malachi 3:16.
85. Acts 3:21; Revelation 11:15.
86. Matthew 19:14.
87. Matthew 13:17.
88. Isaiah 10:3 KJV; Luke 19:44.
89. Malachi 3:16-18.
90. 2 Peter 3:12.
91. Isaiah 9:7.
92. Esther 4:14.
93. Hebrews 11:38–12:2.
94. Romans 8:21b.
95. Isaiah 66:9.
96. Revelation 2:26-27; 12:5,.
97. Revelation 22:17,20.

DEFINITIONS AND EXPLANATIONS OF THEOLOGICAL AND PRESENT-TRUTH TERMS

ACTIVATION

An exercise to challenge God's people to receive the truth and manifest the grace to do what the Bible says they can do. A means of arousing, triggering, stirring, and releasing God's abilities within the Saints. For example, Saints can be activated to speak in tongues, prophesy, or minister healing to one another. Gifts are given by the Holy Spirit but activated by the faith of the believer, just as the gift of eternal life, which is freely given, is not activated within an individual until he or she believes in the heart and confesses the Lord Jesus with the mouth.

A-MILLENNIALISM

See **millennialism**.

ANOINTING / MANTLE

An in-depth study of the word *anoint* reveals that it was used to consecrate people to a particular position or ministry. Prophet Isaiah declared that we destroy yokes because of the anointing (Is. 10:27 KJV). In present-day application, this means the manifest presence of God upon a person to meet specific needs. To say a person has an apostolic or prophetic anointing means that he has the calling to minister at certain times with the supernatural gifting of the prophet or apostle, but it does not necessarily mean the person has the calling or office of a prophet or apostle. *Mantle* has a similar meaning. If someone has prophesied that you have a prophetic mantle, it implies that you can minister in prophetic ministry, to what realm will be determined by time and use (Ex. 28:41; Ps. 2:2; 23:5; 105:15; Zech. 4:6; Heb. 1:9).

APOSTLE

One of the fivefold ministries of Ephesians 4:11. A foundation-laying ministry (Eph. 2:20) which is seen in the New Testament establishing new churches (Paul's missionary journeys), correcting error by establishing proper order and structure (1 Corinthians), and acting as an oversight ministry that fathers other ministries (1 Cor. 4:15; 2 Cor. 11:28). The New Testament apostle has a revelatory anointing (Eph. 3:5). Some major characteristics are great patience and manifestations of signs, wonders, and miracles.

APOSTLES AND PROPHETS IN THE MARKETPLACE

Those called to the fivefold offices of **apostle** or **prophet** who function primarily in business, government, or a "secular" arena rather than inside a local church.

APOSTOLIC-PROPHETIC COUNSELING

One-on-one ministry to help people with scriptural wisdom and insight, but also with the gifts of the Holy Spirit to discover root problems and minister deliverance, inner healing, etc. Apostolic-prophetic counseling serves a little different purpose than the ministry of the prophet, prophetic presbytery, or general counseling. The word of knowledge and discerning of spirits are two key gifts necessary to move in this realm effectively. Allows the counselor to cut through hours of discussion and look beyond the veil of human reasoning to get right to the heart of the matter and bring resolution. This is what makes biblical counseling much more effective than that of the psychologist and psychiatrist who use only human wisdom and psychology. Deals with the root more than the fruit.

APOSTOLIC-PROPHETIC MINISTRY

All methods by which the Holy Spirit makes known the heart and mind of Christ to people. Prophetic ministry includes the ministry of the prophet (the ascension gift office), prophetic ministers (those not called to the fivefold office of prophet but who operate in the gift and anointing of prophecy) and all prophetic Saints (those who have been equipped to hear the voice of the Holy Spirit for themselves). It includes all the ministry and manifestations of the Holy Spirit and all the scriptural ways in which God can be praised. This includes prophetic worship with singing, praising, prophesying, song of the Lord, praise-dance, mime, and sign language. In fact, it includes all dedicated physical expressions which may properly glorify God and edify the Church. Apostolic ministry is moving in the supernatural ministry of signs, wonders, and miracles, while maintaining a proper relationship in the Body of Christ. It includes those called to the office of apostle, those with an apostolic anointing, and all Saints who demonstrate the supernatural works of Jesus in their lives and ministries.

APOSTOLIC-PROPHETIC PEOPLE

Saints who are full of the Holy Spirit and fulfilling the commands to "desire spiritual gifts" and "covet to prophesy" (1 Cor. 12:31; 14:1-2,39 KJV). They believe in, propagate, and support the ministry of apostles and prophets in the Church today.

They earnestly desire and are exercising their spiritual senses to be fully educated and activated in all the gifts of the Holy Spirit that Christ has ordained for them. They are also submitted to divine authority and order (Heb. 5:14; 1 Cor. 12:1,7,11; 15:16).

APOSTOLIC-PROPHETIC TRAINING SEMINARS

Seminars conducted to teach, train, and activate Saints concerning the gifts of the Holy Spirit in order that they may be equipped for the work of the ministry (Eph. 4:13). APT Seminars are open to those called as apostles and prophets, other fivefold ministers who want to enhance their function and relationship with the Saints, and for all Saints who want to operate in their supernatural giftings and callings. Includes impartation of gifts, prophetic presbytery over each attendee, anointed teaching, and practical participation exercises.

ARMOR OF GOD

The supernatural garments of protection and power given to believers in Jesus Christ. Includes the robe of righteousness, the garment of praise, and the full armor of God which protects against onslaughts of the enemy (Is. 61:3,10; Eph. 6:10-18).

ASCENSION GIFT OFFICES

See **fivefold ministers**.

CHRISTIAN INTERNATIONAL BUSINESS NETWORK

A network founded in the 1980s for the purpose of raising up a worldwide network of Saints who practice biblical principles in their vocation and operate in the supernatural power of God. Through chapters in local churches and conferences, the CIBN teaches, trains, activates, and mentors Christian businesspeople and helps advance Kingdom businesses in order to establish the Kingdom of God. The CIBN is not just for those employed in business and government, but for the 98 percent of Saints whose primary function is outside the local church.

CHRISTIAN INTERNATIONAL NETWORK OF CHURCHES

A network of apostolic-prophetic local churches and ministers who are bonded together by a common heart and vision to help bring about the full restoration of the corporate Church. The network seeks to proclaim present truth for the purpose of establishing dynamic, growing local churches, built upon the foundational ministries of the apostle and prophet, that are committed to equip the Saints for the work of the ministry. The CINC was founded to provide a place of relationship and accountability for fivefold ministers, especially those called to the office of apostle and prophet.

COMPANY OF PROPHETS

Today this term refers to the multitude of prophets God is raising up around the world in these last days to usher in the second coming of Jesus Christ. Prophets are being brought forth to be taught, trained, and activated into their preordained ministry of "preparing the way for Jesus to return and establish His Kingdom over all the Earth" as well as "making ready a people for Christ's return" (see Is. 40:3,5; Lk. 1:17). They labor to purify the Church in righteousness and mature the Saints for ministry, bridehood, co-laboring and co-reigning over God's vast domain (Eph. 4:11-12; 5:27).

DISPENSATIONS

Dispensations, covenants, and ages are certain periods of time when God works with mankind according to certain principles and requirements. Church historians have divided the time of man on Earth into eight dispensations. The dispensation of the mortal Church began with the first coming of Christ and will end with the second coming of Christ. Most theologians believe the dispensation of the Church will last about 2,000 years. The Church was birthed after Christ's death and resurrection in A.D. 30. The 2,000 years will be reached in A.D. 2030.

DISPENSATIONALISM

In its basic form, dispensationalism is the belief and teaching of dispensations. In relation to theology and Church history it includes the teaching that there was an apostolic age (or dispensation), within the larger dispensation of the Church, that ended with the death of the 12 apostles. This view teaches that apostles and prophets were set in the Church to write the books of the Bible and lay the foundation for the Church Age. After that was accomplished, apostles, prophets, and all miraculous experiences demonstrated in the first century of the Church were dispensationally deleted from being an active part of the Church. This doctrine was established during the nineteenth century, before the Divine Healing Movement of the 1880s and the Pentecostal Movement restored an understanding of supernatural manifestations back into the Church.

ESCHATOLOGY

From the Greek word *eschata*. In Christianity this term is used to include the doctrine of "last things." All the various teachings by different church groups concerning the end of time, the Church Age, and end of the world as it is now. The timing and way all things will be accomplished and finalized. It includes individuals' future concerning death, resurrection, and God's judgment determining the person's eternal state. It also includes the destiny of the Church, nations, and planet Earth.

EVANGELIST

The traditional view of the evangelist is a bearer of the gospel, or "good news," to the unbelieving world. This is exemplified by modern-day evangelists who preach the message of salvation in crusades. However, Phillip, the New Testament evangelist mentioned in Acts 21:8, demonstrated a strong supernatural dimension to the evangelistic ministry. Philip preached the gospel to the lost (Acts 8:5), moved in miracles (8:6), delivered people from demons (8:7), received instructions from an angel (8:26), had revelation knowledge (8:29), and was supernaturally translated from Gaza to Azotus (8:26,40). As one of the fivefold gifts, evangelists equip the Saints to reach others for Christ (Eph. 4:11-13).

FIVEFOLD MINISTERS / MINISTRIES

The five ascension gift ministries revealed in Ephesians 4:11: **apostle, prophet, evangelist, pastor,** and **teacher.** They are not gifts of the Holy Spirit per se, but an extension of Christ's headship ministry to the Church. Their primary ministry and function are to teach, train, activate, and mature the Saints for the work of their ministries (Eph. 4:12-13).

All fivefold ministers should function in the apostolic and prophetic, meaning they should be able to speak a **rhema** word revealing the mind and purpose of God for specific situations and people (1 Cor. 14:31; 2 Cor. 3:6) and should be able to manifest the miraculous.

GIFTS OF THE SPIRIT

The nine supernatural manifestations of the Holy Spirit that reveal God's heart and mind through vocal expression and demonstrate God's power and wisdom. Listed in First Corinthians 12:8-10: word of wisdom, word of knowledge, discerning of spirits, the gift of faith, healing, miracles, prophecy, tongues, and interpretation of tongues. Verses 7 and 11 declare that every Saint is given one or more of these gifts to bless the Body of Christ and demonstrate the gospel to the world. These gifts of the Holy Spirit are given to believers according to the will of God, but may be activated through faith. They are weapons of warfare for the Saints to destroy the works of the devil and to bless humankind.

GRACE

God's divine, unmerited enablements. God's free abilities (gifts, talents, etc.) being received and demonstrated through a human vessel in spite of sin and human frailties. It is having God's unearned supernatural ability to perform and execute whatever He has willed to the individual Saint (Eph. 2:8-9).

INTERCESSION

Prayer in which a believer acts as a go-between in the spiritual realm between God and another person or situation in order to bring God's will to pass in that situation. Petitions to God to intervene in a situation on behalf of another (Ezek. 22:30).

INTERNATIONAL GATHERING OF APOSTLES AND PROPHETS

A gathering of prophets, apostles, and other ministers and apostolic-prophetic people from around the world. Christian International sponsored the first such conference in the fall of 1987. The events are designed as a vehicle to assist in disseminating apostolic-prophetic ministry around the world that millions might be blessed and that a current consensus of what Christ is speaking to His Church may be attained and acted upon. Christian International conducts an IGAP conference every year in October (usually the fourth week) in Santa Rosa Beach, Florida, to bring maturity, unity, and fruit to the work of restoration God is doing in the Earth, especially dealing with the restoration of apostles and prophets.

KING AND PRIEST MINISTERS

Jesus Christ has made the Saints kings and priests unto God, His Father (Rev. 1:6; 5:10). To clarify and identify where these Saints minister, the author has designated those who minister primarily inside the local church as "priest" ministers of Christ and those who minister outside the local church as "king" ministers of Christ. Saints in the marketplace are the kingly ministers and the Saints who are ordained ministers and church staff are the priestly ministers of Christ's life and power.

LOGOS

One of the Greek words for "word." Logos refers to the unchanging, inerrant, creative, and inspired Word of God. (See Ps. 119:89 KJV: *"Forever, O Lord, thy word* [logos] *is settled in heaven."* See also 2 Tim. 3:16; 1 Cor. 2:13.) The entire written Word of God—the

Holy Bible. It is the complete revelation of God—His personage, character, plan, and eternal purpose—as found in the Scripture.

MARKETPLACE MINISTERS

In the early New Testament Church the word *minister* was not used as the title of a clergy position but of Saints who ministered the life of Christ and power of God in the Church and to the world. Ministers in the marketplace are the Saints whose livelihood is outside the walls of the local church. Every true Saint has the right and authority to manifest the life of Christ and to minister the supernatural power of God. Every Saint will be a minister in the Day of the Saints.

MEMBERSHIP MINISTRY

The specific talents, abilities and callings given by God to each individual member in the Body of Christ. It is important that each Saint find and manifest their membership ministry so that "every joint" will supply according to God's plans and purposes (Eph. 4:16; 1 Cor. 12:7-11; 14:26; 1 Pet. 4:10). Fivefold ministers help educate and activate the members in the Body of Christ into their membership ministries.

MILLENNIALISM

Based on the word *millennium* which means the aggregate of 1,000 years. Revelation 20:1-5 states that after their **resurrection-translation**, the Saints will rule with Christ on the Earth for 1,000 years—a time period known as the millennium or millennial reign. Theologians have developed three opinions concerning this biblical period of time.

A-millennialism is the teaching that the Book of Revelation is a book of symbolism. The 1,000-year period is seen as symbolic of completeness and fullness, not a literal period of time. The time periods mentioned in Scripture regarding the end-times, such as 1,000 years, 7 years, or a certain number of days, are seen as symbolic, not literal. There is only one coming of

Christ at the end of the Church Age, not two. Most historic Protestants and Catholics teach a-millennialism.

Post-millennialism is the teaching that places the **second coming of Christ** after the millennium. The original propagators viewed the "millennium as a period in the latter days of the Church when, under the special power of the Holy Spirit, the work of God shall be greatly revived and the Saints empowered to triumph over the powers of evil. It would be followed by a brief apostasy, the battle of Armageddon and climaxed with the second coming of Christ" (*Baker's Dictionary of Theology* [Grand Rapids, MI: Baker Book House, 1960], p. 353). This belief is held by some Evangelical denominations and some Charismatics.

Pre-millennialism is the view that there are two comings of Christ at the end of this age. It sees Christ coming *for* the Saints (the resurrection-translation or rapture) to take them to Heaven for a short period of time (between a "twinkling of an eye" and seven years depending on the interpretation of end-time Scriptures) and then returning *with* the Saints to establish God's Kingdom over all the Earth for a 1,000-year reign. At the end of the millennial reign of Christ, the devil will be loosed for a period of time and the battle of Armageddon will take place. The devil and his host will be overcome and cast into the lake of fire which will become their eternal state. Most Baptist and Pentecostal denominations propagate pre-millennialism with different viewpoints on the purpose and time of the rapture.

There are four different views of the rapture in pre-millennialism: 1. **Pre-tribulation rapture** rapture before the seven-year tribulation; 2. **Mid-tribulation rapture** in the middle of the seven years (after three and one-half yrs.); 3. **Post-tribulation rapture** at end of seven years; and 4. The **"No-trip" view** wherein the bodies of departed Saints are resurrected and those of living Saints are immortalized, but all stay on Earth to set up Christ's reign. Books have been written on all four views and each gives Scriptures and convincing arguments for their view.

Definitions and Explanations of Terms

Perspective of this book: No attempt is made by the author to prove whether post-, a-, or pre-millennialism is the correct interpretation. The author sees some truth in each viewpoint. For instance, this book presents a portion of the a-mill view which states, "Believers are already in heavenly places in Christ Jesus and reign in life by Him; Satan is a defeated foe and the Saints triumph over him in Christ" (*Baker's Dictionary of Theology*, [Grand Rapids, MI: Baker Book House, 1960], p. 354). It propagates the post-mill view that the Church will grow in power more and more until it demonstrates the fullness of Christ and His Kingdom. It propagates the pre-millennial view that Christ Jesus and His Church will reign for 1,000 years after the rapture of the Church. However, the "pan-mill" view is presented more than anything else: that is, everything is going to "pan out" according to God's pre-ordained eternal purpose regardless of the different eschatological viewpoints that are being propagated by Church preachers and Christian authors.

MIRACLES

Webster's Dictionary says, "An effect in the physical world that surpasses all known human or **natural** powers and is therefore ascribed to **supernatural** agency." **Miraculous** is defined as "performed by or involving a supernatural power; a miraculous cure." Theologically it involves God speeding up the laws of nature or superseding, bypassing, or overriding natural laws.

MONEY

Precious metals stamped and currency printed by governments as a medium of exchange for products and services. Money is the medium of exchange for all earthly things as faith is the medium of exchange for all heavenly things. Like faith, money is neutral and of little practical value unless exchanged for goods and services. Money is not eaten or worn but it can be exchanged for food, clothing, transportation, and anything that mankind can supply. Money represents one's time, talents, and ability to earn and be productive. Jesus put importance on money because He places value on what money represents—one's life, time, and talents.

OMEGA-TRANSITION GENERATION

The word *omega* is the last letter of the Greek alphabet. Transition means passage from one place or state of being to another; a change or process of change. The Omega-Transition Generation is both the last generation of the mortal Church and the one which will experience the transition from mortality to immortality. This generation is predestined to fulfill a purpose of God that only it can fulfill.

PASTOR

In common usage, pastor is the title normally given to the senior minister (or ministers) of the local church, regardless of his or her fivefold calling. In Ephesians 4:11 pastor refers to the fivefold ascension gift that acts as a shepherding ministry to feed and care for the "flock" under their care. The Greek word *poiment*, a shepherd, one who tends herds or flocks (not merely one who feeds them), is used metaphorically of Christian "pastors." *Episkopeo* (overseer, bishop) is an overseer, and *pesbuteros* (elder) is another term for the same person as bishop or overseer (See W.E. Vine, *Vine's Expository Dictionary of Old & New Testament Words* [William E. Vine, Merrill F. Unger, and William White, Jr.]). Responsibilities that appear connected with pastoral ministry include oversight and care of the Saints, providing spiritual food for their growth and development, leadership and guidance, and counsel. Prophetic pastors not only do the things normally associated with pastoring, but also move in supernatural graces and gifts of God (prophesying, word of knowledge, healing) and have the vision and willingness to develop the Saints in their gifts and callings.

POST-MILLENNIALISM

See millennialism.

Definitions and Explanations of Terms

Pre-Millennialism
See millennialism.

Present Truth

Biblical truth that was lost during the Dark Age of the Church, when most biblical revelations and experiences were deleted from being a manifested reality, but has since been restored to the corporate Church through divinely-ordained **restoration movements**. Present truth includes that truth and Christian experience that was restored and reactivated in the most recent restoration move of God. The Prophetic-Apostolic Movement is the most recent restoration movement, and the Saints Movement is the next one on God's agenda.

Priest Ministers
See king and priest ministers.

Prophecy

From the Greek *propheteia*, a noun which "signifies the speaking forth of the mind and counsel of God. The declaration of that which cannot be known by natural means. The forth-telling of the will of God, whether with reference to the past, the present, or the future" (See W.E. Vine, *Vine's Expository Dictionary of Old & New Testament Words* [William E. Vine, Merrill F. Unger, and William White, Jr.], p. 893). New Testament prophecy functions in three realms:

1. Jesus giving inspired testimony and praise through one of His Saints by **prophetic utterance or song of the Lord** (Heb. 2:12; Rev. 19:10).
2. One of the manifestations of the Holy Spirit called the **gift of prophecy** which brings edification, exhortation, and comfort to the Body of Christ (1 Cor. 12:10; Rom. 12:6).
3. The **prophet speaking by divine utterance** the mind and counsels of God and giving a **rhema** word for edification, direction, correction, confirmation, and instruction in righteousness (1 Cor. 14:29; 2 Tim. 3:16-17).

A truly, divinely inspired prophecy is the Holy Spirit expressing the thoughts and desires of Christ through a human voice.

PROPHET

A man of God to whom Christ has given the ascension gift of "prophet" (Eph. 4:11; 1 Cor. 12:28; 14:29; Acts 11:27; 13:1). One of the fivefold gifts that are an extension of Christ's ministry to the Church. An anointed minister who has the gifted ability to perceive and speak the specific mind of Christ to individuals, churches, businesses, and nations. From the Greek *prophetes*, a foreteller, an inspired speaker (James Strong, *Strong's Exhaustive Concordance of the Bible* [(Iowa Falls, IA: Riverside Book and Bible House, n.d.)]; (W.E. Vine, *Vine's Expository Dictionary of Old & New Testament Words* [William E. Vine, Merrill F. Unger, and William White, Jr.], p. 894). A proclaimer of a divine message, denoted among the Greeks as an interpreter of the oracles of gods. In the Septuagint it is the translation of the word *roeh*—a seer—indicating that the prophet was one who had immediate intercourse with God (1 Sam. 9:9). It is also the translation of the word *nabhi*, meaning either "one in whom the message from God springs forth, or one to whom anything is secretly communicated" (Amos 3:7; Eph. 3:5).

PROPHETESS

From the Greek *prophetis*, the feminine of prophet (Acts 2:17; 21:9; Lk. 2:36; Is. 8:3; 2 Chron. 34:22; Jude 14; Ex. 15:20). "Prophetess" is the proper title for a woman with this ascension gift and calling. "Prophet" is the proper title for a man with this ascension gift and calling.

PROPHETIC PRAISE AND WORSHIP

Biblical expressions of praise and adoration (singing, clapping, dancing, lifting of hands, bowing, etc.) that are directed to God, inspired and directed by the Holy Spirit, and which come forth from the heart of man. Prophetic worship is where God's voice is heard and His presence felt as Christ begins to sing and express praise to the Father through His people (Heb. 2:12; Ps. 22:22; Jer. 33:11; Rev. 19:10).

Prophetic dance is physical movements that are inspirational and anointed by the Holy Spirit. Used in praise, adoration, and worship to God. Many times accompanied by song of the Lord.

Prophetic sign is physical expression inspired by the Holy Spirit that uses symbolic gestures such as those used in sign language.

Prophetic dance and sign may be spontaneous or preplanned (the Holy Spirit may inspire the movement during a corporate service or during a practice session for later use in a corporate service). They may communicate divine thoughts, ideas, and purposes—a visible expression of what God is saying (Acts 21:10-11; Job 42:5).

PROPHETIC PRAYER

Holy Spirit-directed prayer. Praying with natural understanding is asking God's help about matters of which we have natural knowledge. Prophetic praying is prophesying in prayer format. It is praying out of one's spirit in one's natural, known tongue, flowing in the same manner as praying out of one's spirit in unknown tongues. The prayer touches specific areas unknown in the natural to the one praying and uses prophetic motivation, word of knowledge, discerning of spirits, word of wisdom, etc. Intercessory prayer is much more effective when it moves into the realm of prophetic praying. In ministering to people in churches who do not understand or promote prophesying, prophetic ministry can still bless the people through prophetic praying. Instead of prophesying, "Thus saith the Lord," or "The Lord shows me that..." one verbalizes by saying, "Lord, we pray for...," or "Jesus, You see what he (or she) has been going through regarding..." etc.

PROPHETIC PRESBYTERY

When two or more prophets and/or prophetic ministers lay hands on and prophesy over individuals at a specified time and place. Prophetic presbyteries are conducted for several reasons:

1. For revealing a Saint's membership ministry in the Body of Christ.
2. For ministering a prophetic rhema word of God to individuals.
3. For impartation and activation of divinely ordained gifts, graces, and callings.
4. For the revelation, clarification, and confirmation of leadership ministry in the local church.
5. For the "laying on of hands and prophecy" over those called and properly prepared to be an ordained fivefold minister.

RAPTURE

Comes from the Latin word *ravio*, which means to seize or snatch. It is the word used by Evangelicals and Pentecostals for the biblical event described in First Thessalonians 4:17 and First Corinthians 15:51-52. Most theologians agree that the bodies of the living Saints will be changed from mortal to immortal in a moment and that the Saints who have lost their bodies through death will have them resurrected and rejoined with their eternal spirit. The differences in viewpoint among theologians are concerning when this event will take place and God's main purpose for activating it.

REGIONAL APOSTOLIC AND PROPHETIC CONFERENCES AND SEMINARS

Events sponsored by Christian International that are held in different regions of the country in order to promote and propagate present truth ministry in that area and to help equip the Saints in the regions where they live and work.

Resurrection-Translation (r-t) of the Saints

The event foretold by First Thessalonians 4:17 and First Corinthians 15:51-52 where the bodies of the Saints who have died are resurrected and made immortal and the bodies of the Saints who are still alive are "translated" from mortality to immortality. Referred to by some as the **rapture**.

Restoration Movement

A restoration movement is when God has the Holy Spirit bring revelation to some men and women of God on some truths and ministries that He wants reactivated into His Church. The "times of restoration" prophesied in Acts 3:21 started in A.D. 1500 and have continued to the present. There have been five restoration movements since 1500. Only two or three restoration movements are yet to take place in order to fulfill apostle Peter's prophecy in Acts 3:18-25.

Rhema

The Greek for "word" that is derived from the verb "to speak" (see Rom. 10:17 KJV: "Faith cometh by hearing, and hearing by the word [rhema] of God"). A rhema is a word or an illustration God speaks directly to an individual or group which addresses their personal, particular situation. It is a timely, Holy Spirit-inspired word from the **logos** that brings life, power, and faith to perform and fulfill it. Its significance is exemplified in the injunction to take the "sword of the Spirit, which is the word [rhema] of God" (Eph. 6:17). It can be received through others, such as by a prophetic word, or be an illumination given to one directly in his personal meditation time in the Bible or in prayer.

The **logos** is the fixed Word of God—the Scriptures. A **rhema** is a particular portion of the logos, and must be in line with it, that is brought forth by the Spirit to be applied directly to something in one's personal experience.

SAINT

A New Testament biblical Saint is a person who has accepted Jesus Christ as his personal Savior by believing for all his sin to be removed by the blood of Jesus. Saints are born again by the Spirit of God which makes them children of the one and only true God, the Father of our Savior Jesus Christ. Saint means a person who is made holy by the righteousness of Christ and who has been set apart wholly for God. A present-truth Saint is a child of God who is walking in all presently restored truth. The Saints who will be used of God the most during the Day of the Saints will be present-truth Saints.

SCHOOL OF THE HOLY SPIRIT

A training time in which God's Saints are discipled in a "hot house" environment to discern the language of the Holy Spirit and manifest the gifts of the Holy Spirit under proper oversight and care. A time and place where the Saints allow the Holy Spirit and Word to operate in them, thereby causing them to exercise their spiritual senses and spiritual gifts. Includes training in discerning between the human soul (mind) and the realm of the Holy Spirit (Heb. 5:14).

Many churches affiliated with Christian International Network of Churches hold regular Schools of the Holy Spirit to equip the Saints.

SCHOOL OF THE PROPHETS

Webster's Dictionary says, "Among the ancient Israelites, a school or college in which young men were educated and trained to become teachers of religion among the people. These students were called 'sons of the prophets.'" Samuel is recognized as the founder of the School of the Prophets, which was continued by such prophets as Elijah and Elisha.

Today this term refers to a group of people who have the calling to prophetic ministry and who have come together in one place to be schooled in hearing and recognizing the true voice of God and in how to properly minister that word with grace and wisdom for the greatest glory to God and good to mankind. For example, Christian International trains Saints and ministers in prophetic ministry through training seminars, our residential Ministry Training College, and our international bases.

Based upon First Samuel 19:18-24, the "school of the prophets" also serves as a covering for the Davidic company (the new order for ministry that God is raising up) to nurture and protect them from persecution by the old religious order (Saul's).

SECOND COMING OF CHRIST

Christ's first coming was when God sent His only begotten Son to Earth to become the perfect sacrifice for the redemption of mankind. Jesus shed His life's blood for the purchase of His Church. Christ's first coming birthed the age of the Mortal Church. His second coming will end the age of the Mortal Church by translating and resurrecting the Saints into the Immortal Church. Christ's second coming will subdue all things on Earth under His dominion, thereby establishing God's Kingdom over all the Earth.

SHARING THE MIND OF CHRIST

The ability of every believer to draw upon the Holy Spirit to receive a sanctified thought for another and then share this thought in everyday language (without using "Thus saith the Lord," "God says," or "The Holy Spirit would say," etc.). The Saints sense the mind of Christ from their redeemed spirit where Christ dwells, not from their natural mind. This activation prepares believers to determine if they have the ability to give an accurate prophecy (1 Cor. 2:16; Rev. 19:10; Rom. 12:6).

SHEEP AND GOAT NATIONS

The nations mentioned in Matthew 25:31-46 and Revelation 21:24. Based on Christ's teaching, sheep nations will be allowed to continue on Earth after Christ Jesus comes to judge the nations. He will place the sheep nations on His right hand, but the goat nations will be placed on His left hand and sentenced to the same fate and place prepared for the devil and his angels.

SONG OF THE LORD (PROPHETIC SONG)

A song that is inspired, anointed, and directed by the Holy Spirit through an individual, usually spontaneous in nature, which expresses the mind of God in musical form. Literally prophecy through song (referred to in the New Testament as spiritual songs—see Col. 3:16; Eph. 5:19). These songs are directed to man for the purpose of edification, exhortation, and comfort or may be directed to God as the Holy Spirit helps us express our deep devotion that we could not ordinarily express by ourselves (Heb. 2:12; Rom. 8:27; Zeph. 3:17 KJV—"The Lord thy God...will joy over thee [or through you] with singing").

> **Songs of Deliverance** are prophetic songs that bring release and freedom to those who hear and receive their message. The words and anointing are an expression of the power of Jesus Christ to break the believer out of oppression, limitation, or bondage (1 Sam. 16:23).

SPIRITUAL WARFARE

> See **warfare praise/warfare prayer** and **weapons of war.**

SUPERNATURAL

The New Webster's Dictionary of the English Language says, "Being above and beyond that which is natural, supernatural phenomena. Abnormal or extraordinary." That which cannot be understood or explained by natural reasoning and human wisdom.

> **Natural** is defined as, "In conformity with the ordinary course of nature; not unusual or exceptional." That which can be experienced by the five senses, understood by the mind, or explained by human reasoning.

TEACHER

An instructor of truth. "All Scripture is given by inspiration of God, and is profitable for doctrine, for reproof, for correction, for instruction in righteousness" (2 Tim. 3:16). One of the fivefold ministries of Ephesians 4:11. A New Testament/present-truth teacher is one who not only teaches the letter of the word, but ministers with divine life and Holy Spirit anointing (2 Cor. 3:6). He or she exhibits keen spiritual discernment and divine insight into the Word of God and its personal application to the Saints.

The Ten M's

Ten English words starting with the letter "M" that Dr. Bill Hamon began using in the early 1980s as a means to discern and evaluate true and false ministers. They are also used to reveal the things that one needs to be mature and to maintain an effective ministry that is pleasing to God. The Ten "M's" are: Manhood (or womanhood), Ministry, Message, Maturity, Marriage, Methods, Manners, Money, Morality, and Motive.

Theologian

From the Greek *theologia—theos* meaning God and *logos* meaning the Word of God as was manifest in Jesus Christ and is now written as the Bible. A theologian is one who has devoted his or her life to studying the teachings of the Bible and the various doctrines propagated by Christian preachers and authors. A spiritual theologian is one who studies the Bible to know how to properly relate himself and others to God.

Tribulation

See **millennialism**.

Warfare Praise / Warfare Prayer

High praises of God that both exalt the Lord and accomplish **spiritual warfare** in the heavenlies (Ps. 149:6-9; Eph. 6:12; 2 Cor. 10:4-6). One of the purposes of praise is to be a **weapon of war** for the Saints to defeat the enemy (Ps. 8:2; 2 Chron. 20:14-22). It is worship that is expressed in obedience to a prompting of God that brings forth a prophetic word, mantle, or anointing that results in the manifestation of God's power (2 Kings 3:15; 1 Sam. 10:5-6).

Warfare prayer is prayer that aggressively takes a stand against any ungodly spiritual forces, such as unbelief, poverty, or infirmity, that may be hindering a person, church, or region from receiving the revelation and blessings of God. Often uses military or warfare terminology such as "defeat," "crush," or "strike" (Gen. 3:15; Mt. 11:11; Ps. 89:20-23; Rom. 16:20).

WEAPONS OF WAR

Supernatural enablements given to the Saints by God in order to lead overcoming, fruitful lives, demonstrate the Kingdom, and glorify God. Includes the blood of Jesus, the name of Jesus, the **gifts of the Spirit**, the high praises of God, and the **armor of God**, especially the sword of the Spirit which is the Word of God (the Bible) (2 Cor. 10:3-5; 1 Jn. 1:7; Rev. 12:11; Acts 2:38; 4:10; 16:18; Phil. 2:10; Ps. 149:6-9; Eph. 6:11-13,17).

INDEX

D

E

F